Praise for *Building Smart Nonprofits: A Roadmap for Mission Success*

"Absolutely, THE collection, of the most important, current, and innovative work happening throughout the country to strengthen nonprofits and expedite organizational potential. A must-read for leaders, board members, and anyone who cares about changing the world." —**Yolanda Coentro**, president and CEO, Institute for Nonprofit Practice

"David J. O'Brien and Matthew D. Craig have produced a work of significant insight for nonprofits. It will be of great value not only to their target audience of small to mid-sized organizations but for the big guys as well . . . and should help all of us achieve a higher level of success as we advance into a very rapidly changing future." —**Clifford Hague**, trustee, San Diego Zoo Global

"The wide range of challenges and approaches that our non-profit sector seeks to address has grown exponentially over the past two decades, while we have simultaneously seen an unprecedented creation of wealth, so it begs the question about how well we are connecting those with this capacity to support those who seek to do good. O'Brien and Craig have created a highly readable, unique, compelling, and timely road map for non-profits to understand this landscape and fulfill their missions." —**John Vasconcellos**, president, Community Foundation of Southeastern Massachusetts

"The landscape of Corporate America is rapidly changing. Governance practices are demanding more emphasis on shareholder values, specifically social and environmental concerns that lean into the 'triple bottom line.' Nonprofits have not necessarily adjusted their corporate governance and business strategy to these changing times. The 'olde tin cup' approach to nonprofit sustainability is over. *Building Smart Nonprofits* is an anthology of best practices and new concepts for the 'new' nonprofits to consider. It is an excellent book, written from a base of experience in the corporate world and nonprofit by the authors: a must-read!" —**Bob Watkins**, vice chair, The Robert David Lion Gardiner Foundation

"This is a book for nonprofit leaders who want to get better at what they do. Starting, operating, and sustaining a nonprofit charitable organization requires leaders to be knowledgable and dedicated to achieving results. O'Brien and Craig honor the hard-earned experience of nonprofit leaders, while offering respectful insights and suggestions that readers will want to put to work." —**Jeffrey R. Pickering**, president and CEO, Indian River Community Foundation

BUILDING SMART NONPROFITS

BUILDING SMART NONPROFITS

A Roadmap for Mission Success

David J. O'Brien and Matthew D. Craig

ROWMAN & LITTLEFIELD
Lanham • Boulder • New York • London

Published by Rowman & Littlefield
An imprint of The Rowman & Littlefield Publishing Group, Inc.
4501 Forbes Boulevard, Suite 200, Lanham, Maryland 20706
www.rowman.com

6 Tinworth Street, London SE11 5AL, United Kingdom

British Library Cataloguing in Publication Information Available

Library of Congress Cataloging-in-Publication Data
Names: O'Brien, David J., 1947- author. | Craig, Matthew D., 1975- author.
Title: Building smart nonprofits : a roadmap for mission success / David J. O'Brien and Matthew
     D. Craig.
Description: Lanham : Rowman & Littlefield Publishing Group, 2020. | Includes bibliographical
     references and index. | Summary: "Based on interviews with over 60 industry thought leaders,
     Building Smart Nonprofits: A Roadmap for Mission Success describes, in practical terms, how
     nonprofits can deploy developing trends and best practices to strengthen operational and
     financial sustainability"-- Provided by publisher.
Identifiers: LCCN 2019056379 (print) | LCCN 2019056380 (ebook) | ISBN 9781538118238
     (cloth) | ISBN 9781538118245 (epub)
Subjects: LCSH: Nonprofit organizations--Management.
Classification: LCC HD62.6 .O267 2020 (print) | LCC HD62.6 (ebook) | DDC 658/.048--dc23
LC record available at https://lccn.loc.gov/2019056379
LC ebook record available at https://lccn.loc.gov/2019056380

CONTENTS

INTRODUCTION

WHY THIS BOOK?

We're going to level with you right up front: This is a book about nonprofit sustainability, and neither of us has worked a day for a nonprofit. At least not as a career. But before you slam the cover in protest and scramble to find your return shipping label, please hear us out. Though we haven't earned a paycheck from a nonprofit, we've served on numerous boards and worked with many who do. Indeed, each of us has participated in the sector for more than twenty years—as board members, volunteers, fundraisers, professional service providers, and citizens of humanity. You get the idea. And we're often frustrated—to watch wonderful, well-meaning, dedicated people struggle every year to keep their organizations' lights on. So we decided to sublimate that frustration (one we found is shared by a lot of other people) into this book, which hopefully shines a light on many of the things that will help nonprofits to continue doing their good work.

The book's working title was *Requiem for the Gala*, a somewhat "snarky" name according to some, and one often met with a knowing nod, nervous laughter, or even the occasional wry smile. From the very start, we knew we'd touched a nerve.

We've all been there: the rubber chicken dinner—more magnanimously known as the *gala*. It's a poor way for a nonprofit to achieve financial sustainability, and to many the poster child for the raft of ineffective and inefficient methods organizations use to fund their operations. Just picture the last gala you attended. Food, wine, and conversations are flowing. Everyone is dressed up in shiny suits or shimmering gowns. Some are bidding on silent auction items or raising their paddle when asked to give money (in full view of their table members for a nice bit of manufactured peer pressure). Then there's the staff members, who toiled tirelessly for months to make sure the event goes off without a hitch. They're exhausted and falling behind in their day jobs. And in the end, their organization often doesn't really raise that much money—especially after all the direct and indirect costs are taken into consideration. But before anyone even has time to catch their breath, it's time to start planning for next year's gala and hope it doesn't rain.

We could substitute the nearly as ubiquitous golf outing in place of the annual gala and the point still holds. But no matter which example we use, is this the most effective way to raise capital? "I would argue no," said Bruce Hoyt, formerly senior vice president of Gary Community Investments in Denver. Rather, Hoyt believes, galas and their ilk work best when organizations are "able to use that venue to showcase the work you are doing to a lot of people and get them involved in other ways."[1] In other words, as several people we spoke with remarked, these events are *friendraisers*, not fundraisers.

Don't get us wrong—we love galas and attend quite a few. And some organizations really can sustain themselves in this manner. Take, for instance, the Robin Hood Foundation, which in 2018 held a benefit in New York that was reported to have raised over $50 million![2] Make no mistake, though: These are the exceptions.

HISTORICAL FUNDING MODELS

So we ask again: Is this any way to sustainably support the organizations we rely on to fix society's most pressing problems? If Apple and Google were forced to finance their operations by relying on unpredictable annual giving by capricious donors, do you really think we'd all be checking Gmail on our shiny new iPhones?

Let's be clear: Overreliance on historical nonprofit fundraising models—be they galas, golf outings, gifts from philanthropists, or grants that won't pay the organization's true costs to provide services—wastes staff resources and impedes long-term strategic planning. Most damning, the practice is unfair to the great many selfless and dedicated people who are working hard to make our world a better place.

Though well-intentioned, these funding models can be insidious and prevent nonprofits from achieving long-term success by:

- Creating difficulties in hiring the best talent
- Curtailing investments in longer-term projects
- Inhibiting risk-taking behaviors
- Allocating scarce staff resources to donor needs rather than mission activities
- Relegating organizations to make do with substandard, outmoded facilities and equipment
- Discouraging open and honest communication about what works and what doesn't
- Elevating the influence of board members who are large donors at the expense of those who may contribute in other ways
- Stifling the creation of measurements that provide evidence of program impact

"THE TIMES THEY ARE A-CHANGIN'"

Now for some good news. Many of these counterproductive ideas are going the way of video rental stores—displaced by a growing adoption of unique and innovative funding and operating practices by the social sector. And they're being driven by a new wave of individual and corporate philanthropists who expect a measurable, sustainable return on their *investments*. Also propelling this trend is the spate of newly minted graduate-degree holders trained in cross-sector disciplines by our colleges and universities. No longer, it seems, are the country's best and brightest minds content to follow the well-trodden path to riches on Wall Street before balancing their fiscal karma much later in life by supporting the charitable sector only after they've made their millions.

Some of these *conscious capitalists* are heading a new wave of companies blurring the distinction between philanthropy and profit. As reported in *The Economist*, "A 'fourth sector' (after public, private, and voluntary) is springing up, consisting of organisations (sic) that straddle the line between business and charity. They call themselves 'low-profit limited liability companies,' 'social enterprises,' and other names."[3] Hybrid businesses that blend the goals and objectives of for-profit and nonprofit organizations are increasingly making meaningful contributions in alleviating society's most intractable issues. These businesses and practices include:

- Social entrepreneurship
- Multipurpose organizations, such as Certified B Corporations, and for-profits pursuing "Triple P" objectives (people, planet, profit)
- Impact investment funds, which invest in organizations with the objective of creating social impact while generating financial return
- Organizations pursuing market opportunities at the bottom of the pyramid to achieve both profits and social benefits
- Major companies renewing their focus on corporate social responsibility objectives

And just as disruptive technologies and ideas drove rapid change in many industries—think of companies like Uber and Airbnb displacing the taxicab and hotel industries in only a few short years—this disruption of third-sector business practices will accelerate. It's our profound hope that future generations will look back at the ways many nonprofits are forced to get by and remark with awe, "They did what?"

LIKE A BUSINESS

A while back we were chatting with Jim Canales about our thoughts for this book. Canales was the James Irvine Foundation's long-serving CEO and now heads the Barr Foundation in Boston. Recognizing the inherent danger in us coming across as the stuffed suits in our ivory tower, he offered an invaluable bit of advice. He suggested we read Phil Buchanan's cautionary works on the subject of "MBA-types" thinking, "If only nonprofits would act more like businesses, all their problems would be solved." Thanks, Jim. Hope we dodged that bullet. And thanks, too, to Buchanan—CEO of the Center for Effective Philanthropy and author of the recently published book, *Giving Done Right: Ef-*

fective Philanthropy and Making Every Dollar Count[4]—for his thought-inspiring writings on the business practices trap and for being kind enough to chat with us. As he explained in a blog post written in 2012, "Thankfully, there are some in business who are keeping it real: who seek to carefully study and learn about the nonprofit sector before generalizing about it—like Jim Collins. In a much-quoted line from his *Good to Great in the Social Sectors* that seems unfortunately not to have been internalized by many in the nonprofit sector or outside it, he makes the point as well as anyone has: 'We must reject the idea—well-intentioned, but dead wrong—that the primary path to greatness in the social sectors is to become 'more like a business.'"[5]

Indeed. Which is why this is decidedly *not* a business book. It's a book of knowledge and know-how distilled from those who are in the nonprofit trenches every day—as executives, leaders, board members, funders, and stakeholders.

Nonprofits are unique in many respects, including their incentives for growth and scaling, sources of funding, and responsibility to society at large rather than shareholders. Thus, they are and should be governed by different standards, practices, and mores than for-profit businesses.

Accordingly, in this book we'll show how nonprofits can improve their sustainability by highlighting organizations and leaders who are taking advantage of cutting-edge trends in the sector and operating in smart, innovative ways. We'll provide practical, real-world examples based on grounded research conducted through interviews with a diverse cross-section of more than sixty industry leaders from fifteen states, representing all social sector stakeholders: philanthropists, foundations, nonprofit organizations, and service providers. These individuals and organizations were selected because of their proven leadership over many years in helping others in the sector to be better. We think their collective insight and wisdom will do the same for you. For us, one of the great joys of writing this book was the opportunity to learn about and meet so many selfless people willing and eager to spread what they've learned to others. Imagine the different response we would have received if we'd called up the CEOs of Fortune 500 companies to ask about their practices! In hindsight, though, it shouldn't be that surprising. After all, service to others is what led most of them to their chosen careers in the first place.

WHO CAN USE THIS BOOK?

There are over 1.5 million 501(c)(3) nonprofit organizations in the United States, the majority of which have annual budgets under $500,000. Only a small fraction—some thirty-six thousand at last count—reported revenues of more than $5 million.[6] Excluding the even tinier number of very large nonprofits, we'll call the group of small and medium-size organizations with revenues from "working on it" to $30 million "Main Street" nonprofits. It's stakeholders of these organizations we hope to reach, and hopefully those just getting started.

Eric Nee, managing editor in chief of the *Stanford Social Innovation Review* since 2006, acknowledged the difficulties those in this group face in trying to deploy alternate funding strategies: "If you're talking about helping small to medium size nonprofits, I would say yes, it's difficult for them to look out beyond the work that they're doing because they have to scramble so much to raise money and they're also probably limited in their ability to provide the services that people really need. The answer, Nee thinks, might be for these organizations to step back and ask, "Are we actually doing the right thing, or is there a way that we can do what we're doing differently?"[7]

In other words, can we start a revolution?

NOW MORE THAN EVER

Our goal is for readers to take away at least one or two ideas that will help them and their organizations in this "stepping back." The development of new sources of capital and the changing mindsets of many social sector stakeholders are heralding significant opportunities for nonprofits to improve sustainability. They can't come soon enough. Continuing volatility in the global economy coupled with recent changes to U.S. tax legislation are amplifying the urgency with which organizations should consider new approaches to how they operate. In a recent blog post, we discussed the possibility that nonprofits may be facing the potential for a "perfect storm," given these warning signs:

- Until very recently, the U.S. stock market had been experiencing the longest period of expansion in its history. (By historical standards we're well overdue for a correction, and one may in fact be underway as you're reading this.) Remember 2008? According to the Russell Sage Foundation and the Stanford Center on Poverty and Inequality, "The Great Recession reduced total giving by 7.0% in 2008 and by another 6.2% in 2009. Although giving increased slightly in 2010 (1.3%) and 2011 (0.9%), it still remains well below the 2007 level."[8]

- According to the Council on Foundations, "The Tax Cuts and Jobs Act will result in a decrease of $16–$24 billion in charitable giving every year, significantly decreasing the philanthropic sector's ability to provide resources and services to people across the United States and abroad."[9] And a July 2019 IRS report estimated that "Taxpayers have itemized $54 billion less in charitable contributions so far this tax season compared to the previous year."[10]
- The Joint Committee on Taxation "estimates that after economic growth is taken into consideration, the GOP tax bill will add $1 trillion to the deficit over 10 years."[11]

So what, you say? Well, if your organization depends on government contracts, grants, or giving to fund operations, these signals should raise eyebrows. Indeed, they augur an environment in which the philanthropically minded may be feeling a little thriftier with their pennies (or cryptocurrency, depending on when you're reading this), and where a ballooning deficit may dramatically decrease government spending on social programs.

To make matters worse, this potential for fiscal headwinds coincides with the stark reality that, even after a decade of economic expansion, many nonprofits are still struggling with financial sustainability. Just how bad is it? "The Financial Health of the U.S. Nonprofit Sector"—a research report written by Oliver Wyman, SeaChange Capital Partners, and GuideStar in 2018—summarized the state of the social sector:

- 7–8 percent [of nonprofits] are technically insolvent, with liabilities exceeding assets
- 30 percent face potential liquidity issues with minimal cash reserves and/or short-term assets less than short-term liabilities
- 30 percent have lost money over the last three years
- 50 percent have less than one month of operating reserves[12]

Some might be inclined to dismiss the importance of these findings as reflective of the belief that there simply are too many small nonprofits—something we weigh in on. However, the study found, "Scale does not always translate into financial stability. Larger nonprofits, which are most often reliant on government funding or service fees, are not financially healthier than smaller ones." In fact, the report adds, "Median operating reserves are approximately one month for nonprofits of all sizes."

As any financial planner worth their salt will tell you, individuals and families should aim to have *at least six or more* months of expenses socked away in reserve. Why should nonprofits be any different? These are the organizations we rely on to make life better for all of us, including our most vulnerable. Apart from the social benefits they provide, nonprofit organizations represent a major portion of our domestic and world economies. As reported by the National Council of Nonprofits, citing data from the World Bank, "If the global nonprofit sector were a country, it would have the sixteenth largest economy in the world."[13] Stateside, the numbers are just as impressive. In 2015, according to the National Center for Charitable Statistics, the nonprofit sector added over $985 *billion* to the U.S. economy, a figure that represented 5.4 percent of the United States' GDP that year.[14]

In addition to the startling economic activity generated by these organizations—to say nothing of the countless taxpayer dollars they save through work governments can't or choose not to do—nonprofits also are one of the largest sources of employment across the country. According to estimates, the social sector represents the United States' third largest workforce (trailing only the retail and manufacturing industries), employing some 11.4 million people. Put into context, that's more than one of every ten American workers![15]

THE CASE FOR OPTIMISM

We'll close this introduction on a hopeful note. Whether or not a recession is imminent, and despite some of the sobering statistics offered earlier, these are heady times to be in the nonprofit world—whatever your role. We're certainly inspired and encouraged by what we've learned over the course of nearly two years of research for this book, particularly that more foundations are making multiyear grants and funding infrastructure and capacity building. Many of those same funders are providing grants to cover the costs of investigating and pursuing collaborations, mergers, and acquisitions. A new and promising capital marketplace, which bridges the gap between philanthropists eager to fund programs that create impact and nonprofits that can prove the efficacy of their programs, is rapidly developing. Real progress is being made to end the use of arbitrary measurements of nonprofits' effectiveness—such as the dreaded *overhead ratio*—which creates a culture of dishonesty in the sector and perpetuates a "starvation cycle" among many of its participants.[16]

Yes, changing stakeholder beliefs, new sources of capital, innovative business models, and new players in a nascent "fourth sector" are all converging to strengthen sustainability and mission impact across the nonprofit landscape. Heady times indeed. We'll detail these exciting developments and much more in the pages that follow. And our sincere hope is that what you'll learn will help those who choose to take that most important and worthwhile journey of living their lives in service to others.

1

FUNDING MODELS AND SUSTAINABILITY

"We Love Our Old Stuff. Does Anybody Else?"

Pop quiz: How do you move a 971-foot, 45,000-ton ship a third of the way across the country—specifically, from the northwest corner of the United States to the tip of Southern California? Perhaps hire a crew, fire up the boilers, and set a course down the Pacific coast? Well, that's a start. But it's going to take more than nautical know-how to get this hulking beast to its new home. It requires massive amounts of logistical coordination, political will, leadership—and, oh, money. Then there's the not insignificant question of what to do with the ship once it's safely in port. Will it just sit there and rust, steadily accumulating barnacles and serving no more noble a mission than to provide a way station for migratory seabirds? Or, might this particular ship be destined for a greater purpose?

Far from being simply a hypothetical exercise, this scenario illustrates precisely the problem a dedicated group of community leaders faced in bringing a fifty-year-old decommissioned aircraft carrier, *USS Midway*, to San Diego Bay and turning it into one of the top five museums in the United States, according to Trip Advisor.

As Scott McGaugh, *Midway*'s director of marketing and one of the museum's founding fathers puts it, "We did our research and found that there were more than one hundred historic ship museums in this country. None were profitable."[1]

Clearly, something wasn't working. The old business model had to be taken behind the barn and put down. To successfully turn the *USS Midway* Museum into the community flagship it is today, McGaugh and his team would have to try something radically different. Which is exactly what they did.

Even the words "business model," when applied to nonprofits, make some people cringe. The concept often conjures up imaginary atrocities, like a pitched battle being waged between capitalism and philanthropy, with nothing less than the soul of humanity at stake. But this doesn't need to be the case. Should nonprofits operate like businesses? Yes. Because they are not-for-profit *corporations*.

Apart from this justification, it's helpful to distinguish between a business model and a funding model. As William Foster, Peter Kim, and Barbara Christiansen of The Bridgespan Group, a nonprofit consulting organization, explain in their work, "10 Nonprofit Funding Models," "a business model incorporates choices about the cost structure and value proposition to the beneficiary. A nonprofit funding model, however, because the beneficiary is frequently not the customer, focuses only on the funding, not on the programs and services to the beneficiary."[2]

In other words, to be financially sustainable, nonprofit leaders must do more than run their businesses in such a way so expenses don't consistently exceed revenue. They also have to make choices about which funding levers to pull to nourish the programs they believe will add value for their stakeholders, and for society as a whole. After all, programs are the lifeblood of any organization.

As if all this wasn't hard enough, nonprofits paradoxically must contend with the persistent debate around whether they should actually earn a profit. You've likely heard the old saying, "nonprofit is a tax designation, not a business plan." Well, it's worth another look. Why is the not-for-profit sector the only industry that defines itself by what it *isn't*? More on this in chapter 2.

Call them what you will—budget surpluses or profits—they remain a divisive topic in the nonprofit world even today. Many of those we interviewed conveyed the sentiment that the more money a nonprofit can make, the greater the impact it can create for the world, while others argued that the pursuit of profits can dilute or even impede a nonprofit's focus on its mission. Those in between explain the controversy as one of degree and definition.

Jonathan Greenblatt, CEO of the Anti-Defamation League (ADL) and former director of the White House Office of Social Innovation, explained it this way: "Remember, part of the reason why nonprofits exist is to fill the gaps between business and government. So you don't want them necessarily running at the same pace as the private sector. We don't want them subject to the same lens as the financial markets."[3]

Likewise, Don Howard, CEO of the James Irvine Foundation and co-author of *The Nonprofit Starvation Cycle*, tried to break the stalemate when he told us, "I think it's somewhat of a false dichotomy. There are a lot of parts about the nonprofit culture and approach that are really important and a lot of elements of running a good business that are important for nonprofits. You've got to do both."[4]

In their widely read article, "Should Nonprofits Seek Profits?," William Foster and Jeffrey Bradach describe the differences among initiatives that seek profits for their own sake with those that are more mission-centered, advising that "executives of nonprofits must ask a critical question: 'Does this venture contribute to our organization's core mission?'"[5]

No matter where you happen to fall along this ideological spectrum, there's no denying the trend of nonprofits looking to create sources of earned income to enhance their financial sustainability. Today's term of art is "social enterprise," and it's all the rage.

Back onboard the USS *Midway*, an F-18 fighter jet has just taken off. The sleek gray fuselage streaks through an azure sky, and then destroys its target with a deft missile shot. Several more targets fall before the pilot completes his mission and lands safely back on deck. Moments later, this newly minted naval aviator emerges wearing a Top Gun T-shirt and an ear-to-ear smile. He's seven years old and has just taken his first ride in the *Midway* Museum's Flight Avionics attraction. A few feet away, two young friends climb into a cockpit and begin to perform somersaults, spins, and other aerial acrobatics in one of several Air Combat 360 flight simulators. The rides cost six to eight dollars per person, in addition to the cost of museum admission, and they're wildly popular among kids and adults alike.

"We love our 'old stuff,'" says the *Midway*'s CEO John P. "Mac" McLaughlin, describing our collective tendency to want to avoid disruption and embrace a business's entrenched way of doing things. When Mac, a retired U.S. Navy rear admiral, and McGaugh were working to bring the *Midway* to San Diego and turn it into a museum, they faced strident opposition from many who saw the addition of "kitschy" attractions like flight simulators as sullying the venerable history of the twentieth century's longest-serving aircraft carrier.

But Mac, McGaugh, and others felt differently. They knew in order for the *Midway* Museum to—ahem—stay afloat, it would need to attract patrons with exhibits and experiences people valued, and as important, were willing to pay for. To Mac and his team, it really didn't matter that some purists thought certain attractions amounted to over-commercializing the *Midway*. It was never about them. From day one, the *USS Midway* Museum was always laser-focused on serving a single group of people: the customers. Someone has to pay to keep the doors open and the lights on, and in Mac's view, that couldn't be achieved with traditional philanthropy alone.

The story of the *Midway*'s journey is remarkable. The ship was decommissioned in 1992 after a nearly fifty-year career serving in conflicts ranging from Vietnam to Operation Desert Storm. After twelve years, thirty-six separate permits, and an application to the Navy that ran in excess of three thousand pages,[6] a group of determined local leaders finally brought the ship to its prime waterfront home in San Diego Bay, where it opened as the *USS Midway* Museum in 2004. Today, the *Midway* welcomes over 1.4 million visitors annually and is consistently ranked among the top ten museums in the United States.

Even more remarkable is the planning that started from the very beginning, which resulted in a funding model that produces exceptional financial success to drive mission impact and sustainability. McGaugh, still with the museum nearly three decades later, tells the story:

> We always approached this idea of bringing an aircraft carrier to San Diego as a business, and [didn't get] overly enamored with the nobility of the vision. We talked about how we didn't want to get into the business of opening a museum and being held hostage to fundraising to make payroll, as so many nonprofits are. So we concentrated on *building the business in order to achieve the mission, not the other way around.*

Mired in the lengthy application and permitting process, McGaugh and his team had a lot of time to think. They tried to consider as many elements as possible, he said:

> Location. Do we have a unique product or service to sell? Pricing. Staffing. What's the unique story we have to tell? We never believed "if we can just get the doors open, people will come."[7]

While the early founders of the *Midway* Museum survived the long planning period with donations (and personal bank loans they backed up with their homes), the museum has been profitably self-sustaining since its opening. Annual revenues are in excess of $30 million, and yearly budget surpluses ($9 million in 2016) are more than adequate to sustain the museum's mission and even fund its own foundation. The latter uses its significant financial resources to support mission-centric activities, including the museum's education programs—which attract more than fifty thousand students each year (many on scholarships) and incorporate K–8 study trips focusing on science, technology, engineering, and math—as well as to provide financial backing for other nonprofits in the San Diego community.[8]

However, the *Midway*'s success is not simply due to its "business-to-support-mission" philosophy. There are two other equally important elements: extraordinary leadership and a supremely dedicated group of volunteers.

As Mac is quick to point out, "All we do as paid staff is develop programs, align resources, and create policies to support those programs." Then, he and his team get out of the way and let the real stars—the *Midway*'s eight hundred–plus docents and volunteers who contribute more than 250,000 hours annually—run their museum.

The possessive is important. *Their* museum. It's the World War II veteran telling firsthand tales of life aboard the *Midway* after the war. It's the former fighter pilot regaling visitors with harrowing accounts of landing his F-4 Phantom on the carrier deck at night in pitch-dark conditions, while standing next to an actual Phantom jet parked on that same flight deck. These are the people who bring *Midway*'s stories to life and create the visitor experience.

Philanthropist Malin Burnham, another of the *Midway*'s founders and its first board chair, frames leadership as stemming from two possible sources: power and persuasion. Power tends to flow from the top down, while persuasion can come from any level within an organization. The difference, as Burnham describes it, is an executive versus legislative model, and it has strong implications for an organization's success, especially in the nonprofit sector.[9]

"The problem with a lot of not-for-profits is they don't give the volunteers ownership of the organization," Mac said. "They allow the volunteers to assist the staff. We've completely reversed that engineering. We tell our volunteers: 'You are the *Midway*. You deliver the product to the customer.'"

That a retired U.S. Navy rear admiral would espouse this type of leadership philosophy may seem strange at first. After all, to paraphrase Gene Hackman's Captain Ramsey in the movie *Crimson Tide*, the military exists to preserve democracy—not to practice it. But Mac learned a valuable lesson from a navy captain while commanding a reservist training program. "Reservists," he said, "are volunteers—not like sailors on active duty who are getting paid to do the work they're told to do. The captain explained to me, 'Mac, if your reservists own the programs you're running, they will raise you to new heights.' And everywhere we went, we had a winning organization."[10]

Know your customers, and provide them the experience they want and will pay for. It's a business maxim as old as, well, business. The magic happens when you successfully infuse pride of ownership within *and outside of* your organization to all stakeholders—leaders, volunteers, and customers. This is what Foster, Kim, and Christiansen call the "Member Motivator" model—where "most of the benefits have a group orientation, creating an inherent collective community to tap into for fundraising."[11] Mac, McGaugh, and others figured this out early. In doing so, they gave a half-century-old warship a second act and brought a piece of living history to San Diego.

MORE CASE STUDIES

Putting the example of the *Midway*'s success behind us, let's examine the funding models of four other successful nonprofit organizations—of different sizes and different domains—and see where they share common elements that foster sustainability and mission impact.

AVID

As you read these words, there's a good chance a group of dedicated professionals are hard at work preparing nearly two million students in eight thousand schools across the United States and internationally for a life of achievement far beyond their wildest expectations. Welcome to AVID, a nonprofit organization founded in 1980 by an English teacher based on a simple core belief—that she could take students from disadvantaged areas of San Diego and teach them the skills they needed to attend college. Only there was one catch. These kids would have to ignore nearly everyone—parents, peers, and, yes, even other teachers—who imposed on them a tyranny of low expectations. AVID founder Mary Catherine Swanson's belief may have been simple, but its fulfillment wouldn't be easy. To succeed and really change their life circumstances, her kids were going to have to want it *for themselves*.

Against that backdrop, the acronym AVID—Advancement Via *Individual Determination*—starts to make a lot of sense. And with the benefit of hindsight, it may seem that AVID's own success—from a single classroom of thirty-two students to a gleaming new office building the organization purchased in 2017 for more than $30 million—was a fait accompli. The truth, however, is that it was much less certain.

There are countless organizations—public, for-profit, and nonprofit alike—engaged in the business of preparing students for success in higher education. Given all the competition and billions of dollars invested by so many, how could one small nonprofit thrive and grow to reach millions of students with 70,000 trained K–16 educators in forty-seven states? The answer is that Swanson and her team created a product that works with a funding model that produces strong financial results: AVID's annual revenues are almost $80 million, and it recently posted an operating surplus of $11 million.

Eighty-eight percent of AVID students apply for admission to a four-year college, with a 90 percent acceptance rate. Of those students who apply, 75 percent qualify for free or reduced-price lunch and 86 percent identify as a race or ethnicity underrepresented in higher education. In short, AVID doesn't cherry-pick students who appear destined for greatness to pad its stats.

Swanson hatched the idea that would eventually become AVID when she was head of the English department at Clairemont High

School in San Diego. While there, she learned her school would soon receive some five hundred new students bused in from a neighboring disadvantaged community as part of a court-ordered desegregation mandate.

"I needed to guide the department as to what we were going to do," Swanson told us, "so I visited the schools that were going to send us these students and found the conditions there to be abominable."

Swanson convinced her bosses to give her one elective class peri-od—what she called AVID—to help students who expressed a clear interest in wanting to succeed, but just didn't know how. She wrote a grant proposal and received $7,000, a relatively small amount even then, but one she stretched out over four years through savvy moves such as hiring former students as tutors. (She paid them minimum wage.)

At the end of those four years, Swanson's school scored thirty-five percentage points higher than any other district school in math, and forty-seven points higher in language arts—incredible improvements for any school, much less one with the third lowest income demograph-ics in the district. [12]

But despite its demonstrable success, AVID was a startup, relying on a great deal of hard work from educators donating their vacations in "summer institutes"—training classes for teachers from many locations held at a local university. Swanson recognized early on that the poten-tial demand for what AVID promised could only be met with a different model, one not wholly dependent on her local school system. In short, she needed a reliable revenue stream.

Now, decades later, Swanson said, "I had worked for a lot of years trying to get grants, but they're mercurial. You don't know if you're going to get them or not." She noted that funders, especially those in education, seem to always be looking for something shiny and new, and "the longer you are around, the harder grant funding is to get, because funders want the silver bullet, and the truth is there aren't any. It's all about hard work."

Seeking other sources of funding to keep AVID alive, Swanson wrote a business plan based on a fee-for-service to be paid for by money from the state of California. The state maintained a budget for profes-sional development, and Swanson thought AVID's mission aligned well. She was building a sustainable source of revenue analogous to those described by Foster and coauthor Gail Fine in "How Nonprofits Get Really Big." In that piece, the authors "identified three important practices common among nonprofits that succeeded in building large-scale funding models: (1) They developed funding in one concentrated source rather than across diverse sources; (2) They found a funding source that was a natural match to their mission and beneficiaries; and (3) they built a professional organization and structure around this funding model."[13]

Part of AVID's curriculum was designed to open up Advanced Placement–level classes for kids who otherwise wouldn't have had that opportunity, something California's lawmakers at the time felt was valuable and were willing to fund. But first the curriculum had to work, and Swanson had to prove it. She said matter-of-factly to her team, "If it's good enough, they'll pay for it and we'll make something, and if it's not good enough we're going to go under."[14]

Fortunately, AVID proved to be a runaway success, and results like the ones Swanson achieved with her first grant were replicated many times over. She knew the best business plan and funding model alone can't bring success. The product has to work, and Swanson was able to continually evidence AVID's impact. This, when combined with another potent key to success—effective storytelling—allowed the organization to scale.

"Our story was out there and the story was telling itself," Swanson said. "I didn't have to do much." Perhaps that's just modesty, but first-generation college-bound students extolling the virtues of your product while donning the colors and logos of their future alma maters certainly make compelling brand ambassadors.

Today, AVID doesn't rest on its laurels. Management consistently solicits feedback from participating school districts regarding what works and makes changes to its curricula as a result. In doing so, AVID creates a virtuous cycle of data collection, storytelling, and publicity—resulting in growth that gives its leaders the comfort to invest operational surpluses for the future. (Like the *Midway* Museum, AVID has a sizable endowment.)

"From the beginning I said, data are our friend in two ways," Swanson recalls. "If you're doing really well you can prove it. If you aren't, you know where you're making mistakes."[15]

Feeding San Diego

The first thing you notice while walking through Feeding San Diego's (FSD) spacious warehouse in the city's Mira Mesa community is, well, the lack of food. To be clear, it's there—stacked and sorted by type and destination. There's just not as much as you would reasonably expect to find in a space large enough to repair an average commercial airplane. But talk with Vince Hall, FSD's enthusiastic CEO, and he'll quickly tell you that's the point.

"We already have more than enough food to solve hunger in San Diego," Hall said. "Our job is to take all the food that is being thrown away and get it to families in need before it enters the waste stream." In other words, what Hall and his team at FSD are working to fix is really a distribution problem.

FSD provides *twenty-six million* meals each year to almost five hundred thousand people, at a cost of twenty-five cents each, with a full-time staff of only fifty people. And we think Wall Street knows how to leverage! How do they do it? They replaced an antiquated "charity" model with one in which the organization is well paid (both in donated food and cash) for services it provides to its charitable partners. And by this point you won't be surprised to learn that FSD, like the *Midway* Museum and AVID, consistently produces annual operating surpluses.

The old model we referred to is how many traditional food banks in the United States still operate. The federal government subsidizes food growers and purchasers and the excess is delivered to food banks, where it's stored until the food can be distributed to families in need, often onsite. The term food *bank* literally was born of its similarity to retail banks, only the former's "vaults" contain food rather than money.

Hall and others like him think that is inefficient. As he explained, "Currently, there's farmland in the U.S. the size of Pennsylvania that's devoted to food waste." Most of the crops that don't make it to food banks end up in landfills. As it decomposes, the organic waste releases methane, which leading scientists say is one of the causes of climate change. This, in turn, has the potential to create future problems for the agricultural sector.

By contrast, FSD practices what Hall calls "food rescue." The organization works with more than 150 food distribution partners in San Diego County, in addition to the one hundred plus sites such as churches and community centers it coordinates. The idea is to meet hungry people where *they* are—in their communities—rather than asking families to commute to a centralized warehouse to pick up food during business hours.

The idea is working. "There's now a waiting list of grocery stores hoping for charitable partners to participate in food rescue," Hall said. "They want to work with us because they are good corporate citizens and recognize we are running a massive food rescue operation for their locations. They perform a great service for which they receive an accelerated tax deduction."

When Hall was interviewing for the CEO position at FSD, he asked a question of the board. "Are you looking to hire a 'fix-it CEO' or a 'don't mess it up CEO'?" They said they wanted the former, and so Hall and his team went to work redefining what a modern food bank could be.

Food banks have been around for a long time, and many are a poster child for the old-fashioned, often harmful moniker of a "charity." As described by Feeding America, "The concept of food banking was developed in the 1960s. A retired businessman had been volunteering at a soup kitchen trying to find food to serve the hungry. One day, he met a desperate mother who regularly rummaged through grocery store garbage bins to find food for her children. She suggested that there should be a place where, instead of being thrown out, discarded food could be stored for people to pick up—similar to the way 'banks' store money for future use. With that, an industry was born."[16]

Under this model, donated food was sent to a centralized warehouse, where those in need could travel—if they had the means—to be fed. Later, food surpluses created by financial incentives directed at the nation's agriculture industry were routed to these warehouses, creating a revenue model that relied heavily on government funding to survive. Another issue stemmed from the fact that this surplus food often wasn't the nutritious, healthy, and fresh product people needed for proper nourishment.[17]

Reflecting on his early days, Hall remembered, "Every time I asked someone what we do, I was hit with this blizzard of acronyms. Every program had eight variations. It was a lot of complexity, and I was simply trying to ask, what is it that we do here? What are the basic elements of our business model that are highly differentiated from each other? With a lot of time spent on the whiteboard, I realized that we can achieve a much greater impact by not having food run through this centralized distribution point."[18]

Armed with knowledge from his epiphany, Hall and his team set their sights on overhauling FSD's business model. Today, 75 percent of the food FSD distributes never reaches a warehouse. Instead, it is rescued and served to individuals and families across San Diego through collaboration with a network of more than 150 partner organizations, including grocery stores, restaurants, farmers' markets, and coffeehouses. (Starbucks is one of FSD's largest partners.) Most of the product is sourced through "food recovery" agreements, wherein FSD coordinates food rescue operations for its retail partners. The prepackaged salad that's a day past its prime, but still safe and nutritious? FSD rescues it and makes sure it finds a second home in hungry bellies, rather than in a dumpster. As Hall put it, "Our mission isn't just to feed people, it's to nourish them." To that end, of the total amount of food FSD distributes each year, over half is produce.

Like AVID and other nonprofits we'll highlight, FSD has created a sustainable funding model by *monetizing its intellectual property*. In FSD's case, this is achieved through using its logistical know-how in return for more than $50 million of food and cash each year. Think of FSD as the FedEx of food rescue. As important, it's also part of a self-sustaining, mutually reinforcing ecosystem. FSD's distribution programs put the organization at the nexus of commerce (its vast network of retail food rescue providers) and consumers (the many thousands of food-insecure families throughout San Diego). FSD reinforces its value to both by helping the former meet its corporate social responsibility goals and earn valuable tax benefits (companies can write off the fair market value of the food they donate, and many share these savings with FSD), while assisting the latter in fulfilling a basic human need.

Our planet may win, too. In rescuing food and distributing it via partners, FSD not only reduces its carbon footprint by minimizing the need for large trucks to transport food to and from a central warehouse, but also keeps tons of organic waste out of landfills. Repositioning food that would otherwise be wasted cuts down on the amount of acreage, chemicals, and fertilizer used in the production of food that is ultimately thrown away—estimated to be some thirty million acres of farmland, four trillion gallons of water, eight hundred million pounds of pesticide, and two hundred billion pounds of fertilizer. [19]

Returning once again to Foster, Kim, and Christiansen, FSD employs what it calls the "Resource Recycler" model, whereby some nonprofits "have grown large by collecting in-kind donations from corporations and individuals, and then distributing these donated goods to needy recipients." [20]

As we've seen with our previous case studies, leadership, too, is a major factor in FSD's ability to continually develop and improve its business model. Hall and his board encourage new ideas and risk-taking. As he explained, "If you don't have a tolerance for failure, you're not going to have a tolerance for risk. And if you don't have a tolerance for risk, you're not going to have the capacity for innovation. So we try to celebrate failures." [21]

Hall compares the importance of FSD's work to a baseball diamond. "First base is hunger," he said. "Second base is housing. Third base is health care. Home base is everything else."

At this point, some of you skeptics may believe we chose the organizations in our case studies to make the point that size—budget and assets—is the sine qua non of effectiveness. We didn't, and it's not. True, the *Midway* Museum, AVID, and FSD all have eight-figure annual budgets, while the vast majority of nonprofit organizations in the United States are far smaller. (Nearly two-thirds have budgets under $1 million, according to GuideStar. [22]) And yes, growing income and assets beyond a mere subsistence level can allow an organization the flexibility to do many things, such as expand its programmatic reach. But too often, nonprofit leaders (and their donors) incorrectly equate size with effectiveness.

Trista Harris, former president of the Minnesota Council on Foundations and author of *FutureGood*, described the confusion as a misguided quest for growth and scalability. She said, "It's important for foundations and nonprofits to remember that bigger isn't always better. You have to be the right size and the right scale to do the work you're built to do." [23]

Jan Masaoka of CalNonprofits adds that a singular focus on growth can have the unintended consequence of commoditizing an otherwise unique idea or program. Masaoka uses the analogy of McDonald's. She acknowledges that by any objective metric, the restaurant chain has successfully scaled its operations. "But," she asks, "are McDonald's restaurants the nicest? Do they serve the best food?" In the nonprofit world, Masaoka believes, "Size isn't the right metric—impact is."[24]

Barrio Logan College Institute

With that thought in mind, let's now travel south of downtown San Diego to the city's Barrio Logan neighborhood. A slowly gentrifying mélange of low-slung art studios, leafy residential streets, and austere industrial warehouses, the community proudly displays its deep Latin roots. At its heart is Chicano Park, a nearly eight-acre gathering space punctuated by brightly colored murals celebrating the rich history of San Diego's Mexican American population.

It's here we find another nonprofit organization that's preparing young students for college—one much smaller in size than AVID, but with equally outstanding impact. With an annual budget under $2 million, the Barrio Logan College Institute (BLCI) is a power-puncher in a small package. Led until recently by its perpetually sunny CEO, Jose Cruz, BLCI takes disadvantaged kids—many of whom are the first in their families to move beyond high school—and turns them into successful college graduates.

"We serve a primarily Latino community near downtown San Diego that struggles with low educational attainment and high poverty rates," Cruz said, adding that he's keenly aware of the fact that a lack of educational opportunity is linked with higher rates of crime, low civic engagement, and poor health outcomes. As Cruz describes the Barrio Logan community, "Only 38 percent of adults have a high school diploma, 3 percent have a bachelor's degree, and the average household income for a family of four is $25,000."[25] And yet, despite these strong socioeconomic headwinds, *100 percent of the students who attend BLCI enter college*.

This outstanding achievement stems in large part from BLCI's rigorous after-school and summer programs—starting when students are in the third grade—which include tutoring, identity development, course election, and guidance through the often complex college-admission process. Tuition at BLCI is free, but parent engagement through regular volunteering is mandatory. The key, as Cruz sees it, is to cultivate positive reinforcing relationships among all stakeholders—students, families, corporate and education partners—who have a vested interest in BLCI's success. To that end, Cruz and his team work with participating companies and universities to regularly conduct efficacy studies on BLCI's programs, ensuring students are learning the skills they'll need to do well in school and in the workplace.

Like AVID, BLCI is successfully monetizing its intellectual property through government grants, revenue provided by colleges (including several of San Diego's major universities), fee-for-service contracts with local community organizations, private donations from individuals, as well as a large base of corporate supporters. And, as we've seen, the ability to prove impact is critical to BLCI's diverse funding model. "We haven't struggled too much with convincing people that this is a worthwhile investment," Cruz said. He cites BLCI's grant-approval rate of 37 percent—pretty good when compared to other organizations'. The success rate is "usually around the high 20s to 30 percent for most nonprofits," Cruz said. "We attribute the difference to the demonstrable effectiveness of our programs."[26]

Other organizations, too, have taken notice of BLCI's results. It recently completed a merger with Yalla, a similar nonprofit, but one that serves a different community with its own unique culture. As with any successful merger, the BLCI/Yalla marriage was based on a set of complementary visions and values: "gives and gets." Each organization contributes to and receives benefits from the other partner. In this case, BLCI gained access to Yalla's sports-oriented curriculum, and Yalla received BLCI's programing, strategy, and fundraising expertise.

Today, in an effort to further monetize its intellectual property, BLCI's leadership is investigating the possibility of developing a "consulting division," through which others would pay for access to its college preparation know-how, perhaps through such avenues as licensing its proven curricula. All of this is based on a three-part philosophy Cruz has steadfastly embraced since the very beginning. "It's the *Do It, Prove It, Share It* model," he said.[27]

DOES SIZE MATTER?

The issue of a nonprofit's size is a core concept of "Everyone a Changemaker," created by Ashoka, an organization whose mission is to identify and support leading social entrepreneurs across the globe. Ashoka's founder, Bill Drayton, explains the difference to us between the goals of a for-profit corporation and those of a nonprofit social entrepreneur by saying, "Every social entrepreneur is a mass recruiter of local Changemakers. He or she has no interest in capturing a market and then digging a moat. Instead, the goal is to change the world."[28] Drayton's point is that seemingly smaller nonprofits can create an outsize impact—by sharing their knowledge with others through selfless and effective collaboration.[29]

Phil Buchanan, CEO of the Center for Effective Philanthropy, echoes this sentiment. He believes nonprofits should simply abandon the idea of trying to be like their for-profit counterparts, such as McDonald's, which strive to build more and more outlets, to the point that, Buchanan says, "It becomes an end in and of itself, and the real question is, to what end?" Rather, he suggests, for many nonprofits, "the best way to achieve impact is to do their work quietly or step off the stage and let someone else have the spotlight."[30]

Buchanan provided an example of an organization he works with whose mission is to break the cycle of gang membership. Because gangs, by their nature, are rooted in a particular area, the organization's leadership sees no value in scaling its programs geographically. It recognizes its model wouldn't necessarily work in another city. Instead, it achieves impact in two ways: by going deeper in its own community—extending services not just to gang members, but also to members' families—and collaborating with complementary organizations through such initiatives as the establishment of teaching and learning centers where groups can share knowledge and best practices.

Buchanan's example makes the point that *scale* can describe many things other than growing to serve a larger population. It can also mean expanding within an existing constituency to provide additional services, or disseminating what's been learned to others so *they* can expand to other populations. In short, the reflexive belief that a nonprofit must grow if it has an effective program is often a fallacy. What makes an organization successful in one market might not translate well to another.

Stanford University professors Huggy Rao and Robert Sutton call this the "Buddhism-Catholicism continuum" in their book, *Scaling Up Excellence*.[31] They explain that business leaders must decide whether and how to scale a particular venture by first asking, "Is it more like Catholicism, where the aim is to replicate preordained design beliefs and practices? Or is it more like Buddhism, where an underlying mind-set guides why people do certain things—but the specifics of what they do can vary wildly from person to person and place to place?"[32]

As an example of this distinction, the authors cite the foray into China by two "do-it-yourself" home improvement giants, IKEA and Home Depot. Encouraged by its considerable success in the United States, Home Depot chose to take the more rigid "Catholic" approach. Its slogan at the time said it all—"You Can Do It. We Can Help."—and the company never deviated from this approach, even in a vastly different cultural market. But what executives failed to realize was that many Chinese eschewed the DIY model. They wanted more than just help with their home improvement projects; they wanted a company that would offer to do the work for them. This was the "Buddhist" strategy IKEA employed through such services as product delivery to customers' homes and a fee-based assembly option. In 2012, six years after Home Depot made a major acquisition of twelve stores in China, the company announced it would close its remaining outlets there. That same year, IKEA posted double-digit sales growth at its eleven stores in mainland China.[33]

Common Elements

Despite the uniqueness of their respective missions, the four nonprofit organizations we've held up as examples of how to operate in a smart, sustainable way share some common elements. The first is that they've all figured out how to get paid for activities that are part of their DNA. The *Midway* Museum solicits feedback from its customers. Nearly everyone at the museum prefers the word "guests," a term that invites comparisons to the hospitality industry, which Mac and his team firmly believe they're part of. The aim is to truly understand what customers value before creating experiences and activities they'll pay for. AVID rigorously collects data on student performance to quantify the benefit its curriculum provides, so school districts that financially support the organization can easily see the value of their investments. FSD uses its logistical know-how in creating a more efficient food distribution system to build a network of profitable partnerships. And BLCI cultivates diverse stakeholders—governments, colleges and universities, corporations, even other nonprofits—and aligns them behind a common goal of preparing students for higher education. Whether you call it social enterprise or something else, these organizations have *matched mission with money*, a critical step in ensuring long-term sustainability.

Intellectual Property

In a broad sense each organization has also successfully monetized their intellectual property (IP), which Merriam-Webster defines as "property (such as an idea, invention, or process) that derives from the work of the mind or intellect."[34] In our discussions with industry leaders across the country, we were surprised at how many believe most Main Street nonprofits don't really have much IP. Some felt the reason for this is since nonprofits exist to fill the voids left by government and the private sector, those with valuable IP would be replaced by for-profit businesses. However, this assumes organizations are limiting their definition of IP to more traditional interpretations, such as patents and trademarks. When we broaden it, as Merriam-Webster does, to include *ideas* and *processes*—anything an organization knows how to do that others value—we start to see numerous opportunities for nonprofits to get paid for their "secret sauce."

Still, some believe it would be unseemly or inappropriate for nonprofits to derive financial rewards in pursuit of their missions. After all, if your goal is to put an end to homelessness, and you've created a better way of doing it, why wouldn't you just give away that knowledge for free?

Then there are those like Bruce Hoyt, formerly senior vice president of Philanthropic and Impact Investing at Gary Community Investments, who take a more balanced view on the topic. Provided the activities are mission-focused, Hoyt believes, "There are so many nonprofits that are so experienced and have learned to do things a certain way to drive impact. They have brilliant leaders and they have a ton of intellectual property that is not being monetized directly."[35]

In fact, many organizations—such as those in health care and higher education—have made the practice of monetizing their intellectual property into a science. Patient revenue, tuition payments, and research grants—not to mention more esoteric funding mechanisms, such as technology-transfer arrangements—permeate these industries and allow most people to benefit from the monetization taking place within their organizations. Why should this phenomenon be limited to hospitals and universities? Is it because much of their IP lends itself to commercialization? Perhaps. Or, does management and staff participation in the rewards of monetization drive greater activity?

Let's be clear: We are not advocating that organizations in the citizen sector start up licensing departments to seek royalties in an attempt to pursue earned income ventures that, in the words of Foster, Kim, and Christiansen, account "for only a small share of funding in most nonprofit domains," and where "few of the ventures actually make money."[36] Indeed, to that latter point, John MacIntosh of SeaChange Capital Partners views social enterprises as potentially vulnerable to for-profit ventures that incorporate a social component into their business model. His belief is that it's hard for many nonprofits to compete when they're constrained by their mandate to provide a social benefit. While MacIntosh is less sanguine about social enterprise in general, he does feel most nonprofit organizations have some form of monetizable IP that could help them earn additional income at the margin even if it cannot support a stand-alone business.[37]

That's really the point. We're simply suggesting that more nonprofit organizations look at their unique know-how as a possible source of revenue, and more nonprofit funders respect the right of the organizations they support to monetize their intellectual property. The objective isn't purely to seek profits. Rather, it's to be, as Dace West, vice president of Community Impact at the Denver Foundation, described to us, "not a business, but a strongly functioning organization."[38]

Diversification

Another trait the organizations in our case studies share is the diversification of their sources of revenue. No funding model should put all its eggs in one basket, an aphorism that's particularly relevant today given the potential for combined negative impact from new tax legislation, an eventual economic recession, and reduced government funding. However, no matter what's happening with the economy or political landscape, income diversification can be key to long-term financial sustainability.

This view is shared by Carrie Hessler-Radelet, CEO of Project Concern International (PCI), who described her organization's strategy to diversify a revenue model that for most of the past half-century has been primarily funded by government grants. For more than fifty years, PCI has successfully pursued its mission, "to empower families and communities to enhance health, end hunger, and overcome hardship" in sixteen countries, serving over twelve million people last year alone. Thus, it's no stranger to the world of government-funded fee-for-service programs—nor is Hessler-Radelet, who prior to joining PCI in 2018 was director of the Peace Corps.

"International development nonprofits are facing a challenging environment, with significant fluctuations in policy priorities around the world," Hessler-Radelet explains. "We have seen proposals that go as far as a 32 percent decrease in the international affairs budget—a major source of our funding."[39] This reality has led Hessler-Radelet and her team to explore several exciting new efforts—including partnerships, collaborations, joint ventures, and other innovative and creative opportunities to help ensure PCI's sustainability. Facilitating all this, she hopes, will be steady, market-derived earned income that helps smooth out the lumpiness and uncertainty of government grants. It also makes budgeting easier and encourages risk-taking, as the organization knows it can count on a regular, consistent stream of income.

PCI is not alone in this. Many nonprofits doing wonderful work are subject to the vagaries of government funding. Even those that aren't still must contend with accelerating rates of change in our world. Remember the book *Future Shock*? Alvin Toffler's words seem especially prescient and definitely should be considered when thinking about diversification in funding models: "To survive . . . the individual must become infinitely more adaptable and capable than ever before. We must search out totally new ways to anchor ourselves, for all the old roots—religion, nation, community, family, or profession—are now shaking under the hurricane impact of the accelerative thrust. It is no longer resources that limit decisions, it is the decision that makes the resources."[40] And that was written in 1970!

FutureGood's Trista Harris brought these thoughts up-to-date when she discussed the potential impact of recent changes to the tax laws. "I think a lot of gifts that have gone to nonprofits in the past will actually go to more direct crowdfunding efforts," she predicts. Indeed, Harris says, we've already begun to see the democratization of philanthropy take shape, as such sites as GoFundMe are being used in lieu of insurance to defray a significant percentage of individuals' health care expenses. This model now competes with traditional nonprofits for scarce funding dollars. Harris continues by saying, "I think we're hitting a time of exponential change, and that's happening for a lot of reasons, one of which is tremendous growth in technology. As a result, I think the time of a five-year strategic plan for a nonprofit organization is completely dead. Instead, you need to have a flexible strategic framework, and consistently realign your strategy to help you get to your audacious goals."[41]

Diversification can take many forms, and seeking alternative funding streams in a random or haphazard fashion can be fraught with negative consequences. Much has already been written on the perils of nonprofits chasing the holy grail of unrestricted earned income. For example, Foster, Kim, and Christiansen argue that pursuing earned-income ventures that are not "mission-centered . . . jeopardizes those who benefit from their programs . . . and harms society itself, which depends for its well-being on a vibrant and mission-driven nonprofit sector."[42]

Even if they are mission-aligned, some earned-income initiatives can still be harmful if they drain too much of an organization's valuable—and finite—resources. In making this determination, nonprofit leadership should always consider the opportunity costs of not deploying these resources, including their staff's time, toward other endeavors. Many organizations find that an earned-income venture, however appealing it may initially appear, would actually operate at a net loss when these opportunity costs are taken into consideration. One particular organization we know of used to boast about the strength and sustainability of its funding model because it comprised five diverse (though not really mission-related) sources of income—all from earned revenue. On the surface, each seemed to generate positive cash flow. However, upon closer inspection, several of these disparate initiatives were really siphoning money and effort away from the organization's core activities—and exhausting the staff! This created high turnover, causing leadership to further lose focus as it scrambled to fill open positions. Given that most nonprofits, including this one, spend the majority of their budgets on personnel costs, high levels of staff turnover can truly cause problems.

Is our example an isolated incident? Well, as Foster and Bradach found in their research, "when we examined how nonprofits evaluate possible ventures, we discovered a pattern of unwarranted optimism. The potential financial returns are often exaggerated. Most important, commercial ventures can distract nonprofits' managers from their core social missions and, in some cases, even subvert those missions."[43]

Further underscoring this point is "A National Imperative: Joining Forces to Strengthen Human Services in America," a comprehensive report on the financial health of community-based organizations (CBOs) partially funded by the Ballmer Group and the Kresge Foundation. The authors, from Oliver Wyman and SeaChange Capital Partners, list understanding the true costs of activities as one of five significant "North Star" initiatives for the sector. They say "it is critical that financial expertise enable CBOs to account for and understand the full costs of delivering services, so that they can position themselves for financial success."[44]

Unfortunately, many Main Street nonprofits often are too busy on what Buchanan calls "the hamster wheel"—trying just to keep their organizations afloat with limited resources—to take a hard look at determining the full costs of diversification activities. Most basic bookkeeping software does a fair job of allocating direct costs to programs, but to truly account for all the resources that go into a certain endeavor, more sophisticated systems and a sharply analytical eye are required. As we discuss in this book, there are many technology and human capital resources available to nonprofits of all sizes, some at little or no cost, to assist them with understanding and monitoring the full costs of their funding models.

Once nonprofit leaders put their activities under the full-cost accounting microscope, they might find a few sacred cows (looking at you, annual golf outing) that need to be euthanized. That's okay. No, that's great. Walk away from events that sap too much time and energy from staff. Just say "no" ("thank you") to grants and funders that don't include money to cover the total cost—including *overhead*—of delivering programs in their contracts. Sure, there may be certain exceptions, such as an event or program that raises brand awareness of an organization and thereby enhances other surplus-generating components of its funding model. But even these should be scrutinized. The fact is every business—nonprofit, for-profit, or otherwise—has limited time, talent, and treasure, so these resources need to be used wisely.

It's not enough just to operate profitable programs. Well-run organizations also have to be smart about what they do with their excess cash. Antony Bugg-Levine is CEO of Nonprofit Finance Fund, a community development financial institution (CDFI) that provides consulting and financing to nonprofits and their funders. As he explains, "It's common practice to say to nonprofit leaders, 'you should be budgeting to surpluses.' We would argue that it's really important that they pay attention to liquidity. If you truly want to be an organization that over time can deliver greater results, you've got to pay attention to your balance sheet as well. And so we do a lot of work encouraging nonprofits and their funders to understand when we say full costs, it's not just the marginal cost of delivering on the program, it's recognizing the need to build reserves over time. It is often incredibly difficult for nonprofits to build reserves and secure flexible funds."[45] In Bugg-Levine's view, generating unrestricted reserves is one of the best ways nonprofits can facilitate long-term investment and encourage risk-taking activities like program expansion or M&A—activities that can lead to exponential growth in impact.

But how, exactly, should nonprofits diversify their funding models to increase the likelihood of being able to generate reserves? Should they start a social enterprise to add a source of unrestricted revenue? Or concentrate on an existing core activity, but "go deep" in building relationships with donors/grantors who are interested in that cause? The answer, of course, is "it depends." Clearly, organizational size is a consideration given the demands that maintaining multiple mission-aligned services can place on nonprofits' already stretched financial and human resources. As Eric Nee, of the *Stanford Social Innovation Review*—a leading source of information on a wide range of topics affecting the nonprofit and social sectors—told us, "[Often nonprofits] have never stepped back to really think hard about what the best funding model is given their missions. There is a common belief that the more revenue streams you get the better you will be, because if you lose one of them the others will make up for it. Sometimes that may be true, but often that isn't an excuse not to fully understand where your natural funding sources are and to double down on those."[46]

Nee also stressed the need for more cross-sector collaboration to achieve better social impact. The private, nonprofit, and government sectors all have important roles to play in addressing complex issues, and to successfully do so they need to work together to create virtuous ecosystems.

In *How Nonprofits Get Really Big*, Foster and Fine report that in their study of 144 nonprofits (excluding those in higher education and hospitals) that reached $50 million in revenues, "Most of the organizations did so by concentrating on one type of funding source, not by diversifying across several sources of funding."[47] But this concentration can be dangerous, especially for Main Street nonprofits. (The study sample represented "less than one-tenth of 1 percent of the nonprofits founded since 1970."[48]) Remember PCI? Its focus on government grants was quite successful for fifty years, until changes in the government's funding priorities made efforts to diversify the organization's revenue a necessity.

Indeed, as Foster and Fine point out in their study, although most of the organizations they surveyed "relied on a single source for the bulk of their funding, they did not rely on a single payer. Organizations achieved diversification and mitigated their funding risk by securing multiple payers of the same type to support their work. For example, not just government funding but also state government funding; not just individual donations but also small individual donations; and not just corporate donations but also in-kind corporate donations."

In his conversation with us, Foster stressed that, above all, nonprofits must really work to know themselves and then align their revenue-generating activities with where they're likeliest to get sustainable funding. As examples, he cites the tendency for state and local governments to fund human services organizations, while nonprofits with a focus on the environment are more apt to secure funding from like-minded individuals. The key, Foster says, is to match your mission with complementary funding sources, and then make sure you have the operational capacity to achieve that funding.

The good news is that today multiple large funders are giving unrestricted money to nonprofits for capacity building. This is a very welcome development to many in the sector who believe, as Foster does, that donor-imposed restrictions—either temporary or permanent—can serve as an implicit tax on the donations. Ultimately, though, growth and scale shouldn't be the goal nonprofit leaders are striving for. Doing great work should be. As Foster stressed to us, you can be sustainable, impactful, and small![49]

LEGAL STRUCTURES

No discussion of planning and executing a business model would be complete without first pondering a fundamental question—one Nee at the *Stanford Social Innovation Review* raised during our interview: Should you even be a nonprofit? "Sometimes," he said, "what you're trying to accomplish actually lends itself better to being a for-profit or a hybrid corporation." What organizations really should ask themselves, Nee argues, is "what is the right legal structure for what we want to do?"[50]

Given the phenomenal rise of many hybrid structures, such as Certified B Corporations, Benefit Corporations, and Flexible Purpose Corporations, as well as unprecedented interest in the myriad forms of social entrepreneurship, it's useful to examine how the use of different corporate entities may improve organizational sustainability and mission impact. Would, for example, creating a for-profit subsidiary facilitate new sources of capital, partnerships, or collaborations?

In addition, impact investing—which we introduce in the next chapter: "Wall Street for the Third Sector"—has the potential to unleash huge amounts of fresh capital to the citizen sector—from foundations, philanthropists, and individuals with investments in traditional securities that want to earn financial and social returns on their money. As a result, nonprofits may be able to structure some of their activities in for-profit or hybrid entities to increase the availability of capital and other resources to support their missions.

Gary Community Investments (GCI), an organization that brings together business and philanthropy to serve Colorado's low-income children and their families, illustrates this relatively new way of thinking. GCI combines a Certified B Corporation with a private foundation, and recently took the further step of changing its legal status to become a Public Benefit Corporation. Why? One reason is that this structure provides GCI tremendous flexibility and access to a spectrum of resources in pursuit of its mission. As Bruce Hoyt explained, "We're very unique in a number of ways. Not only coupling the B Corporation with the foundation, but also with an organization that is intentionally sunsetting, combines to create the power in our model. [GCI founder Stan Gary] did this so that we could play across the capital continuum—we make grants, we can make program-related investments, mission-related investments, for-profit investments with a social impact, and credit enhancement guarantees. We can really now think of each investment we make and decide what form of capital can maximize the impact to the institution we're investing in over the long run."[51]

PCI, too, is considering multiple corporate structures as Hessler-Radelet and her team pursue options for revenue diversification. "We are changing technically everything about the way we work. Right now we're a 501(c) that is structured in a way which allows us to complete government cooperative agreements," she explained. Yet, the rules vary by country, and given the international nature of PCI's operations, a one-size-fits-all corporate structure makes it difficult for the organization to enter into productive partnerships overseas. "So," she continued, "we are diversifying our corporate structure into separate nonprofits to perform other kinds of work. We're also considering other examples of social enterprise, such as incubating PCI Social Ventures, which will be a for-profit."[52]

We recognize we've laid a lot on you in this chapter. At this point, you'd certainly be justified in asking, "Okay, so what's the bottom line?" Well, here you go: Sustainability starts with a diversified, mission-aligned funding model that's based on the full cost of services, creates reserves, supports risk-taking, and is dynamic enough to allow for flexibility in our ever-changing world. If that's too complicated, just remember the "three Ms," as outlined to us by Bridgespan's Foster. In the end, he said, there are only three pathways to long-term sustainability: the marketplace, the mission, and the mandate. The first involves selling things, social enterprise, for example. The second means your mission must be embraced by enough people who will give to the cause. And the third speaks to an area where the government has a clear mandate—as with charter schools—to support the organization's activities.

2

WALL STREET FOR THE THIRD SECTOR

Financing Philanthropy

Mention Wall Street and some people reflexively conjure up Gordon Gekko's power-suited, pomade-coiffured visage smugly spouting "Greed is good."[1] And to be fair, many latter-day Gekkos and his ilk haven't done much to disabuse skeptics on Main Street of this notion. From the 2008 financial crisis that gave rise to the worst economic downturn since the Great Depression to today's widening wealth gap and income inequality, the image of rapacious corporate machines squeezing every last drop of productivity from the working class isn't entirely undeserved. As of this writing, businesses—especially the largest multinational corporations—are enjoying record profits. Meanwhile, according to a 2018 Pew Research Center article, "today's real average wage (that is, the wage after accounting for inflation) has about the same purchasing power it did 40 years ago. And what wage gains there have been have mostly flowed to the highest-paid tier of workers."[2]

So the concern is certainly justified. But too often the well-documented excesses of the financial sector overshadow the importance of what, at its core, Wall Street was designed to do. Specifically, its focus is on providing access to efficient capital markets that enable the creation of vibrant economies and, ultimately, wealth. Wealth, in turn, supports social benefits.

At least it should. Yet a common refrain is that the inability of the nonprofit sector to access capital markets for loans or money for long-term investments is a major impediment to organizations achieving sustainability. As with most generalizations, however, this view obscures some of the reality of what's actually happening. For example, many nonprofits regularly issue debt obligations to help fund their operations and pay for assets, such as equipment or real estate. Much of this debt comes in the form of tax-exempt bonds that are issued through intermediaries, called "conduits." And lest anyone think tools like these are beyond the pale for Main Street organizations, "pretty much any nonprofit has the legal authority to borrow in the tax-exempt bond market,"[3] according to a guide published by the nonprofit advocacy agency CalNonprofits. Additionally, as we've discussed, some nonprofit organizations participate in the capital markets through for-profit subsidiaries and other hybrid entities.

Still, the fact remains that the vast majority of social sector organizations—*public benefit corporations*—cannot raise permanent capital by selling equity securities in public or private markets. And, given the often episodic and fragile nature of their cash flow, many are unable to meet lenders' underwriting standards required to borrow money. The confluence of these two realities can leave nonprofits at a distinct disadvantage relative to their for-profit counterparts. As author Terry Lane points out, "There are a few states that let nonprofits sell shares of stock that entitle the owner to some management control of the nonprofit, but unlike corporate stock, these shares don't include dividend rights or the ability to share in profits."[4]

In his widely read (and somewhat controversial) book, *Uncharitable*, Dan Pallotta observes, "With no mechanism (in the social sector) for offering a return on investment capital, all the investment capital goes into the for-profit sector." Further, Pallotta asks, "What would happen if we were to open a market for social change that would provide a *financial* return on investment to this market for financial investors?"[5] That was written in 2008. Fast forward more than a decade, and just such a market is developing—with increasing momentum—driven by investors seeking both a financial and social return on their money. Although still relatively small when compared with all charitable giving in the United States (estimated at over $410 billion in 2017 by Giving USA[6]), this market—what we'll call Wall Street for the social sector—is opening doors to entirely novel sources of capital for nonprofit organizations. As noted in the *New York Times* when announcing the recent creation of one such financial instrument—an Impact Security—"By some estimates, if just 1 percent of the money in the portfolios of wealthy individuals in the United States was directed to nonprofits through new financial instruments . . . the nonprofit world would be sitting on $1 trillion."[7] It's hard to overstate the potential benefits a new generation of socially conscious investors could bring to the sector. But for this to take place, everyone first has to make sense of a bafflingly complex alphabet soup of financial jargon.

SRI, MRI, AND PRI (OH MY!)

In our many discussions with leaders from across the nonprofit and financial sectors, it quickly became apparent that these new and exciting products and services suffer from inexact, confusing, and overlapping terminology. As Eric Nee of the *Stanford Social Innovation Review* told us, "I read a story the other day that stated that something like one-third of all investing can now be lumped under the terms 'social investing' or 'impact investing.'"[8] He went on to explain that the article included in its broad definition of impact investing, individuals and organizations investing with a social conscience, such as avoiding investments in tobacco or oil companies, as well as the myriad Corporate Social Responsibility (CSR) activities performed by for-profits and hybrid organizations (such as B Corps). Even municipal bonds were included. Summarizing Nee's point, overgeneralization does nothing to aid in people's understanding.

Even if the impact investing universe is contracted to include only investments made by foundations and philanthropists directly to nonprofits, there still are no universally recognized definitions. This is confusing to people in the nonprofit sector as well as to those working outside it, and has the potential to create uninformed opinions on the part of both funders and recipients, such as, "We don't fit that mold."

Let's try to cut through the haze. Many people with means would be pleased to devote a portion of their investment portfolio to investments that generate a financial return—even if at below-market rates—and support social causes they care about. This is the crux of what's known as *socially responsible investing* (SRI), and it has taken off. By some estimates, in early 2016 "socially responsible assets under management reached $8.72 trillion in the US and $23 trillion globally."[9] These figures equate to roughly twenty cents of every dollar under professional management and include "conventional" investments like stocks and bonds, which investors may choose because a particular company represents a cause they believe in. Someone who's passionate about the development of green energy technologies, for example, might choose to buy stock in SunPower, a company that designs and manufactures solar electric systems. The good news is people no longer have to sacrifice their portfolio's performance to invest with their conscience. Thanks to Big Data and the creation of new securities, the universe of socially responsible investment options is larger than ever. Today, nearly anyone can construct a well-diversified portfolio that hits their investment return targets and allows them to sleep at night. And that's a very positive development, especially among those in the millennial generation who, as countless studies have cited, increasingly demand more values-based investment options. In fact, according to a report published by Ernst & Young, "Millennial investors are nearly twice as likely to invest in companies or funds that target specific social or environmental outcomes."[10]

Now let's narrow our funnel a bit to what's called *impact investing*. According to the Global Impact Investing Network (GIIN), a nonprofit membership-based knowledge exchange, "Impact investments are investments made with the intention to generate positive, measurable social and environmental impact alongside a financial return."[11] If socially responsible investors are the qualitative, starry-eyed poets, impact investors are their quantitative, data-driven cousins. They want to see the *specific, measurable* impact of their investments. For example, private and community foundations may make impact investments in the form of loans or grants to an organization to further its specific mission (commonly known as *mission-related investments*, or MRI) or fund a particular program (*program-related investments*, or PRI) to achieve a desired (and measurable!) outcome. These investments can be made at or below market rates, with funds from the foundations' grant budgets or endowments, and generally include mechanisms to quantify their social results. Although some foundations have been making impact-type investments for many years, it's only been in the past decade or so that the term impact investing has officially entered the lexicon. Said to have been coined at the Rockefeller Foundation's Bellagio Center in

2007, the moniker has given rise to "an industry that started with a few forward-thinking risk takers, then grew to attract mainstream investors and philanthropists."[12]

Just how big is this industry now? In its 2018 Annual Impact Investor Survey, the GIIN reported that, "229 of the world's leading impact investing organizations, including: fund managers, banks, foundations, development finance institutions, pension funds, insurance companies, and family offices . . . collectively manage over $228 billion in impact investing assets, a figure which serves as the latest best-available 'floor' for the size of the impact investing market."[13] And the cumulative effect of all this capital is likely much larger still. According to Bridgespan's William Foster, "impact investing brings a level of discipline and focus to an organization's underlying economic model. It shines a light on impact, and by doing so creates the potential to attract other sources of funding to specific programs that are shown to be effective."[14] Wall Street has a term for this too: *leverage*.

To really understand the significance of impact investing, let's start by examining how traditional foundations have tended to operate in the past. Historically, foundations "warehouse" their capital by putting all their investible assets into conventional investments—think stocks, bonds, and cash—to earn a targeted rate of return. They then distribute at least 5 percent (the legal minimum required) of the assets each year—mostly in the form of grants—to fund nonprofits' missions and programs. If annual earnings on a foundation's investment portfolio averaged 7 percent, management could pay out the required 5 percent in distributions while still having 2 percent left over to cover expenses and leaving the remaining investments (called the *corpus*) intact to ensure its long-term sustainability. According to Candid (formerly Foundation Center and GuideStar), "about 86,000 charitable foundations hold more than $890 billion in assets. In 2015, they gave out a total of $62.8 billion, averaging 7 percent across the industry. What to do with the rest of that money—$827.3 billion—has presented both problems and opportunities."[15]

The opportunities center on the potential to unleash—and leverage—this huge amount of capital to create social good, while the problems primarily involve roadblocks put up by both the Internal Revenue Service (IRS) and well-entrenched investment dogma. The latter refers to a long-standing belief—supported until very recently by IRS regulations—that using a charitable foundation's corpus to make investments that by their nature may entail greater risk and lesser returns should be anathema to those who espouse good fiscal stewardship. Fortunately, these so-called prudent-man restrictions were eased by new guidelines issued by the IRS in late 2015, which provide that "when deciding how to invest the foundation's assets, a foundation manager can factor in how the anticipated charitable outcomes from the investment might further the foundation's mission in addition to the financial returns that are typically considered."[16]

Still, some hardliners maintain that mixing mission objectives with investment policies is not judicious, arguing that conventional investment practices can "do better" over time. But let's take another look at this concept. First, historical financial returns from "conventional" stocks and bonds are no guarantee of future performance. Markets run on demand and supply, and we—along with others—would maintain that portfolios screened for SRI criteria may outperform "conventional" investments in the future—because of greater demand coupled with liquidation of investments that don't pass the screens. As this book went to press, Laurence D. Fink, founder and CEO of BlackRock—the world's largest investment manager, with some $7 trillion in investments—announced the firm "would make investment decisions with environmental sustainability as a core goal . . . and would begin to exit certain investments that present a high sustainability-related risk, such as those in coal producers."[17] Apart from the economics, directors/trustees of nonprofits have a duty of obedience to the mission: "faithfulness to the organization's charitable purposes and goals." For example, if a nonprofit's mission is to save the rainforest, shouldn't the portfolio be screened to exclude oil companies and those that contribute to global warming? If not, are the directors/trustees violating their duty?

The recent proliferation of socially conscious investing options has made the historical tradeoff between "doing well" and "doing good" largely an anachronism. What's more, the significant growth in impact investing is due to a realization on the part of many philanthropists that today's intractable social problems require bigger solutions—and more money. As the Heron Foundation explained in 2012, "The urgency and size of the problems we face require that we work differently. Everything at our disposal is now a mission-critical resource. Philanthropy's financial tool kit should include every investment instrument, all asset classes, and all enterprise types."[18] Backing up this rhetoric with action, in late December 2016 the Heron Foundation achieved its goal of investing 100 percent of its endowment—some $270 million—as well as other forms of capital in support of its mission.

The use of the phrase "all enterprise types" underscores a key point—specifically, the conviction that mission results can be enhanced by investing assets not only in the social sector, but also in the full range of legal entities, including socially minded for-profits, hybrid organizations, and special-purpose entities, such as Limited Liability Corporations (LLCs). When billionaire Facebook founder Mark Zuckerberg and his wife, Dr. Priscilla Chan, established the Chan Zuckerberg Initiative in 2015 to advance the couple's philanthropic priorities, they registered the corporation as an LLC rather than as a more traditional foundation, à la Bill and Melinda Gates. Vehicles like LLCs offer greater control over assets relative to other legal structures, a feature valued by many younger philanthropists who, unlike the Carnegies and Rockefellers of yesteryear, likely will be steering their fortunes for good across many decades. As the *New York Times* reported, "The L.L.C. structure gives Mr. Zuckerberg and Dr. Chan more flexibility in investing in for-profit social enterprises and also supporting political causes, allowing them a freer hand. That is because an L.L.C. has fewer rules than a traditional foundation, such as the 5 percent requirement."[19]

Increasingly, foundations are using more than just grant money to provide financial support to organizations. Many are offering credit enhancements, loan and performance guarantees, and other similar arrangements that capitalize on the relative strength of their balance sheets without the need to expend assets. If, for example, a nonprofit isn't able to qualify for a loan on its own, a foundation could step in and offer to guaranty the loan, thereby giving the nonprofit access to needed funds without the foundation having to cut a check.

In recent years, numerous large foundations have announced the dedication of major portions of their grant budgets or endowments to impact investing. These include such household names as the Ford Foundation ($1 billion), the Bill and Melinda Gates Foundation ($1.5 billion), and the John D. and Catherine T. MacArthur Foundation, which announced, "In addition to our traditional grantmaking of about $250 million each year, we have expanded our impact investing strategy, working in new ways and tapping a dedicated pool of $500 million to help make the global impact investment marketplace more inclusive, efficient, and effective."[20] And this trend isn't limited to mega institutions.

In 2017, the Rhode Island Foundation (RIF) created an impact investing fund with a promise to allocate 5 percent of its endowment assets to community-based projects. The fund will make investments ranging from $200,000 to $2 million to organizations working within RIF's strategic focus—education, healthy living, and economic security—including nonprofits, for-profits, and hybrids. The aim of the fund is to earn both a financial and measurable social return. Two of the foundation's early investments are worth highlighting in view of their structures, sizes, and relatively simple methodologies used to measure impact.

The first involved purchasing $300,000 of "preferred stock" in a new eight-thousand-square-foot community-owned grocery store located in a federally recognized inner city "food desert," Urban Greens. As Jessica David, RIF's executive vice president of strategy and community investments explained to us, structuring the investment as preferred stock enabled the store to issue a challenge to other investors to match RIF's purchase, which David says they did. By contributing "equity" rather than debt, the "preferred stock" model also increases an organization's net assets, allowing it to leverage its balance sheet to generate access to future capital. David adds that the impact criteria were centered on customized, mutually agreed-upon metrics, such as co-op membership, sales of food to low-income customers under the supplemental nutrition assistance program (SNAP), and hiring employees from the local community.[21]

RIF's second impact investment was a $1 million loan to help a local nonprofit radio station, Rhode Island Public Radio, purchase and relocate broadcasting transmitters that would increase the station's potential audience. Ultimately, the station would collect $6 million during a capital campaign to fund the project, but it needed money in the interim. David says that creating the impact metrics was informed by the station's response to her team asking why it wanted the equipment and how would it further the station's mission. The station's answers to those questions yielded dual requirements that it report on its expanded listenership and the resulting increase in financial support. "We try to be clear and upfront with the client as to what they are aiming for and develop the metrics they can report to us," David said.[22]

Stories like these pop up all over the place. During the course of our research, every community foundation we spoke with told us it has committed at least a portion of its assets to impact investments or was actively planning to launch a dedicated impact *donor-advised fund*.

A *what*? Sorry, we fell into the jargon trap again. Let's back up. A donor-advised fund, or DAF, is an account a donor sets up at a public charity—such as a foundation—that allows the donor to receive an up-front tax deduction on the amount given to the DAF, without having to immediately direct the funds to a beneficiary. Technically, the charity that sets up the DAF has control of the assets in it and has the legal say as to where the money is distributed. In reality, however, grants from DAFs are typically made in accordance with the original donor's wishes. To illustrate, imagine you're a wealthy individual who wants to reduce the taxable value of your estate, but you don't yet know which nonprofit (or nonprofits) you would like to receive your charitable gift(s). Or you have an organization in mind, but you just don't want to give it all the money at once; you'd rather direct smaller gifts to it over time. A DAF can help with this.

The use of—and amount of funding directed to—DAFs has grown considerably in recent years. According to the Institute for Policy Studies, DAFs now represent "the fastest-growing recipients of charitable giving in the U.S.," with donations increasing "from just under $14 billion in 2012 to $23 billion in 2016—growth of 66% over five years."[23] But this growth has also given rise to some criticism. Since DAFs are not required to distribute their funds within a certain time period (not even the 5 percent minimum required of foundations' assets), some have claimed this results in "warehousing wealth"—allowing donors to receive a tax deduction on funds that remain undistributed, sometimes for many years. Also, though DAFs are primarily held at community foundations, they are increasingly being sponsored by banks, investment firms, and other Wall Street financial institutions (known as "FIDAFs" when held by these companies). For comparison, community foundations held about $30 billion in assets in 2016 versus roughly $45 billion kept at national organizations, mostly FIDAFs. This causes concern among some who believe community foundations can't effectively compete with the low fees offered by many FIDAFs. Thus, they fear future charitable dollars will gravitate toward the predacious maw of "Big Finance" at the expense of local community foundations that are meant to provide deep personalized services in assisting donors with sourcing and qualifying grant recipients. Critics further argue that FIDAFs offer little in the way of such services and suggest they may even have a vested interest in encouraging low payout rates to increase the value of their assets under management.

What does this have to do with impact investing? For one, the crescendo of criticism likely will result in reforms to the administration of DAFs. Indeed, proposed regulations to mandate minimum payout rates already are afoot. If passed, this would almost certainly add to the amount of money available for funding impact investing initiatives. Equally important is the potential effect of increased scrutiny on where DAFs are established and held. The selection, planning, and monitoring of new funding vehicles such as impact investments presents a tremendous opportunity for community foundations to use their local knowledge and expertise to compete with FIDAFs.

As Dace West of the Denver Foundation explained, "Impact investing serves as a competitive advantage for community foundations over [brokers and other financial services firms] that aren't on the ground in local communities."[24] West and her team at the Denver Foundation are currently working to launch a $3 million pooled impact fund that will allow donors to direct their DAFs to support impact investments in affordable housing and small businesses in the Denver area.

The potential for impact investing to continue growing is huge, if only because there is a surfeit of would-be investors lining up to deploy their dollars for the greater good. No less a voice than Larry Kramer, president of the William and Flora Hewlett Foundation (and himself *not* a fan of foundations using their endowments for impact investments), predicts as much. "There is considerably more money looking for concessionary (below market) impact investment than there are such investments,"[25] he said. Whether or not these investments deliver "concessionary" rates of return remains to be seen. What's clear, however, is that the universe of impact investment options is expanding. Let's look closer at some of what's driving this change.

PAY FOR SUCCESS

There are several interpretations of the concept known as pay for success (PFS), but they all center on "an approach to contracting that ties payment for service delivery to the achievement of measurable outcomes."[26] In these arrangements, social benefit programs are funded by private investors, who bear the risk that their investments may or may not yield certain agreed-upon performance benchmarks. If they do, the investors are repaid (with a return on their money) by the contracting party, typically a government agency. If the benchmarks aren't hit, investors may receive only part of their money back—or none at all. Hey, all investment carries risk. Yet, as the U.S. Federal Reserve Bank reports, "Undercapitalization of nonprofit organizations and years of seemingly stagnant results in addressing certain social problems have led many to hope that [pay for success financing] will bring solutions in the form of new capital to support program delivery, improved accountability, and increased rigor in performance measurement."[27]

The concept of paying nonprofits for providing services based on the achievement of measurable outcomes isn't all that new. The first PFS project began in the United Kingdom in 2010, and the United States followed several years later with the launch of its first deal. Stateside, however, the prevalence of these projects—sometimes also called social impact bonds—has been limited. The reasons for this are manifold, though it's likely due in large measure to the commonly held belief that pay for success "is appropriate only for a narrow cohort of nonprofits that meet two related criteria: they must be able to effectively deliver and measure their social impact; and they must be able to translate that impact into financial benefits or cost savings that are traceable to the budgets of one or more institutions or government departments."[28] In addition, early applications of pay for success were constrained by the complexity and expense of administering the multiparty contracts, which usually meant only large deals made financial sense to pursue. As a result, most smaller, Main Street nonprofits stayed away.

But the evolution of two critical elements of PFS funding promises to open the door to greater demand for projects. The first is the growing ubiquity of private investors who are increasingly concerned with earing a dual return—financial *and* social—on their money. And the second is the rise in foundations, philanthropists, and grant makers who demand evidence of performance and impact, and seek to link their investments with mission.

We'll talk further about how PFS arrangements have become less cumbersome later in this chapter, but for now let's see what we can learn from examining one of the largest PFS projects ever completed.

Roca

For more than thirty years, Roca—a Massachusetts nonprofit with about $12 million in annual revenue—has embraced a simple mission: "to disrupt the cycle of incarceration and poverty by helping young people transform their lives."[29] The pithy tagline on its website says it even better: "Less Jail, More Future."

Roca's PFS project—officially known as the Massachusetts Juvenile Justice Pay for Success Initiative—"is a $28 million partnership between Roca, the commonwealth of Massachusetts, the intermediary Third Sector Capital Partners, and a host of private investors."[30] To date, it's the largest PFS initiative in the United States, according to the organization. Over a five-year period that began in 2014, various criminal justice agencies from across the state will refer more than one thousand high-risk young men to Roca, with the goal of helping them avoid the recidivism trap through consistent employment and development of productive life skills. Given the high cost of keeping these individuals behind bars, Roca estimates that by reducing incarceration rates by 40 percent—the project's target—Massachusetts taxpayers will save $21.8 million. A 65 percent reduction would boost that figure to $41.5 million.[31]

Under the project's structure, private investors and foundations provide 85 percent of the funding, which is repaid with interest by the state if agreed-upon goals are met (as measured by independent evaluators). So, in keeping with the theme of this chapter, let's now examine this transaction using a typical Wall Street tool: the "Gives & Gets" (see Table 2.1).

Upon first glance, the term *quasi-equity* appears rather unusual when applied to the financing of a nonprofit. After all, "equity" implies ownership, and nonprofits don't have owners—at least not in the traditional sense. But many industry experts we interviewed drew comparisons between the funding Roca received and *equity* as it's used in the

Table 2.1.   Gives and Gets

	Investor	Roca	Massachusetts
Gives	Funds 85 percent of intervention with loan	Performs intervention; funds 15 percent	Repays loan and interest if impact achieved
Gets	"Double" return if criteria is met	Multiyear funding *Quasi-equity	Reduced cost of incarceration; surety of impact

for-profit sector. It's an apt analogy. Both are sources of money that don't have to be repaid, and both provide a known quantity of multiyear funding that can be used to build the business. However, Roca's financing has to be directed in support of the organization's programs. It isn't completely unrestricted, like equity in the for-profit world. So, we'll call it quasi-equity.

John Grossman, senior fellow at the nonprofit advisory firm Third Sector Capital Partners, who helped structure the Roca deal, explained he thinks the allure of the pay for success model to nonprofits is self-evident. "Knowing you've got a five-year contract, for many nonprofits [that's] so unusual. They're thinking 'You mean to tell me I'm going to be able to serve [a number of people] each year for the next five years and you're promising me I'm getting paid for that?' From a sustainability point of view, that's important to folks."[32] Grossman added that the multiyear, reliable funding available through PFS transactions—often thought to be too complex and costly to pursue—can actually be quite favorable when compared to the cost, effort, and uncertainty of trying to stitch together ad hoc year-to-year grants.

This sentiment was echoed by Yotam Zeira, until recently Roca's director of strategy and external affairs, who believes the many benefits attached to his organization's PFS initiative were well worth the time and energy invested, especially when compared with less certain, more restrictive forms of funding.[33]

PFS programs are often criticized—or, worse yet, nonprofits assume, "they're not for us"—because they can appear too complicated, burdensome, and expensive to implement, or are believed to be practical only for huge programs, like public health, that are funded by governments or international nongovernmental organizations (NGOs). As such, many Main Street nonprofits still don't consider PFS as a funding source. But, increasingly, this model is proving its effectiveness for programs and organizations of all sizes—provided there's ample data to demonstrate impact.

Bruce Hoyt equates evidenced-based outcomes with "the base of the pyramid of success for a nonprofit." Further up the pyramid is organizational and programmatic scaling, while the peak represents revenue. This is where, in Hoyt's view, successful organizations should seek diverse and consistent income sources, rather than rely on only one or two, such as grant funding. He adds, assuming nonprofits have the data to back up their effectiveness, many funding options are on the table, including a "social [enterprise] model, a pay for success model, or at this point, a direct government payer, because you've proven your intervention is so successful that the government has agreed that they should step in and start paying for it."[34] Get all this right and you've gone a long way toward sustainability, he says.

Hoyt acknowledges the view that the shift toward evidence-based programs can be daunting to start, but he believes, "The value-add [to nonprofits and their stakeholders] has been pretty significant. And like any new [worthwhile] investment product that comes out, they are very complex and hard at first." But, Hoyt adds, as you gain experience with these programs, "the standardization and the models get a little easier and more routine, and you can drive down the transactional cost."[35]

Another often-heard drawback of evidence-based funding, particularly with PFS, is the difficulty of creating relevant impact metrics. No doubt this was true years ago—even in the recent past—but today we're awash in data points. They're *everywhere*! And thanks to advances in technology, information is easier and less expensive to collect than ever. You just have to figure out what to measure and how. Sorry, we have to drop in a couple of clichés here. Ready? "Don't reinvent the wheel!" Often the data you're looking for—or at least a very relevant proxy— already exists. Use it! And (last one, we promise), "Don't let the perfect be the enemy of the good." Rather than wasting valuable time and resources trying to capture the perfect data, just pick a metric—or two—that accurately showcases your organization's effectiveness and run with it. (More on this in chapter 7.) More and more, funders are working with nonprofits to develop customized, simplified measurement criteria, and—even better—many are providing financial assistance to help organizations build the necessary infrastructure to capture the data. All this represents a shift to what Third Sector's Grossman calls a "provider-friendly" model, wherein funders and nonprofits recognize and work to support their mutual interests. [36]

As Hoyt explained, "We have what we call an impact term sheet we create on every investment over $50,000, where we agree with our investee what impacts we are going to achieve with the investment and how we're going to measure it." [37] Hoyt admits that assessing impact in the nonprofit sector can be hard. After all, you can't simply Google a nonprofit's stock price to see how the organization is doing. By their nature, social returns are messier and more difficult to quantify than financial returns. But if all stakeholders really put forth the effort to try, it can be done. And in an increasingly data-driven world, it's table stakes for funding.

At this point you may be saying to yourself, "Okay, most nonprofits don't have a shovel-ready $28 million project sitting around. How can PFS help my organization?" Glad you asked. Let's look at a smaller one—coincidentally in the same domain, prison recidivism, but on the other side of the country in San Francisco.

The Last Mile

If you look at the statistics, the United States punches far above its weight in terms of the number of people we lock up in prison. With roughly 5 percent of the global population, we house 25 percent of the world's inmates. [38] The Last Mile (TLM) hopes to change that. Like Roca, TLM provides successful job training programs that aim to break the cycle of incarceration. Inside California's San Quentin State Prison, TLM's staff train inmates for careers in software engineering and technology. Its curriculum works, but it also costs money. In 2018, TLM received $800,000 from a group of eleven impact investors who put their money into a unique new investment called an *Impact Security*. Created by NPX, Inc., an innovative nonprofit finance firm, Impact Securities allow nonprofits to "issue performance-based debt to investors and make required payments on the debt over time with donations from the established donor fund." [39]

The model is straightforward. Investors put up their "risk capital" in advance by purchasing the Impact Security—essentially a bond—issued by the nonprofit. The bond is created from a pool of cash pledged to the organization by donors, the proceeds from which can be used for program development, scalability, or a host of other purposes depending on the needs of the nonprofit. Though investors' money is out the door, the donors' funds don't move until certain impact metrics—which are agreed upon by all parties, and measured and audited by an independent impact auditor—are achieved. Donors receive a tax deduction on their donation along with the certainty of knowing their dollars will be used to create measurable good. Investors aim to benefit from both a financial and social return on their money. If the expected impact milestones are met, money is released from the donor fund to pay back the investors with interest. If not, investors stand to lose some or all of their money, and donors can simply redeploy their funds toward another charitable purpose.

NPX is a new player in the field of socially conscious financial service providers that is offering a novel way for both donors and investors to change how they fund nonprofits. The uniqueness of its Impact Securities compared to Social Impact Bonds is in the legal structure of the security and strategy to focus on private donors rather than the government as the source of outcome-related payments. According to NPX, "By making this Impact Security a standardized debt security, instead of a bespoke agreement, it is readily transferable, able to have an identifier, able to be held in a brokerage account and able to trade and settle through clearing houses. If issued by a nonprofit, the offering of the security is exempt from Securities and Exchange Commission registration requirements, which means the securities can be offered publicly, opening it up to the broadest possible range of investors."[40]

The implications of this and other emerging impact-based funding mechanisms for nonprofits are enormous. As the Virgin Group's Richard Branson said about NPX's concept, "Innovation is crucial to keep industries moving forward. Companies are continuously evolving and innovating, the same should be true for nonprofits and the communities they serve. The NPX team has taken this approach to philanthropic giving and its innovative solution will help nonprofits to raise more funds and their profiles at the same time."[41]

Returning to TLM, let's review the structure of that transaction in more detail. Again, a Gives & Gets table (Table 2.2) may help visualize the various players and their roles.

Table 2.2. Gives and Gets

	Investor	The Last Mile	Donor	NPX Advisors	Evaluator
Gives	Funds the program in the form of a loan	Performs work	Repays loan and interest if impact achieved	Structures and brokers transaction	Audits impact
Gets	"Double" return if criteria are met	Multiyear funding *Quasi-equity	Charitable deduction; surety of impact	Fees	Fees

Wait. There are now five participants, and two of them are charging fees. So how, exactly, is this an improvement over the old PFS model? Lindsay Beck and Catarina Schwab, co-founders of NPX, say their goal is to simplify the complex, opaque process of funding nonprofits based on their results. Beck and Schwab explain, "It's really important that the nonprofit know and drive what they're going after, the impact they are trying to achieve, how long it will take and how much money is required. So the amount raised and the timeline of the deal are led by the nonprofit. And the same is true for the impact reporting—everything is structured on units of impact."[42] In other words, under NPX's model repayment isn't an all-or-nothing proposition. It's not binary. Over the three-year life of the TLM project, partners will determine its impact by measuring the cumulative number of hours inmates work, with a goal of 18,000 hours worked by program graduates. If the goal is met, investors will be repaid up to $900,000 (the maximum return is 12.5 percent if impact is achieved in year one).[43] But the amount investors ultimately receive can vary based on the actual number of hours worked. An outside party helps to determine a "fair market value" for each hour of work, and reports the results, which will then be used to calculate how much money is returned to investors. That number may be the amount they put in, plus the maximum return of 12.5 percent. It could be nothing. Or something in between. Investors stand to lose part or all of their investment if TLM fails to achieve its goal, in which case the project's sixteen donors would direct their committed funds toward other charitable purposes. Either way, transaction cost and complexity are kept to a minimum by the Impact Security's simplistic unit of measurement structure.

Oh, and one more thing. For those who may balk at the prospect of donors paying 12.5 percent to help a nonprofit achieve its mission, we'd kindly draw your attention to a study of the two hundred thousand largest nonprofits conducted by McKinsey & Company. It found their average fundraising costs to be about 18 percent, despite what they may have claimed.[44]

Nonprofit Merchant Banks

Anyone who has even wandered into an Econ 101 class is probably familiar with the twin pillars of economics: supply and demand. These are the forces that also drive Wall Street. Suppliers of capital seek places to put their money to work. Organizations demand capital to run their operations. And then, of course, there are intermediaries whose job it is to design, service, and broker a never-ending stream of new products. In short, these are the experts and firms that make sure supply and demand don't unknowingly pass each other in a crowded bar without first sitting down for a drink. It's no different in the world of capital and funding for the social sector, where a new breed of specialists is performing these roles and enabling the growth of new markets. As we close out this chapter, we'll highlight two such firms, called nonprofit merchant banks, because they use their own money as well as OPM (other people's money) to do deals. Both companies provide assistance to the nonprofit sector by offering loans and grants, as well as consulting, advisory, and support services.

SeaChange Capital Partners is a firm whose very name promises profound transformation. As envisioned by its founders—former senior partners at Goldman Sachs—the core of SeaChange is to encourage and support transactions among nonprofits and their stakeholders. The firm was initially funded in early 2008 with backing from major foundations (Bill & Melinda Gates Foundation, Omidyar Network, and the William and Flora Hewlett Foundation, to name a few). Today, it makes grants, loans, and investments that help nonprofits with a variety of strategic pursuits. Investigating a possible merger with another organization? Want to collaborate with like-minded nonprofits? Need assistance with financial modeling for a new program? SeaChange can offer money and advice. The company also provides consulting services to organizations exploring a planned dissolution or restructuring, which, as SeaChange partner John MacIntosh explained to us, is a natural part of many nonprofits' lifecycles.[45] He also pointed out that by helping facilitate activities like mergers, collaborations, and partnerships within the nonprofit sector, his firm creates opportunities for funders to multiply the impact of their investments. SeaChange manages three funds to facilitate collaboration, including mergers and acquisitions. Money from these funds also covers the cost to bring in consultants who advise on some of the thornier issues that can crop up whenever one organization joins forces with another, including board and leadership integration and financial co-mingling (see chapter 4). This type of funding, too, is "particularly valuable for the nonprofits involved because of [the funds'] timing, their flexibility, their ability to catalyze giving by others, or because they otherwise offer the prospect of being many times more valuable than the typical funds received by the organizations."[46]

Nonprofit Finance Fund (NFF) was born from crisis. It was 1980, and double-digit inflation caused the price of heating oil to spike to levels many property owners couldn't afford. Particularly hard hit were low- to moderate-income housing nonprofits in New York City that were having trouble paying their residents' heating bills. The solution: a loan from NFF to purchase more efficient boilers, saving the organizations enough money to continue operating throughout the frigid winter months. NFF is what's known as a Community Development Financial Institution (CDFI), a type of organization that provides access to credit and other financial services to underserved populations. NFF goes a step further by focusing on holistically serving the social sector through consulting, training, technical assistance, and advocacy on behalf of a broad range of nonprofits. Nancy Jamison, the former CEO of San Diego Grantmakers, calls it her "go to place" for resources.[47]

NFF's tagline is "Where Money Meets Mission"—a succinct turn of phrase that aptly describes what it does. In addition to funding, the firm also provides advice on how best to strategically deploy it. NFF has provided $875 million in direct financing to support almost $3 billion in projects for thousands of organizations nationwide. CEO Antony Bugg-Levine describes his organization by saying, "There are three legs to our stool: lending, consulting, and advocacy. It's always been our ambition to use what we learn from our clients as a consultant or a lender to advocate for how the system of solving social problems should be changing."[48]

NFF also helps organizations evolve in ways that drive long-term sustainability and success, such as developing new revenue sources. These changes require money, different from program funding and general operating support, that Bugg-Levine calls "change capital." It's "a specific investment you make in a specific timeframe with an understanding that at the end of that investment you will have done something that makes your business model more stable," he said. [49]

As we highlight in chapter 10, SeaChange and NFF provide great resources for the sector, with countless reports, seminars, webinars, and educational materials available on their websites.

So what's the message for Main Street? We've seen in the preceding pages how Wall Street is slowly but assuredly making its way into the social sector. The next generation of nonprofit leaders, investors, and service firms are participating in a bold new financial marketplace—not out of greed, but from a desire to leave the world a better place than they found it. Let's call it conscious capitalism. If you'll excuse us taking a little liberty with an overused phrase, will this rising tide lift all nonprofit boats? Probably not. But the momentum is growing every day. And those who have long wondered what could happen if only the social sector could participate in the capital markets on equal footing with their for-profit sisters and brothers may soon have their answer. Who knows? Even Gordon Gekko might smile at that.

3

EQUAL PAY FOR EQUAL WORK?

The Social Sector Compensation Gap

For many centuries, the vows of chastity, obedience, and poverty have been a widely accepted part of Western religious dogma. Their roots are noble and, among a certain set of devout practitioners, serve to bind adherents together in a shared sense of humanity. But for nearly as long, one of these vows—poverty—seems to have slipped the confines of the spiritual domain and suffused into a more secular order: the nonprofit sector.

Okay, perhaps "poverty" is too strong a word. Of course there are many—most, in fact—who work for nonprofits and are far from destitute. But we needed to get your attention. Because, with the possible exception of certain nonprofit professions (those in health care, scientific research, and postsecondary education, for example), it's well understood and generally accepted that if you want to follow your passion for good work, you'll likely earn less than you would at a comparable job in government or a for-profit company. The question of exactly how much less we'll leave to the quant jocks and statisticians. And yes, the gap widens or narrows depending on whether we're talking about executives or worker bees.

Frankly, we're not here to argue dollars and cents as much as shine a light on the blatant inequity inherent in the unspoken *expectation* that those in the nonprofit sector will be paid less than they might otherwise earn by working elsewhere. That's sadly ironic, given that we rely on the third sector to solve some of society's most difficult and pressing problems that government and for-profit institutions are unwilling or unable to address. For a large portion of you, this reality won't be news. For some, it may hit close to home. However, as with many of the topics covered in this book, new ways of thinking are beginning to create noticeable change. Will the nonprofit sector ever achieve perfect compensation equality? Should it? Perhaps not. After all, history shows us bad things can happen when companies hire people whose prime directive is money. (Nonprofit Enron, anyone?) But there's a fine line between reasonable sacrifice and financial martyrdom.

As Nancy Jamison asked, "Why is it often assumed that you are supposed to be poor when you work in the nonprofit sector? If people decide they want to contribute to positive community impact, should it really be the accepted truth that they make less money? In many ways this in fact seems counterintuitive!"[1]

Based on our research, we have reason to hope—in fact, believe—that perception will change. In a 2015 blog post reporting the results of its annual survey of nonprofits from across the United States, the Nonprofit Finance Fund (NFF) stated: "A human capital crisis is brewing. From fundraisers to leadership to front-line direct service workers, nonprofits report difficulties attracting and retaining top candidates. Many nonprofits are monitoring competitive wage indices and are concerned about their inability to offer attractive compensation packages. Additionally, many organizations recognize and understand that offering a living wage is mission critical and aspire to adequately compensate staff."[2]

To be clear, we're not suggesting that compensation in the nonprofit sector rise to reach the excessive levels often seen among executives in other industries. A recent analysis concluded the average CEO/worker pay ratio at Fortune 500 companies is 339 to 1![3] Mirroring this practice would undoubtedly distance leaders in the social sector from the very people and communities they strive to serve, as well as tarnish many of the admirable, mission-centric qualities of those who choose to make the betterment of society their life's work. But *greater* equality is necessary—in fact, critical—to grow and maintain a vibrant and effective nonprofit sector.

THE COMPETITION FACTOR

Why is this issue so important? One reason is that competition among the sectors for resources continues to increase, while differences between for-profit and nonprofit organizations become harder to distinguish. Nonprofits routinely compete with for-profits for contracts to supply goods and services, labor, and financial resources from funders and customers. This is true across the sector, whether the organization is involved in social services, education, or arts and culture. A nonprofit museum competes with restaurants, movie theaters, and sports teams for the leisure time of its patrons. Government agencies, by far the third sector's largest funding source, frequently request bids for lucrative contracts from nonprofits and for-profits alike. Nonprofits attempting to diversify their revenue sources by creating a social enterprise for earned income often face stiff competition from other companies engaged in the same line of work. As the *Stanford Social Innovation Review*'s Eric Nee, observes, "Capitalism is an amazingly creative system for providing goods and services, but it can also be cold-hearted, weeding out enterprises that aren't efficient users of capital, ideas, and labor, in favor of those that are, regardless of a company's social mission."[4]

Fair or not, most things are fungible.

And it's not just for-profits that nonprofits are competing with. With the phenomenal growth of social entrepreneurship, philanthro-capitalism, and hybrid organizations such as "B Corporations," distinctions between the sectors continue to diminish. *The Economist* described this trend as "a 'Fourth Sector' (after public, private, and voluntary) . . . consisting of organizations that straddle the line between business and charity. They call themselves 'low-profit limited liability companies,' 'social enterprises,' and other names."[5] Besides *competing* with these new types of organizations, nonprofits must also *collaborate* with them—creating partnerships that maximize effectiveness by allowing each party to do what it does best in a collective effort to solve social problems.

As industry lines blur, "sector switching" among workers will increase. But for nonprofits to compete on equal footing with their for-profit counterparts in the marketplace for human capital, they must continue to address the issue of compensation inequality.

The nonprofit Community HousingWorks (CHW) gets this. For more than thirty years, CHW has successfully competed head-to-head in the highly lucrative arena of multifamily real estate development. The organization maintains more than 3,300 apartments throughout California, providing stable housing to some 9,000 low- to moderate-income residents. How? "The organization has to make an intentional decision to invest in our people," said Brian Kay, CHW's chief financial officer since 2012. Himself a sector switcher from the for-profit world, Kay adds that this investment also affords CHW "the benefits of having business-savvy, intelligent leaders who think in terms of social enterprise and entrepreneurial techniques in addition to purely just doing whatever it takes or working all hours just to meet the mission."[6] Such acumen is critical for running an organization that maintains multiple sources of revenue, including developer and asset management fees, resident service fees, and contributed income. Besides generating reliable operating surpluses, CHW's robust earned income business model has the added benefit of helping the organization avoid the potentially negative perceptions of spending on employee compensation—something so many nonprofits face from donors and other funders.

Opponents of greater pay parity among sectors generally maintain that higher staff salaries drain finite resources that should be spent on direct services. They often support their views with inaccurate or misleading interpretations of laws and tax regulations centered on the role of the nonprofit as a public benefit corporation. While we fully disclose that we're neither lawyers nor accountants, a brief review of certain IRS provisions (also followed by many state and local jurisdictions) is useful in examining these arguments.

Let's first deal with the notion that the IRS imposes specific limits on compensation levels for nonprofit employees. It doesn't, and confusion on this issue stems from the misinterpretation of a critical IRS regulation, specifically the prohibition of "unreasonable benefits" paid to "insiders" (e.g., directors, officers, key employees) of a nonprofit organization.[7] Make no mistake: violations of this regulation can carry severe penalties (and just to get our attention, in certain circumstances the IRS can also impose them on board members and trustees). But though compensation of key personnel is subject to IRS scrutiny, nonprofits are in fact permitted to pay "fair and reasonable" wages to their employees based on a "market rate."[8] Enter the shades of gray. Absent a universal standard for what exactly constitutes a *market rate* of compensation, we're left with the IRS's somewhat amorphous definition of *reasonableness*: "Reasonable compensation is the value that would ordinarily be paid for like services by like enterprises under like circumstances."[9] Everyone clear? No wonder many organizations choose to "round down" compensation packages just to stay in the tax man's good graces.

It's worth bearing in mind, however, when looking at organizations that are comparable in terms of size, scope, and services, nonprofits should certainly include companies in the for-profit and government sectors. Furthermore, IRS guidelines also provide a type of "safe harbor" for organizations. By following certain documentation practices, nonprofits receive a "rebuttable presumption of reasonableness," which, in effect, places the burden of proof that compensation is excessive on the IRS.[10] (One recent exception: The major tax legislation passed in late 2017 makes paying nonprofit executives over $1 million more expensive by imposing a 21 percent excise tax. But to be clear, this does not limit salary amounts. And, interestingly, the legislation excludes health care providers.)

Media, too, can cloud the issue. Well-publicized allegations of egregious conduct by a relatively small number of nonprofits has further put the topic of compensation under a microscope (see CharityWatch's Hall of Shame for a sample).[11] Whether or not the allegations are warranted, the potential for negative press coverage (often accompanied by significant donor fallout) is cited by some as justification for curtailing compensation, even when such compensation would otherwise be reasonable when subjected to market tests.

In 2002, Pallotta TeamWorks, the eponymous nonprofit founded by Dan Pallotta to help produce events including the Avon Breast Cancer 3-Day walks and AIDSRides-USA, folded amid a firestorm of adverse publicity and "criticism of its high fees and Pallotta's handsome compensation."[12] From his perspective, Pallotta argues in his book *Uncharitable* and later through another nonprofit he founded, the Charitable Defense Council, that arbitrary limits on nonprofits' expenses, including marketing and compensation, are detrimental to the sector.[13]

Clearly, examples of extravagant practices and excessive compensation exist. They always will. And the media, as well as other watchdogs, are absolutely justified in calling out bad behavior whenever they see it.

The public trust (and money) placed in our nation's nonprofits demands nothing less. As the charity rating agency GuideStar points out, "Like religion, politics, and sports, nonprofit executive compensation often evokes strong emotion. Donors, journalists, state officials, and members of Congress frequently express outrage at the salaries nonprofit CEOs receive, especially if the organizations they head are public charities that rely on donations from the public."[14] But let's be careful to not conflate the misdeeds of the few with the beneficence of the many. Some nonprofits act improperly, just as myriad abuses can be found in other sectors. Cherry-picked examples of wrongdoing only serve to hinder meaningful discussion of the compensation gap and obscure the very real issue of pay inequality—an issue that can be traced back to America's founding.

A brief history lesson is probably in order. The entrenched belief that nonprofit businesses are—and should be—fundamentally different from their for-profit and public sector counterparts is rooted in Native American culture. As author Stephan Katzbichler writes, "The Native approach of 'helping and generously assisting others' is still today the fundamental idea behind American philanthropy and was the origin for developing America's non-profit sector in the next centuries." This belief was furthered by the Pilgrims, for whom, Katzbichler continues, "philanthropy was not a private alternative to public action," but rather a crucial attitude of serving "the general good . . . of the colony."[15] Over time, a long-standing cultural orientation toward public service also came to encompass a tradition of sacrifice—including one's compensation—that persists to this day.

Simply boosting pay, however, isn't a complete solution. Nonprofits, and the people they attract, really are different. In *Good to Great and the Social Sectors*, a manifesto accompanying his best-selling book, *Good to Great*, Jim Collins offers a keen observation about that. In his view, nonprofits can satisfy a uniquely singular motivation for many who choose to work in the social sector: "desperate craving for meaning in our lives." Collins adds that, "Purity of mission—be it about educating young people, connecting people to God, making our cities safe, touching the soul with great art, feeding the hungry, serving the poor, or protecting our freedom—has the power to ignite passion and commitment." Because of these values, traditional incentive plans based primarily on financial compensation often are not effective—and can even be counterproductive—in nonprofits. In fact, those who have followed their hearts into public service many only be doing what, as humans, we're hardwired to do. Dozens of studies over many decades "have conclusively shown that people who expect to receive a reward for completing a task or for doing that task successfully simply do not perform as well as those who expect no reward at all."[16] "Money by itself can never attract the right people," Collins writes. "Money is a commodity; talent is not."[17]

At this point, it may just be easier to throw up our hands and conclude that because many who work for nonprofits believe so strongly in "the mission," they've simply resigned themselves to earning less. But, as one observer asked, "Why does a willingness to accept lower wages . . . seem to be an indicator or qualification for one's job in the nonprofit sector?"[18] In a rational and perfect world, shouldn't this commitment be rewarded with more than just a "warm glow"? To some, the emotional benefit of doing good for others represents a form of noncash compensation, and therefore we should expect it "to lower the actual cost of wages for nonprofits."[19] *Really?* Try suggesting to the next social worker you meet that she should simply use her abundant existential satisfaction to put food on the table or pay the rent. There's a reason Abraham Maslow put the physiological needs of sustenance and shelter at the base of his hierarchical pyramid—below esteem and self-actualization.[20]

Yet, many still maintain that the benefits of paying market salaries—such as attracting and retaining a capable and diverse pool of human talent—are diminished by the potential impact on donor relations and an organization's ability to scale. They're not wrong. In *Building Non-profit Financial Capacity*, coauthors Grace Chikoto and Daniel Gordon Neely conclude, "Large expenditures for executive compensation negatively affect nonprofits' potential for financial growth."[21] Sad, but true. However, these views, too, are slowly beginning to change.

A growing chorus of experts increasingly believe many of the "tried and true" (and, we'd add, arbitrary) measurements long used to assess nonprofits' health and effectiveness are effectively useless. Worse yet, insidious metrics, such as the percentage of funding that goes directly to programs, may actually be harmful, hindering an organization's incentive to hire the best and brightest, take risks, make long-term investments, and use leverage to scale mission-related activities. Punishing nonprofits for spending money on salaries is counterproductive and part of what at least three influential charity rating agencies have termed *The Overhead Myth*.[22]

THE YMCA STORY

Let's look at one nonprofit organization—or more accurately, a group of organizations—that serve as an example to support many of the arguments for compensation equality. The YMCA (the "Y", as it's more commonly known) comprises a network of some 2,700 health and fitness clubs operating across the United States.[23] Similar to many nonprofits, the Y runs a business that collaborates and competes with the for-profit sector; in this case, its competition is the multibillion-dollar personal fitness industry.

As lifelong members of the Y in multiple cities, we can say firsthand that its facilities, equipment, scope of programs, and staff competency are every bit the equal to its competitors' in the private sector. Membership dues are reasonable and sufficient to pay for most of the organizations' operating costs and mission-related activities. When we visit our local Y a few times each week to break a moderate sweat, swim a few laps, or try out that new yoga pose, we expect to receive a high level of professional service delivered in a well-maintained, clean, modern, and attractive facility that incorporates the latest fitness technology. And as consumers, that's really where we stop. We have no interest in the Y's overhead ratio or some whimsical formula that supposedly tells us whether it's doing a good job. Our (hopefully) shrinking waistlines tell us that.

Furthermore, we wouldn't expect the Y to provide the services it offers by paying its people substantially less than market wages. (It doesn't, by the way. Our own analysis of 2016 data available on GuideStar showed the CEOs of the three largest regional YMCAs each earned an average of over $650,000 in total compensation.) Would our views change if we were donors rather than consumers? Unlikely. To the contrary, as donors we would be delighted to know the Y runs a mission-centered, competitive business that produces enough income to support its philanthropic activities while providing a living wage to its employees.

METRICS—AND COMMUNICATION

By now, we hope we've at least persuaded you a little that, though well-intentioned, the use of arbitrary, shortcut metrics such as *overhead* as barometers of nonprofit effectiveness are unhelpful at best and harmful at worst. So why are they so popular?

A few reasons. One is that donors and grantors frequently seek expedient ways to evaluate organizations they might support. This certainly is understandable. Meaningful assessment of effectiveness requires deep, time-consuming analysis, as well as significant resources. Another concerns trust. Or rather a lack of it, fueled to a great extent by media reporting of the abusive practices of a relatively few bad actors. And this mistrust permeates the entire sector, from donors and nonprofits to the public at large. The *Stanford Social Innovation Review* reported on a Brookings Institution survey that found that 70 percent of Americans believed "charitable organizations waste 'a great deal' or a 'fair amount' of money. Only 10 percent thought charitable organizations did a 'very good job' spending money."[24]

Which points to a broader issue: nonprofits in general do a poor job of communicating what resources they need to succeed. This is due in part to a lack of time and staff resources, but it also has roots in the same sense of mistrust many nonprofit leaders feel has long been directed at them and their organizations. They fear negatively impacting relationships with funders and donors they've worked so hard to attract by having candid discussions about how much money it truly takes to keep their organizations going. Some even exacerbate the problem by deliberately mischaracterizing spending to meet their funders' expectations. This perceived power imbalance means it's often simply more expedient to "give in" to funder demands and accept whatever has been offered, no matter how harmful it may be to long-term success.

Indeed, according to the NFF's 2018 State of the Nonprofit Sector Survey, the second biggest concern among respondents was receiving funding for the *full cost* of program services, including salaries and other indirect expenses. And the problem appears to be getting worse. The percentage of nonprofits that identified "full cost funding" as a top operational challenge rose from 19 percent in 2015 to 57 percent in 2018. Yet, the report finds, "the number of nonprofits reporting being paid less than 10 percent for indirect costs, despite laws to the contrary, remains virtually unchanged, at between 49 and 60 percent, depending on whether grants or contracts are with the federal, state, or local government." In case you're curious, the survey respondents' top concern: "financial sustainability."[25]

All this feeds what Ann Goggins Gregory and Don Howard coined *The Nonprofit Starvation Cycle*, which leaves too many nonprofits with inadequate and outdated systems, equipment, and facilities; underpaid staff; and high turnover. "The cycle starts with funders' unrealistic expectations about how much running a nonprofit costs, and results in nonprofits' misrepresenting their costs while skimping on vital systems—acts that feed funders' skewed beliefs," the authors write.[26] "Organizations that build robust infrastructure—which includes sturdy information technology systems, financial systems, skills training, fundraising processes, and other essential overhead—are more likely to succeed than those that do not."[27] Appropriate and fair compensation allows nonprofits to employ the human resources necessary to support all of those endeavors. Fortunately, as Don Howard told us, "A lot of progress has been made. I think the foundation funder community is much more sensitized and there are a lot of examples of folks changing their behaviors to properly or better support the kind of infrastructure needs that we talked about in the starvation cycle piece. Probably the most consequential was the guidance by the Federal Office of Management and Budget that federal dollars, even when granted by a state or county, need to fund a minimum ten percent indirect rate, and if a nonprofit can demonstrate a higher amount, they have to fund it."[28]

Another of the headwinds plaguing the nonprofit sector is the relative scarcity of readily accessible performance benchmarks akin to those used by other corporations to justify executive pay. For-profits enjoy the ability to communicate results to investors in clear, crisp financial terms like *operating margins*, *return on equity*, and *earnings per share*. Of course, nonprofits use financial metrics, too, but they often fail to convey the same measurement of organization or program effectiveness. While research has found considerable overlap in the leadership skills needed to succeed in the two sectors,[29] differences in corporate structure—such as a lack of ownership benefits (stock options, for example)—complicate the payment of incentive compensation to nonprofit executives and staff. But it can be done. Employees in the sector can be paid based on mission-focused performance benchmarks as a replacement for net profits.[30] In fact, using nonfinancial pay-for-performance targets is not unique to nonprofits. Many corporations tie incentive compensation to the achievement of more nebulous objectives, such as *customer satisfaction* or *market share*.

At least two nonprofit industries—healthcare and higher education—seem to have cracked the compensation conundrum in their executive ranks. It's not at all uncommon for college and university presidents to command huge salaries (to say nothing of the rich contracts signed by many head coaches, but we'll leave that third rail alone). Likewise, CEOs of many of the nation's hospitals and health care conglomerates routinely earn seven-figure salaries. According to a recently published study, the average CEO compensation at twenty-two "major US nonprofit medical centers" jumped from $1.6 million in 2005 to $3.1 million in 2015, a 93 percent increase.[31]

We're not here to pass judgment on that. And believe us, if we someday find ourselves in need of the services provided at one of those hospitals, the last thought running through our minds would be, "Hmmm, I wonder what the boss of this place is pulling down." We're also not economists, who no doubt could explain the salary phenomenon with heady terms like *price elasticity* and *moral hazard*. (Check out *The Economist* if you're inclined to geek out on more economics.) As we've said, our question is more philosophical: Why is it generally accepted that personnel at some nonprofits are well compensated, while that same level of compensation is objectionable at others? So we asked industry leaders—over sixty of them—for their thoughts. The vast majority felt the dichotomy was due, at least to some degree, to the close personal relationship between donors and the institutions they support. This visceral link: "You cured my cancer," or "You made my career possible," is part of what William Foster, Peter Kim, and Barbara Christiansen describe as the "Beneficiary Builder" funding model. "Donors are often motivated to give money because they believe that the benefits they received changed their life,"[32] the authors write. Echoing this sentiment, one person we interviewed explained, "I have a very close relationship with [my university and hospital] compared to when I'm giving money to someone who's feeding people in Africa. I don't see those people every day. I don't have that really close relationship."

While the donor-nonprofit relationship partially explains this paradox, other leaders we spoke with believe there are two equally important factors at play. The first is that philanthropy represents a much smaller share of certain nonprofits' income sources. To be clear, we're not saying compensation equality should be limited to organizations with earned revenue. But it does seem those nonprofits that have more robust funding models can avoid at least some of the blowback from paying higher salaries. A second reason concerns the fact that many organizations—universities and hospitals among them—face fierce competition for human resources from for-profit companies. Of course, economists have an explanation for this, too: *the law of supply and demand.*

There's no denying the nonprofit sector is different in many respects, not the least of which is its paramount responsibility to the betterment of society above shareholders or corporate owners. And therefore nonprofits are and should be governed by different standards, practices, and mores. But at the same time, adherence to these unique standards shouldn't preclude them from paying more competitive wages. Each organization, too, is unique, and thus needs to tailor its particular compensation plan to meet the specific requirements of its mission. As author Matthew T. Journy writes, "Charities need to balance their overall tax-exempt objectives with their need to hire and retain skilled management to accomplish those objectives, their future growth with their financial constraints, and their desire to compensate exceptional service with the public perception of corporate greed."[33] If that conjures up images of playing three-dimensional chess with Mr. Spock, we sympathize. It's tough work. But, candidly, without the ability to hire and retain the most capable human talent, nonprofits cannot succeed over the long term. Eventually, their effectiveness will deteriorate, or worse. After all, these are the people who are tackling some of society's most intractable problems: poverty, homelessness, hunger, and mental health, among many others.

They can't do it alone. Refreshingly, there's been an uptick in cross-sector collaborations among nonprofits, governments, and for-profit corporations. However, this only underscores the need to reduce the compensation gap. Absent a skilled workforce able to commit its time and talent to the mission without overly burdensome personal financial concerns, the nonprofit sector can't be an effective—and equal—partner in these collaborative efforts. It's disingenuous for us to expect otherwise. If soda manufacturers can pay market wages, why can't organizations that protect our most vulnerable populations do the same?

Unfortunately, there are no silver bullets. Main Street nonprofits, many of which rely on philanthropy for at least a portion—if not most—of their resources will continue to have difficulties narrowing the compensation gap. But based on our research and experience, we can offer some suggestions that may help.

FUNDING MODELS

The evidence is clear: Nonprofits that rely less on philanthropy and charitable giving enjoy greater freedom in their compensation practices. Therefore, creating more diverse funding sources through earned income ventures like social enterprise, monetization of intellectual property, or other models can improve an organization's ability to attract and retain human talent. As an example, employees of nonprofit research organizations and universities are highly incentivized to create valuable intellectual property by sharing the financial benefits of monetizing their inventions. Although this practice is still somewhat controversial, its prevalence has grown considerably since the passage of the Bayh-Dole Act of 1980, which enabled universities to maintain ownership of government-funded research.[34]

How the purse is ultimately split is a matter to be worked out by the interested parties. Malin Burnham, a philanthropist whose support and leadership was a major factor in establishing the highly successful Sanford Burnham Prebys Medical Discovery Institute, told us, "The general rule we use in dividing up intellectual property [IP] rights is to split the IP, with one-third going to the individual scientists, one-third to [the research institute], and one-third to the business subsidiary." In Burnham's experience, this arrangement usually seems fair to everyone and allows projects to continue their momentum without "a lot of squabbling over ownership." He adds that apart from helping the institute attract and retain talent, allowing people to individually and collectively share in the upside of their discoveries creates an environment in which everyone "works together, not for themselves but for the common good."[35] *Good to Great*'s Collins calls this "legislative leadership" in the social sector, a system that "relies more upon persuasion, political currency, and shared interests to create the conditions for the right decisions to happen."[36]

Legal Structure

There are a number of reasons an organization may wish to consider alternative corporate structures beyond the common 501(c)(3) designation. We'll go over these in a future chapter, but there is at least one potential advantage worth mentioning here. As with diversifying funding models, evaluating different legal formations can add flexibility to how an organization pays its people. For example, a nonprofit can create a wholly or partially owned subsidiary in a variety of forms, including benefit corporations (B Corps), limited partnerships (LPs), or limited liability corporations (LLCs). In these cases, the subsidiary can conduct mission-related activities (or not) with the full range of available compensation practices—including stock options and other incentives that are often difficult for a nonprofit to pull off. Reduced disclosure requirements for the subsidiary in the nonprofit's Form 990 tax return may also help diffuse potentially negative donor perceptions of market-based compensation. Since salaries of subsidiary employees aren't necessarily required to be listed on the 990, organizations can avoid what one nonprofit executive called itemized compensation "for God, country, and the world to see."[37]

Storytelling

This last suggestion is a bit, well, squishier, but every bit as important. We're talking about storytelling—an art *every* successful nonprofit we know of has mastered. In his highly popular TED Talk, "How Great Leaders Inspire Action," author Simon Sinek explains, "People don't buy what you do, they buy *why* you do it."[38] The *why* creates empathy; the *why* hits the heartstrings. Nonprofits that persuasively communicate their *why*, and back it up with demonstrable impact data, can change the narrative around compensation levels to one that supports aligning pay with mission results. It's too commonly accepted in the nonprofit world that competitive incentive plans are difficult to implement because organizations lack readily available and compelling performance metrics. For-profits are awash in this information, but impact data exists in the social sector, too. Organizations just need to figure out ways to quantify and extract these metrics, and then use the data to craft compelling stories. Will doing so generate a world of equal pay for equal work in the nonprofit sector? Maybe not. But we believe it can help bridge the compensation gap, and go a long way toward achieving better outcomes for all stakeholders—including employees.

In case you're still skeptical, we close this chapter with an example of how one of America's largest counties has used carefully created performance metrics to improve the lives of its residents and of those who work tirelessly to serve them.

King County Outpatient Treatment on Demand Initiative

With a population of 2.1 million and spanning thirty-nine cities, King is Washington State's largest county. And, as in numerous other major metropolitan areas, many who live there struggle with mental health and addiction issues. By some measures, at least fifty thousand county residents receive outpatient behavioral health care annually. But this number should be higher. That's because, according to at least one nationwide estimate, nine out of ten people who need help dealing with addiction never get it.[39] And of those patients in King County who were able to receive needed care, many had to wait weeks just to secure an appointment.

"When someone is shooting up heroin several times a day, there are a few points when they might say to themselves, 'I've really got to stop this,'" said Molly Carney, executive director of the nonprofit Evergreen Treatment Services, located in Seattle. The key is to make help available during those fleeting moments. But in King County, as elsewhere, funding often isn't sufficient to allow treatment facilities to provide on-demand care—and it's not just patients who suffer. According to Jim Vollendroff, director of the county's Behavioral Health and Recovery Division, staff turnover at many of these facilities is a big problem.[40] "Nobody gets rich in this business," Carney said. "We spend so much time trying to keep our doors open that it's exhausting."[41]

In 2017, King County decided to try something different. With the help of Third Sector Capital Partners, the nonprofit advisory firm that collaborates nationwide with governments, funders, and service providers to address social needs, and funding from the Ballmer Group, the county launched a new program to make available $1.4 million in funding for *incentive payments* to providers that meet specific service benchmarks. Among these are measurements of how long it takes a patient requesting care to initially be seen (the target is within a day), and the number of days between a patient's first appointment and a follow-up visit. The King County Outpatient Treatment on Demand Initiative, as the program is known, soon grew to include twenty-three independent local health-care organizations.

It's still in its early days, but preliminary results are encouraging—for patients and providers. In addition to helping improve access to on-demand health care, much of the project's funding went toward staff salaries, with the goal of aiding in employee retention. As Third Sector's John Grossman explained, the initial incentive payments were designed to be "provider friendly." That means they were paid in advance, so service providers could hire additional staff and make structural adjustments to gear up for changes, knowing if they hit their benchmarks, future incentive payments would be available.[42]

Beratta Gomillion, executive director at the Center for Human Services in King County, believes the on-demand initiative has been a "win-win-win" for her organization, its patients, and staff. "The consumer benefits because it eliminates long wait times for an assessment [and] allows us to strike while the iron is hot and provide services when the consumer wants it," she said. "Clinicians love it because it eliminates no-shows, freeing up their time to do other tasks. Our management loves it because it improves clinicians' productivity. My only wish is that we had implemented this years ago."[43]

Equal pay for equal work? Unlikely that compensation in the third sector will—or even should—reach the levels of their for-profit brethren. But increased use of alternative funding models and legal structures, storytelling, and the (hopefully) demise of the Nonprofit Starvation Cycle can assist in at least reducing the gap.

4

ARE THERE TOO MANY NONPROFITS?

A Look at Strategic Restructuring

If you're really keen to get a rise out of somebody—especially someone connected to the nonprofit sector—ask them this: "Are there too many nonprofits?" A simple question, yes, but one that's bound to elicit passionate responses from people on both sides of it. According to Guide-Star, there are over 1.6 million nonprofit organizations registered with the IRS, and nearly two-thirds of them have annual revenues under $1 million.[1] Most are *way* under. In fact, only 10 percent of the country's nonprofits take in even $500,000. Think about that. Then consider that the average McDonald's store brings in over $2.5 million. Every. Single. Year.[2] "Hold on a second," you say. "What's a nonprofit have to do with a McNugget?" Absolutely nothing. We only bring up the comparison for the same reason you should always include people in your photos of Niagara Falls: to show scale.

Now back to some statistics. In our home county of San Diego, there are more than 11,000 registered nonprofits. Only 2,500 report having *any staff*.[3] At all. Of those that do (and have at least $50,000 in gross receipts), each must file a Form 990 tax return with the IRS, which means they'll also likely need to hire an accountant. And a lawyer. Not to mention someone within the organization to ensure it remains in compliance with a host of complex regulatory requirements. So let's just definitively conclude there are too many tiny nonprofits that can't afford to operate, and most of them should simply allow themselves to be acquired or go out of business. Next chapter. Right?

At this point, that faint murmur you're hearing might be the sound of your blood boiling. See, we told you this was a charged issue. But maybe we're not asking the right question. Perhaps, rather than debate whether there are too many nonprofits, we should instead ponder a different question—one Jan Masaoka of CalNonprofits put to us during our interview with her: "Are there *too few good ones*?"[4]

Okay, we probably didn't ratchet down the temperature much with that question, either. But Masaoka makes a valid point, which is it's tough to expect an organization—*any* organization—to change the world with next to no financial resources. And that's not a knock on those who try. It is, however, a clear-eyed admission that each dollar directed at one organization is a dollar another often more efficient organization doesn't have to put toward its mission. Every nonprofit leader we've ever known has a surfeit of passion for their cause. Far too many don't have the money or other resources they need to go the distance.

Before we completely depress you, let's say something unequivocally positive: Nonprofits of *all* sizes can provide valuable services to the sector and to society. We firmly believe this, and the sentiment was shared by nearly everyone we spoke with during the course of our research. Even those small organizations we just singled out frequently add a lot of value—in many cases because of their deep knowledge of and connections to the communities in which they work. As the Denver Foundation's Dace West explained to us, "Sometimes an organization's size is important, but often it's not. Small, grassroots organizations can be very effective."[5]

To maximize that effectiveness (and stay in business), however, under-resourced nonprofits need to concentrate on what they do best. Often this means also joining forces with other organizations to leverage assets and reduce costs. "Many nonprofits are subscale to accomplish what they are trying to do—both in terms of mission impact and operating as a sustainable organization," said Don Howard of the James Irvine Foundation. He believes this argues for consolidation or some other approach to resource sharing, noting, "How can you benefit from the back office of a larger nonprofit and still retain the storefront appeal of a smaller nonprofit? If there were some way to incentivize collaboration in the back office, I think we'd be a better sector."[6]

In *The Necessary Revolution*, organizational systems guru Peter Senge and his coauthors make the case that today's world is a complex and interconnected web of governments, businesses, and nonprofits that must work together to address a common set of sustainability problems.[7] While it still might be too early to call this a revolution, many experts we consulted believe collaboration in the nonprofit sector is crucial to improving financial sustainability and mission impact. But sometimes even collaboration isn't enough. Pick any point along what nonprofit strategy expert David La Piana calls the "continuum of mergers, joint ventures, consolidations, and joint programming,"[8] and the message is the same: Sometimes one organization just has to take a leadership role.

Dr. Gary Weitzman knows this well. As president and CEO of the San Diego Humane Society, he oversees a nonprofit that has completed four acquisitions in as many years, even going so far as to hire a full-time staffer to handle the integration of multiple cultures from the legacy organizations. The results have been undeniably positive. "If you're going to be responsible with the public's money, then you have to look at where economies of scale and new opportunities are most possible," Weitzman said. Reflecting on the San Diego Humane Society's history of mergers and acquisitions, he added, "I can't see why anybody wouldn't do it."[9]

The reality, however, is that most don't. Why? Why is a tool commonly used among for-profit companies anathema to so many in the nonprofit sector? It turns out there are a lot of reasons.

One is a lack of the same external drivers and incentives we often find in the for-profit world. As the ADL's Jonathan Greenblatt explained, "In a for-profit, you either have investors who are seeking an exit or pressuring the business to try to make sure it's constantly pushing limits and boundaries. Nonprofits really don't have the same pressure. I just don't think the incentive structures are there for more people to exit. They are satisfied with a status quo that offers job security and they don't necessarily see the value in change."[10]

John MacIntosh of SeaChange Capital Partners agrees, adding that, "In public companies, if a shareholder or a competitor really thinks you should merge, they can take certain actions to strongly encourage you to consider that. [In the nonprofit sector,] it's more a matter of self-discipline."[11]

There's also the issue of personal incentives. Owners and executives at for-profit companies are frequently enticed to pursue mergers or acquisitions by the promise of lucrative stock options and other "golden parachutes." There's no such equity to cash in at nonprofits. While exit compensation arrangements can and do exist in the social sector, they are constrained by the fear they might be considered "private inurnments" by the IRS. Before you go looking up that last term, let us cut through the haze and simply say: It's bad. Think potentially heavy excise taxes, personal liability for directors, loss of tax exempt status, and other punishments. Like we said, it's bad. Even if they don't run afoul of IRS regulations, exit compensation arrangements at nonprofits can have materially negative impacts on donor relations and public perception. And on top of all this, payouts are nowhere near as lucrative as in the for-profit sector.

Resources, too, play a significant role in the dearth of nonprofit mergers and acquisitions (M&A). Many organizations, particularly smaller ones, are busy enough just keeping the lights on. They just don't have the staff or financial wherewithal to pursue a time-consuming and expensive investigation of the merits of a possible M&A deal. Transactions also require specialized, sophisticated expertise from investment bankers, facilitators, and other intermediaries. Though growing, the availability of these types of professional services in the nonprofit sector is still limited. But for the sake of argument, let's say an organization did manage to close a merger deal. Now the surviving leadership has the herculean task of figuring out how to successfully combine two possibly disparate corporate cultures. And, if the missions are not closely aligned or complementary, the merger is likely doomed to fail. This stuff isn't easy. Bridgespan partner and former Tides Center CEO Willa Seldon observed, "People often don't want to give up their brands."[12] One reason relates to a term you probably have heard of: *founder's syndrome*. For the uninitiated, it isn't a medical malady, but rather an attitude or belief held by an organization's founders, leaders, staff, or even board members that, "We built this. We are the secret sauce. Nobody else can do it better." More on this in chapter 5.

Finally, there's the fear of upsetting current or prospective donors. Nonprofits are often reluctant to address consideration of M&A opportunities with donors out of concern it may delay or impede future grants. They're also worried that mergers may decrease overall funding. For example, donors may reckon, instead of "giving to two we'll give to one."

Most nonprofit mergers are considered for cost reduction, not for mission impact, and therefore often viewed, as Bridgespan noted in an in-depth report, "as a route out of financial distress or leadership vacuums instead of . . . as an effective growth strategy."[13]

Well, then. That's certainly a long list, isn't it? No wonder we don't see more consolidation in the nonprofit sector. And that's unfortunate, since a growing body of evidence points to a relatively high rate of success with nonprofit mergers and collaborations. (Conclusions on the long-term success of mergers in the for-profit space are mixed at best.) At the very least, resource sharing should be more prevalent. In financial terms, SeaChange's MacIntosh said, "nonprofits pay almost nothing to collaborate other than transaction costs, which generally are a small fraction of the potential benefits."[14] However, he added, it's counterproductive for major funders to suggest collaboration to a nonprofit without first achieving complete buy-in from the organization's board, leadership, and staff.

The bottom line is the world is hard and nonprofits need help. More than ever, today's problems truly take a village to solve. Whether we assemble that village by merger, acquisition, collaboration, or consolidation isn't really the point. Rather, it's that organizations need the support of all stakeholders—especially funders—in pursuing opportunities to leverage and conserve their resources. The yield is precious: greater financial sustainability and improved mission results. The for-profit world has long used the alchemy of capital and expertise to elevate these techniques to an exalted art form. But nonprofits are catching up. Increasingly, there is help available to organizations wishing to navigate the mutuality minefield. This includes support from forward-thinking foundations and philanthropists, as well as a growing number of consultants and advisors who can assist in planning and executing transactions. It turns out demand from within the nonprofit community has been growing, too. As far back as 2014, a study by Bridgespan and the Lodestar Foundation determined, "The notion that collaboration strengthens a pursuit isn't new, but it's certainly become hot in the nonprofit world." The authors were surprised by the degree of collaboration they discovered in the sector, as well as how successful those collaborations were overall. In addition, they noted, "Both funders and nonprofits wanted more of all types, in particular shared support functions and mergers."[15]

But it takes money. One of the key (if self-evident) conclusions reached in a report issued by the NFF was that, "Nonprofits need dedicated resources for mergers and collaborations. Partnerships are resource intensive, yet most nonprofits operate in a resource-constrained reality." Many costs are involved, "from the opportunity costs of senior staff dedicating time and attention to a partnership, to the cash expenditures of consulting fees, systems integration, benefits and compensation reconciliations, and work or program space changes." Although in some cases funders or donors offered some support to help defray expenses related to these transitions, "often the collaborating partners shouldered the burden of additional costs themselves."[16]

SHOW ME THE MONEY

So just how does a Main Street nonprofit find the resources—human and financial—to investigate possible partnership opportunities, much less close a deal? As we've said, a growing number of funders are recognizing the power of collaboration and appreciating the benefits that accrue to participating organizations.

The SeaChange-Lodestar Fund for Nonprofit Collaboration is one such example. Itself a collaboration between the Lodestar Foundation and SeaChange Capital Partners, the fund was set up in 2009 to help nonprofits cover the costs of exploring, evaluating, and closing cooperative transactions with other organizations. *Seed grants* of up to $5,000 "pay for the organizations to convene key parties and/or retain outside experts to educate those parties on the general technical and logistical aspects of collaboration."[17]

The fund's expectation is that its seed grants will more often than not bear fruit and lead to an exploratory phase. Here, the stakes are higher, and both organizations' leadership, including key board members, must fully support the idea of a potential partnership. Also required is a clear articulation of the desired outcomes each organization wants to achieve from a merger or strategic collaboration. Since the services of outside consultants and other intermediaries are often needed, grants of up to $25,000 are available to help pay for these expenses. Assuming a deal is greenlit, the fund then provides additional money to cover the myriad costs associated with implementation. Some are "unavoidable but uninspiring . . . such as IT integration, rebranding, severance costs, and lease-breaking"[18]—prosaic expenses to be sure, and ones that might cause many funders to balk. Over the past decade, according to SeaChange's statistics, the fund has looked at some 375 opportunities and bankrolled more than ninety-five transactions. John MacIntosh, for one, would like to see those numbers go even higher. "If nonprofits fully explored the various ways they can work together," he said, "which certainly could be through a merger, but could also include back office sharing or even divesting a program to an organization that might perform better, they would do it more."[19]

One of the fund's namesakes, the Lodestar Foundation, devotes a significant percentage of its own grantmaking to backing consolidation via mergers and collaborations. These grants—which range from $5,000 to $3 million (most being $10,000–$40,000)—are designed to support "nonprofits that have made the joint decision to explore and/or implement permanent relationships."[20] True to its name, Lodestar also has helped create a trove of resources to assist the sector, including Candid's Nonprofit Collaboration Database, which contains searchable information on more than 650 alliances.[21] Think of it as Tinder for nonprofits.

SeaChange and Lodestar aren't the only players. With support from the Boston Foundation, the Hyams Foundation, the Kresge Foundation, LISC Boston, and United Way of Massachusetts Bay and Merrimack Valley, the NFF created and managed the Catalyst Fund for Nonprofits, a half-decade cooperative effort to explore possibilities for mergers and partnerships among organizations in the Boston area. (You have to concede there's just something beautifully symmetric about a group that chooses to collaborate to identify more opportunities for collaboration.) In its five years of operation, the Catalyst Fund worked with over eighty nonprofits and funded twenty partnership ventures, including thirteen mergers. It also produced a host of useful resources for like-minded organizations, such as step-by-step guides, practical examples, and suggestions from a detailed report on the project's key findings. Tellingly, all of the Catalyst Fund's initial backers remain active in supporting M&A and other collaborative ventures through transaction support, advocacy, and funding.

In fact, many foundations we spoke with said they provide grantees financial resources, in a variety of forms, for the pursuit of consolidation activities. This isn't a new development. In a piece published by the *Stanford Social Innovation Review*, author Jean Butzen advises organizations that, "Even if your current donors do not specify that they fund merger and partnership expenses in their guidelines, if they are invested in your development as a nonprofit they may be willing to consider a one-time request from you for merger or partnership costs. Now, more than ever, donors are showing interest in nonprofits merging."[22] That was written in 2009. In the intervening decade, however, despite our previous examples to the contrary—and perhaps because of the litany of reasons we outlined earlier in this chapter—merger momentum still hasn't fully gained steam.

Another reason for this might simply be lack of awareness among nonprofits of the extensive toolkit available to them. (There's a reason we're writing this book, after all.) In a previous chapter, we discussed the importance of what we termed nonprofit merchant bankers—consultants and financiers who, in addition to raising funds and brokering transactions, design, structure, and provide advice on strategic partnerships and M&A activities. In short, not much would get done in the capital markets without them. And yet, a goodly number of nonprofits don't know these services exist. Industry insider and author Bhakti Mirchandani explained that, "Executives at nonprofit potential and target acquirers may not have the time or the specialized skills to focus on an M&A transaction. Due diligence, negotiating affiliation agreements, and integration are all time-consuming activities that require specialized skills. Thankfully, there are nonprofit merger specialist consultants and advisors."[23]

We've already looked at a couple of them, and there are many others. The Bridgespan Group—itself a nonprofit—is an international consulting organization started in 1999 by former partners of the white-shoe consulting firm Bain & Company. Though Bridgespan specializes in serving mid- to large-size nonprofits, the organization's website is a rich (and free) collection of articles, podcasts, videos, and case studies on a wide variety of topics, including strategic restructuring. (There's so much information, we had to interview three Bridgespan partners just to make sense of it all.)

The aforementioned David La Piana founded La Piana Consulting more than twenty years ago with support from the David and Lucile Packard Foundation, the James Irvine Foundation, and the William and Flora Hewlett Foundation. Its mission—"to improve leadership and management practices throughout the sector for greater social impact,"[24] —has led the firm to advise "hundreds of nonprofits in negotiating mergers, joint ventures, and other strategic partnerships, and [help] many more assess their readiness for such collaborations."[25]

La Piana also has literally written the book on strategic partnerships. Among his many published titles are *The Nonprofit Strategy Revolution, The Nonprofit Mergers Workbooks I* and *II, Play to Win,* and *The Nonprofit Business Plan.*[26]

You get the idea. There's help available for those organizations open to strategic collaboration to improve financial sustainability and mission impact. The growing interest in partnering up among nonprofit leaders and the funding community has been accompanied by similar growth in the number of experts who provide advice on evaluating, structuring, and closing transactions.

For those just beginning to dip their toes into the somewhat murky waters of formal collaboration, the terminology can be confusing. The following information outlines some of the more common arrangements, laid out based on the degree of integration required by the participating organizations.[27]

Four types of collaboration can be arrayed on a spectrum based on level of integration, from less—associations and joint programs—to more—shared support functions and mergers:

- Associations (includes coalitions and collaboratives)

  - Works together over an extended period of time to accomplish shared goals
  - Joins by formal agreement
  - Governs separately
  - Works separately

- Joint Programs

- Works with another organization to deliver a program over an extended period of time
- Integrates and agrees upon contract
- Governs separately

- Shared Support Functions

  - Shares administrative functions (such as accounting, human resources, and IT)
  - Contracts for administrative services or hiring a third party to provide those services

- Mergers (includes affiliate and subsidiary structures)

  - Legally links the governance of two organizations
  - Integrates into one entity, or establishes an affiliate or subsidiary, or creates a new entity

Not to belabor semantics, but there's also an important difference between *collaboration* and what's known as *collective impact*. John MacIntosh at SeaChange described this distinction:

- **Collaboration:** A merger, acquisition, joint venture, or programmatic alliance in which two or more parties *combine* some or all of their important activities in a long-term formal way
- **Collective Impact:** A strategy for creating a very particular type of collaboration whereby nonprofits, government, business, and the public coordinate around a common objective to address a complex social problem[28]

Okay, let's get out of the weeds now. Rather than bog you down with nomenclature, we'll simply say that all the arrangements we've mentioned can carry significant benefits to the nonprofit sector. Collaboration—in any form—is a powerful tool not only for marshaling scarce resources, but also for reducing the burdens on overworked staff, eliminating duplicative back-office and information technology systems, and building scale to leverage administrative and executive talent. The key is for leaders to put ample thought into which system makes the most sense given their organization's unique circumstances.

WHY GO IT ALONE?

Let's take a look at some of this in action, starting with shared support functions and outsourcing. Depending on your views and experience, that last term may be somewhat controversial. But it shouldn't be—at least not here. When we talk about outsourcing, we aren't saying people should lose their jobs. Rather, they should have *fewer* jobs. No joke—we once received a business card from a nonprofit employee that noted her title was, "Director of Development, Finance and Human Resources."

At the risk of offending any of our similarly overworked readers . . . ah, who are we kidding? Anyone with that many jobs doesn't have time to *read*! So here goes: If your business card has more titles than the Library of Congress, you're probably not great at any of your roles. And you know what? That's not your fault. You simply have too much you're responsible for and you're stretched too thin. Anyone would be! The nonprofit employee we just mentioned is one of the most capable, responsible, caring, and selfless people we know. She just has way too much to do. *She* knows it. And, we suspect, if this paragraph is describing you, you know it, too.

It's not just the labor pool that's overburdened. We're often shocked to learn how much money Main Street nonprofits spend on non-core back-office activities that could easily be outsourced. And none of this takes into account the disruption that occurs when someone gets sick, takes parental leave, or—another real-life example—the finance department can't close the books because they have to help out with the annual gala. Apart from the obvious potential cost savings, outsourcing some or even most back-office functions can provide other important benefits, such as access to the latest business tools and technologies. (Everything always seems to work fine, until your system crashes.) Look, when we have a toothache we don't drill our own teeth. We go to a dentist. And not to a dentist/auto mechanic/veterinarian. So why are so many organizations operating in a manner tantamount to representing themselves in court? Come to think of it, legal representation is something nonprofits are already outsourcing—along with payroll, audits, tax returns, and perhaps more. In fact, every rote, repetitive function should be considered a candidate for outsourcing and subjected to rigorous cost-benefit analysis. Start by asking, "Is this the highest and best use of my or my staff's time?" It's a mind-set. Just as when thinking about collaboration, nonprofits should concentrate on doing what they're really, really good at.

But don't just take our word for it. This sentiment was echoed in a blog by McKinsey & Company, "Eight Business Technology Trends to Watch," in which they noted, "As more and more sophisticated work takes place interactively online and new collaboration and communications tools emerge, companies can outsource increasingly specialized aspects of their work and still maintain organizational coherence. Much as technology permits them to decentralize innovation through networks or customers, it also allows them to parcel out more work to specialists, free agents, and talent networks."[29] This movement has been afoot for a while. Way back in 2010, an article appeared in the *Stanford Social Innovation Review* extolling the virtues of "radically modifying the way that non-profits manage their business functions," and observing that, "To compete and succeed over the long term in this new environment, many visionary executives are choosing to outsource part or all of their back-office functions to outside providers."[30]

If you're eager to get started, check out *A Nonprofit Guide to Outsourcing*[31] and a searchable database of potential vendors.[32]

But what if your organization is really small? Or it's just starting out and doesn't yet have critical administrative infrastructure in place. Maybe it hasn't even received a tax-exempt designation from the IRS. What to do in these cases? An arrangement called *fiscal sponsorship* may be a solution. Though these partnerships have existed for a long time, they're often misunderstood. According to TSNE MissionWorks, a nonprofit provider of consulting and training services that has been sponsoring organizations for decades, "Fiscal sponsors are 501(c)(3) charitable corporations that give unincorporated groups whose missions are aligned with their own a tax-exempt home."[33]

Although legally under their patron's corporate umbrella, sponsored organizations and programs nonetheless retain a high degree of autonomy. They chart their own strategic course, build relationships with funders, and often even maintain independent advisory boards. For their part, fiscal sponsors can provide a wide range of services, including imputing tax-exempt credibility to nascent nonprofits looking to establish their bona fides with prospective donors. Some, such as San Francisco-based Tides, do a whole lot more. Envision, if you will, a high-tech startup company in the for-profit world. Domiciled in a millennially hip yet spartan office space, the firm and its ambitious progenitors are surrounded by other like-minded entrepreneurs and coached by leading domain experts: lawyers, investment bankers, and top technology talent. This is fertile soil for collaboration. Tides and organizations like it are this milieu's nonprofit equivalent.

Founded in 1976 by social entrepreneur Drummond Pike as a response to what he perceived as a paucity of guidance in philanthropic giving, Tides today is a nonprofit that provides a host of services to the social sector. Among them are grantmaking, managing donor-advised funds, impact investing, and fiscal sponsorship. Through its furnishing of collaborative workspaces, as well as providing support and advocacy assistance in keeping with its mission to "accelerate the pace of social change,"[34] Tides has sponsored more than 1,400 nonprofit projects over its four-decade history. In 2017 alone, "[Tides] managed essential support services for 170 social ventures, employing 760 staff, and collectively managing program budgets totaling almost $153 million."[35] For this, Tides charges its clients 9 percent of project revenues. If that figure strikes you as a bit high, compare it to the 20–30 percent often spent by nonprofits on administration and overhead. The turnkey services Tides provides include financial administration, human resources, benefits management, governance, compliance, and risk management. Now, imagine you are a lean startup nonprofit. Would you want to tackle all that yourself? But it's not just about organizational capacity or financial savings. It's also surrounding yourself with similar souls, giving your team access to a network of potential funders and collaborators, and freeing up your staff to focus on their collective core competencies.

Short of outright outsourcing, sharing services and resources with other organizations is an alternative way to potentially lessen burdensome overhead costs. We say *potentially* because to work—to create a whole that's greater than the sum of its parts—collaboration really has to be driven by the right motivations. Many of the people we interviewed during the course of our research had the same dire warning: Corporate allegiances of any kind—mergers, acquisitions, partnerships, or collaborations—simply will not succeed if they are purely centered on saving money. Because of their relative permanence, mergers can be particularly fraught. "One really important observation [about mergers]," said the NFF's Antony Bugg-Levine, "is they're successful when driven by a recognition that the merged entity can better serve its clients and its mission, and not by cost savings."[36] Indeed, whether in the nonprofit or for-profit sector, anticipated savings from M&A very often don't materialize until farther down the road, if ever. Therefore, in any shared arrangement, the impetus has to be delivering value and providing more effective service to stakeholders. Or, as Robert Foster, director of Impact Investing at San Diego Grantmakers, put it: convene your collaborative ecosystem around *outcomes*. Ask, "What do we want to accomplish together?"[37] Then, make sure all involved thoroughly understands their role.

When they do, the result can be symbiotic kismet. Philanthropist Joan Jacobs gave us the following simple yet powerful example that illustrates this concept of mission-based resource sharing: The nonprofit La Jolla Playhouse operates in several theaters located on the University of California San Diego's beautifully verdant campus. The university grants the playhouse use of its theaters at no cost, and, in turn, La Jolla Playhouse supports several much smaller theater groups in the community. The collaboration provides facilities for the performances of these groups, which, as Jacobs describes, don't have aspirations of building their own facilities. "They are happy doing their six performances a year and both organizations are satisfying the community in keeping with their missions."[38]

A NEW KIND OF ECOSYSTEM

While describing other examples of organizations coalescing around a shared objective—what MacIntosh dubbed collective impact—several people kept using a common term. Let's see how quickly you can spot it. Ready? First, from Eric Nee of the *Stanford Social Innovation Review*: "We need private, social, and government sectors to address complex issues, and to do so they all need to collaborate and create virtuous ecosystems."[39] Second, here's the Denver Foundation's Dace West: "The first step in being a good partner in a virtuous ecosystem is rigorous, deep self-assessment. Ask 'why do I want to be a partner—what do I bring to the table?'"[40] Find it yet? *Virtuous ecosystems*. Well done, you! This delectably apt turn of phrase kept popping up over and over during the course of our research and interviews. We love it because, at its heart, it's describing a self-reinforcing system in which each participant is encouraged—*required*, in fact—to concentrate on what it does best. Precious resources aren't needlessly squandered. Everyone's purpose is complementary and valued. And the results are accretive. As Project Concern's Carrie Hessler-Radelet explained, "The key to good partnerships is recognizing what you're good at and what your partners are good at to create a one plus one equals three scenario."[41]

Just two steps—an organization determining its "special sauce," that is, what it brings to the table, coupled with an awareness of others who could augment the partnership—form the basis of collective impact. Sometimes these arrangements are obvious, but not always—even when perhaps they should be. John Vasconcellos, CEO of the Community Foundation of Southeastern Massachusetts, describes a successful collaborative effort that developed with a $15,000 grant to help facilitate regular meetings among several organizations running after-school youth programs in New Bedford, Massachusetts. "There was a real coming together with positive results," he said, "such as when one organization helped to overcome transportation issues which prevent attendance by providing buses for kids and staff." In hindsight, Vasconcellos is surprised this seemingly simple solution wasn't discovered earlier. "These folks were all from the same community, knew each other socially, but just had never worked together," he said.[42]

Other attempts at collective impact are more complex due to the nature of the problems they want to solve, such as homelessness, and therefore require a broader approach. Seldon at Bridgespan believes nonprofits "do a lot of light collaborations." However, she continued, to really put a dent in society's gnarliest issues, organizations have to take time and make the effort to foster what she calls "deep collaboration" across multiple sectors. On this, she sees room for improvement, noting, "I think more often we are meeting rather than collaborating."[43]

With so much at stake and so many potential obstacles to partnership, it may seem easier just to maintain control and head out alone. But a bit of planning and forethought can go a long way. As West explains, "it's really important to slow down and talk through some of the things that might trip up collaborations and partnerships further down the line, when the initial excitement has worn off and people may start not to like each other as much. Basic things like 'What's our decision-making structure?' 'What happens if we have a disagreement?' 'Do we fundraise together?' 'How are we communicating about the work we're doing?' 'Do we all get credit?'"[44]

Before we wrap, let's take a look at one more example of a virtuous ecosystem in action: Colorado Resource Partners' WORKNOW initiative.

Sam lives in Denver. Looking through one of his tiny apartment windows, he sees gleaming new buildings and serpentine highways being built all around him. The infrastructure economy is literally humming with activity. But Sam is stuck flipping burgers for minimum wage. Best he can do, because Sam's been in prison. Besides, he has to watch the kids when his wife is working. He doesn't even own a car, let alone have the money to pay for gas and insurance. Pretty bleak, right?

Enter WORKNOW, a robust new workforce development program designed to help Denver families living in areas experiencing gentrification train and find employment in the construction industry. (It won't surprise any of our readers who have been to the Denver metro area recently to learn there are *a lot* of these projects going on.) Launched in October 2017 with a $1 million seed capital grant from Gary Community Investments, WORKNOW is the brainchild of Colorado Resource (CORE) Partners, a cross-sector coalition of fifteen regional organizations representing governments, nonprofits, and for-profits alike.

Through its alliance of partners, this innovative program trained Sam and found a job for him in the construction industry—where he now earns two to three times the minimum wage, before overtime. That's not all. When Sam needs daycare for his kids, there's a CORE organization ready to help. Bus passes to get him to the jobsite? Covered. Money to pay for work clothes and tools? Check. Everything Sam needs to succeed is provided by coalition partners. Oh, and after the initial million is spent, who pays? Private employers—eager to fill construction positions with skilled and motivated candidates. In its first year alone, WORKNOW has found, trained, and placed 190 "Sams" in stable, good-paying jobs.

In a press release delivered on the eve of WORKNOW's one-year anniversary, Katrina Wert, director of the Center for Workforce Initiatives at Community College of Denver, summarized what she believes brought this ambitious project to fruition: "The early success of WORKNOW confirms the need for increased collaboration among families in the community, construction contractors, and regional economic development projects so that the entire Denver metro community can thrive. The breadth of this collaboration demonstrates a shared commitment to increasing economic stability through employment and career advancement opportunities."[45]

Now, if that doesn't convince you of the merits of strategic partnership, well, we suppose you should just return this book to the library. Kidding, of course. We really hope you bought a copy. Joking aside, in our conversations with industry leaders, all expressed major interest in and support for the various types of collaborative initiatives we've described in this chapter. Nonprofit executives see the potential to transform their sector through improved mission impact. Funders expressed the need to incentivize strategic restructuring through greater support of exploratory activities, deal facilitation, and post-event integration. To be clear, not everyone is sanguine on the idea. Some, including funders, are still reluctant to initiate transactions—viewing such overtures as "bad philanthropy" by encouraging "shotgun weddings." That perspective should augur more initiative being taken by nonprofits themselves. As Bridgespan's Seldon told us, "There are some funders who will invest in helping to foster collaboration. But I think organizations could be bolder in creatively pursuing ways to collaborate, and then searching for funding together."[46]

In the end, though, it takes collaboration—from all stakeholders—to encourage collaboration. Everyone must buy in. Organizations have to seek out opportunities and consider the cultural impact of a merger or partnership. Funders have to get over their fears that one plus one will be less than two and commit resources toward various collaborative efforts. And board members, who represent a multitude of industries, have to help break down silos and foster collaboration among different sectors.

But the best advice might just be what we call the Partnership Golden Rule: Be someone you would want to collaborate with, and others will find you. Look for shared values, and you will find opportunities to work together.

5

THE TWIN ENGINES OF THE PLANE

Boards and the CEO

Before you read any more, we feel we owe you full disclosure. Hey, you've been with us this far, right? So you should expect nothing less. Here goes. This is a chapter about *leadership*. There, we said it. Feels really good to get that off our chest right up front. Why the concern, you ask? Because, with the possible exception of love or *Harry Potter*, arguably no other subject in the literary canon has commanded the volume of shelf space leadership has. Seriously. A lot of smart people have already said a lot of smart things about it. What could we possibly add? Maybe not much. (Leadership lesson number one: under-promise and over-deliver.)

We at least hope to put a somewhat unique spin on an otherwise familiar topic, since we're going to be talking about leadership from the twin perspectives of nonprofit executives and their boards. Because, as we hope you've seen in previous chapters, both have the capacity to greatly affect their organization's mission impact and sustainability.

We've already shown how leadership can help nonprofits build sustainable funding models and create virtuous ecosystems. In fact, the need for strong leadership winds its way into every chapter in this book. It's that important! But where does it come from? How do you get it? Some say, "You'll know leadership when you see it," or "Great leaders will emerge from the crowd." Maybe. But if you're running an organization now, can you really afford to wait?

BOARD OR BORED?

Let's take a look at that paragon of good governance and fiscal steward-ship: the board of directors. Without question, having a high-quality board is paramount to a fully functioning organization. However, if left unchecked, overemphasizing a board's (admittedly important) legal re-sponsibilities to ensure compliance with myriad regulations can often leave little time for broader, equally important activities. Taken to an extreme, this can extinguish members' passion for the cause that led them to join the board in the first place.

It's well recognized under a plethora of state and federal laws, as well as by custom, that as stewards of assets owned by John Q. Public, nonprofit board members must exercise three "duties" in their role as directors/trustees:

- **Obedience:** Requires faithfulness to the organization's charitable purposes and goals
- **Loyalty:** Requires members to work unselfishly for the benefit of the organization and not for personal gain, and prohibits (with some exceptions) conflicts of interest and appropriation of the nonprofit's assets
- **Care:** Requires familiarity with all available information before taking action with attentiveness and care under the circum-stances[1]

Important stuff, all, and for lots of reasons—not the least of which are the significant reputational risks and personal liability that can come with violating any of those duties. But as many an overworked and underappreciated board member has silently mused during yet another endless round of committee reports (please read them in advance, peo-ple!), hyper-focusing on mundane legalities can make the boardroom table a pretty boring place to be. Over time, members justifiably may begin to feel like traffic cops, and start to *manage* rather than *lead*. If you're unclear on the difference, *management* starts with the head. *Leadership* starts with the heart. People at all levels have to be inspired! If they're not, bored board members may still show up—because they love the mission—and do what they can, but they'll feel underutilized, frustrated, and disenfranchised. Given many members' vast experience, resources, and relationships—what a waste! Yes, fiduciary fealty has its place, but it must be balanced with a sense of inspiration and purpose for an organization to thrive. After all, you can have the best set of books in the world and still go bankrupt.

While researching their seminal book *Governance as Leadership: Reframing the Work of Nonprofit Boards* (required reading for board members, by the way), authors Richard Chait, William Ryan, and Barbara Taylor found that in many organizations, "the board's work becomes so predictable and perfunctory as to be tedious and monotonous."[2] Sure, it can't all be rainbows and unicorns—sorry, one of us has a three-year-old daughter—but the authors maintain that boards need to give *equal time and effort* to all of what they refer to as the three modes of governance.[3]

Liz Shear, longtime professor of nonprofit leadership at the University of San Diego, summarizes the interplay of these three modes in what she calls "The Kaleidoscope of Governance,"[4] with each mode viewed as a different lens. When turned, they lead to infinite and ever-changing patterns of performance:

- **Fiduciary:** The goals are good oversight of operations, legal compliance, and stewardship of assets. It's about organizational efficiency, not effectiveness, and boards must ask, "What's going right and what can go wrong?"
- **Strategic:** Here, the concern is with the creation and evaluation of organizational impact. The goals are to move the organization wisely into a preferred future, shaping the work to meet it and offering technical assistance along the way. Boards must partner with the organization's leadership team to answer the key question: "What's the future of this organization and what's the strategic plan to get there?"
- **Generative:** This is idea mode. Creativity flourishes and organizational roots are used to foster new growth consistent with core values and the mission. Here, the goals are to identify and use present and past experience, values, culture, challenges, and assumptions to shape decisions about future directions, policies, and programs. Board members must ask, "What are the right questions we should be asking?"

Learning to deftly turn this kaleidoscope confers important benefits to the organization and its board. As Chait and his team explain, successfully toggling the work of the board repositions its role from that of traffic cops to co-leaders with the organization's executive team. And individual board members feel revitalized and reengaged because they are encouraged to contribute their specialized skills to improve sustainability and mission impact.

TIME, TALENT, AND TREASURE

Since we're clearly on a roll with threes (three duties of board members, three modes of governance), we're just going to keep it up. Here's a (third!) group of threes you've likely heard before: time, talent, and treasure. The "three Ts," as they're often called, have long been used as a wish list for board member recruitment. But as with most shortcuts, there are limits to this one's utility. Overreliance on a few alliterative traits can filter the spectrum of capable prospective board members through too narrow a prism. Other nonprofits may create "skill grids" as a template for filling board seats, but if not carefully crafted, these, too, can be overly restrictive and not cover all the skills needed on a particular board *at a particular time*. Boards, like the organizations they serve, are protean. They're movies, not snapshots. Neglecting to keep members relevant and up-to-date will severely limit the board's potential to fulfill its co-leadership role. Let's look at a couple of the more well-known board member archetypes: the Big Check Writer and the Worker Bee.

Pretty hard to find much fault with someone who consistently supports your organization year after year, right? After all, what nonprofit wouldn't want a board member with a fat wallet and a generous spirit? And we're certainly not saying deep-pocketed members can't serve a very valuable purpose. But context matters. Many of you likely have served on boards with people who viewed their checkbook as their sole contribution, otherwise preferring to maintain MINO status. That's pronounced like the fish—minnow—because, well, it's cute and easy to remember. It stands for *member in name only*. You know board members like this. Some, especially those with a certain degree of notoriety or community cachet, can suck all of the oxygen out of a room—often at the expense of their less-well-heeled colleagues' potentially amazing skills and ideas. An organization's executives, too, might be overly deferential to wealthy board members, handling them with kid gloves, lest they upset their golden egg–laying goose. And let's not forget the lessons we've learned about the importance of diverse revenue sources for sustainability. If you're counting on board member beneficence to make budget, you're opening up your organization to a lot of risk in the event those members take their charitable inclinations elsewhere. Board members shouldn't be looked at as a nonprofit's primary funders. If so, your "customers" change every time the board turns over. To be clear, however, we believe all board members should financially support their organization. If members aren't putting their own money— no matter how small the amount—behind a cause, how can they reasonably expect an outsider to do so? But we also believe before board members can be engaged in fundraising, they first have to be engaged as board members. This means creating an atmosphere of inclusivity, where everyone's contributions—financial and otherwise—are valued.

Then there are the Worker Bees, those dutiful and diligent denizens of the board. You probably know one of them, too. Heck, maybe you *are* one of them. If so, let us be the first to give a heartfelt *thank you*. Why? It's likely that no matter how much you think your efforts are cherished, you are in fact quite *underappreciated*. Because you say "yes" to everything. You *do* everything. You are your fellow board members' go-to person. For everything. Too often, you pick up the operational slack for others. (See MINOs discussed earlier.) Your time to think and create is constrained, and you're left with little energy to work in the strategic and generative modes so critical to board success and your own personal development. And for all your trouble, you eventually flame out. This may happen because you're stretched too thin, but it can also result from being pigeonholed into a very narrow range of responsibilities based on your background or professional skill set. Are you the CPA on your nonprofit's board? Don't serve as the organization's accountant, too. Not only is it a potential conflict of interest, but it's also a sure road to board member burnout. You do this stuff all day for a living. Do you really want it to consume your off-hours, too?

Of course, we've had to generalize with these examples. But we think you may have recognized more than a kernel of truth in both the Big Check Writer and Worker Bee archetypes. And our point is simply to emphasize the importance of organizations setting up their boards in such a way that maximizes each member's unique gifts of time, talent, and treasure. This takes a lot of strategic planning and foresight, because once constructed, boards can't be quickly changed like tiles in a game of Scrabble. It's about getting members in the right seats on the bus, so they can contribute in ways that fulfill both the person and the mission.

Some strategies can help. One is to build *alternative boards*, such as an advisory board comprising representative stakeholders—separate from your elected board—who can give you insights into the efficacy of your mission and programs. Nonprofits fortunate enough to have the requisite resources can also consider creating endowment or foundation boards—especially for those members who prefer simply to write checks. In fact, give them an honorary position, too, such as *Director Emeritus*. Hey, big egos like big titles. Members who are less inclined to get their hands dirty in the trenches of the full working board can be shifted to another one better suited to their desires and inclinations. The *USS Midway* Museum, as an example, maintains two equally important boards: a foundation board where members manage investments and grants, and a working board for strategic and operational accountability. Back to our bus analogy, the key is to delegate, tinker, and yes, *talk with* your board members until everyone is in the right seat to best serve the organization. Some people thrive on the lofty visionary work of long-term planning and loathe mundane, detail-oriented tasks. They're perfect for a board's strategic and generative functions, but terrible for the fiduciary jobs. Okay, you get the idea: Use board resources where they can make the greatest contributions.

Another option to consider (and, frankly, one we don't see considered enough) is term limits for board members. Maybe the reason for the relative disuse of this practice is the negative perception that the imposition of term limits simply is a way to pare deadwood. Yes, it can serve that purpose. But term limits are also a great way to infuse diversity and "new blood" into a board. After all, how can you expect your organization to stay current if your board isn't? There are downsides, of course. An obvious one is the potential loss of institutional memory and team cohesion. The trick is to strike the right balance between time-tested teamwork and the risk of stale, entrenched viewpoints. You don't want to tip from *awesome* to *ossified*.

It's a slippery slope, but there are some tactics that can help. A few of these are lengthened—but still limited—terms, "penalty box" provisions (after a certain number of terms, members must sit out for a period before rejoining the board), and asking valuable members who have termed out to chair committees or special projects rather than occupy a formal board seat. Also, requiring potential board candidates to serve on committees or advisory boards prior to officially joining the full board can augment the nonprofit's institutional memory, and is a great way for everyone to "test drive" the relationship. There are highly skilled people out there who are happy to serve in these roles in lieu of committing to a board seat.

Much has been written on the subject of board development in the decade and a half since Chait and his coauthors published their groundbreaking work. We'll provide additional resources later in the book, but one of these deserves a quick mention here as another "go-to" organization: BoardSource. This nonprofit's mission is to support organizational governance and board/staff leadership development through education and training, consulting, research, and myriad publications. Main Street nonprofits: if you don't yet know this group, you should.

PERFORMANCE REVIEWS AND PROFESSIONAL DEVELOPMENT

Let's jump back to the title of this chapter for a moment. We think the analogy of an airplane's twin engines for a nonprofit's executive and board of directors is apt. Stay with us. Each engine operates with its own system of indicators and alerts that monitor the engine's effect on safety and performance. For the plane to operate flawlessly, both engines have to be finely tuned and working in concert. For nonprofits, this fine-tuning starts with regular (at least annual) 360-degree performance reviews of board and staff, and continuous professional development. Larger organizations tend to do this well. Smaller ones, sadly, not so much. In fact, almost never. If these nonprofits were airplanes, we would think long and hard before agreeing to ride in one.

You just can't neglect performance reviews and maintenance and expect to function well—no matter what industry you're in. There are many reasons this exists in the nonprofit sector, including *founder's syndrome* (more on this in a minute) and boards that are stuck in fiduciary mode. Strikingly, though, it's most often because reviews and development simply have never historically been part of an organization's culture.

Inga Ingulfsen, research manager of global projects and partnerships at Candid, which aggregates and makes available to other nonprofits an expansive trove of funding data from foundations and other grant makers, stressed the importance of unrestricted funding for leadership development. This is especially critical, she says, in mid-level leadership positions, which can serve as an organization's executive pipeline. Without one, this lack of bench strength can put organizations at significant risk when there is turnover—something that happens frequently in the nonprofit sector.[5]

Diversity

As with motherhood, apple pie, and puppies, it's hard to find anyone who would utter an unkind word against diversity. It's easy to see why. Availing yourself and your organization of the full marketplace of ideas is crucial for sustainability. The National Council of Nonprofits agrees: "Having a board with diverse perspectives is critically important," it writes. "Each person will bring his or her own personal and professional contacts and life experiences to their service on a nonprofit board." This collectively broad perspective, the authors continue, puts organizations "in a stronger position to plan for the future, manage risk, make prudent decisions, and take full advantage of opportunities. A diverse board that is also sensitive to cultural differences is usually one that has a stronger capacity to attract and retain talented board members—as well as to be in touch with community needs."[6] Malin Burnham, the philanthropist and venerable long-serving member of numerous boards, puts it more succinctly. "Board diversity of knowledge, experience, and perspective is the key to success," he said.[7]

So why do so many boards still look like the honor wall at a 1950s country club? According to BoardSource's latest survey, "84 percent of board members report as Caucasian," and 27 percent of boards said they have precisely zero people of color. For you statistics junkies out there, that's *100 percent white*. Just as troubling, in the more than twenty years since BoardSource has conducted its survey, "the levels of board diversity have largely remained unchanged, with people of color and ethnic minorities never representing more than 18 percent of board membership."[8] Women, too, tend to be grossly underrepresented on corporate and nonprofit boards.

Yes, it's not all boards. Some make diversity a priority in recruitment. In fact, we recently attended an event for a local nonprofit and were pleasantly surprised when a young lady who was clearly not past her fourth decade introduced herself as a member of the organization's board. But far too many boards are still what we call (with more than a touch of irony, it must be said) *awesome.* That's spelled OWSM, which stands for *old, white, stale, male.* Now, before some of you dust off your typewriter to complain to our editor, you should know that one of us is a white male senior citizen, so we hope we can get away with this comment.

Slow but real progress is being made. However, nonprofit leaders need to know they're taking significant risks, including potential loss of funding, by being (or even appearing to be) out of touch with the changing times and evolving needs of their stakeholders. More than ever, board members should represent and reflect the communities their organization serves. Let's think about this. If minorities and twenty-one- to thirty-four-year-olds are not on your board, you're excluding 30 to 40 percent of the population. Is that representing your community? And the latter group probably have skills—like being comfortable with technology—that the older crowd may not have.

So why are so many boards OWSM? Dr. Ray Ashley, CEO of San Diego's Maritime Museum, believes it's because, like viruses, "boards tend to replicate themselves. Members recruit other like-minded members." To combat this inertia, he says, organizations "must work harder to create intentional diversity—of background, socioeconomic status, and thought."[9] Think of your board composition as a Facebook group. If each comprises only people with similar upbringings, education, accomplishments, environment, and culture who see things the same way you do, you'll never expand beyond your own echo chamber to get a diversity of opinions that can widen your worldview.

Beware: Toxic Leadership and Founder's Syndrome

These are nasty little bugs that can creep into any organization and leave it with a debilitating illness that's hard to cure. Sometimes, the behaviors that ultimately sink a nonprofit are subtle. Other times, those inside and outside of the organization can see the fall coming a mile away. And in either instance, the maladies of *toxic leadership* and *founder's syndrome* can manifest themselves at both the executive and board levels. So how can these diseases be diagnosed? In a recent article, Elizabeth Schmidt of George Mason University described the following symptoms of founder's syndrome:

- Sense of grandiosity—that the organization is the founders', and it exists to serve their egos (or pocketbooks)
- Inability to delegate—poor management on the part of the founders
- Inability to make a smooth transition from the founders to new leadership
- Unwavering dedication to the original vision for the organization[10]

Founder's syndrome is but one example of a broader pox known as toxic leadership, which, if left untreated, can have a disastrous impact on mission success and organization survival. Colonel George E. Reed (U.S. Army, Ret.) is dean of the University of Colorado, Colorado Springs' School of Public Affairs, and someone who knows a thing or two about leadership from his civilian and military careers. (Prior to his current position, Reed was associate dean of the School of Leadership and Education Sciences at the University of San Diego, and his last active duty assignment was as director of Command and Leadership Studies at the United States Army War College.) Reed sees evidence of toxic leadership exhibited in three district traits, which can occur with the CEO or one or more board members:

- An apparent lack of concern for the well-being of subordinates
- A personality or interpersonal technique that negatively affects organizational climate
- A conviction by subordinates that the leader is motivated primarily by self-interest[11]

As Reed explains, "Many perceive toxic leadership as stemming from a specific behavior such as bullying, but that is too narrow a perspective." In his experience, any behavior, regardless of how well-intentioned, that creates or perpetuates a belief that those in authority don't value the welfare of others in the organization can result in a toxic environment. This includes CEOs who view their boards as people to manage rather than co-leaders, or boards that try to micromanage their CEO's activities. Some of the negative effects are obvious—like high rates of turnover—but some are less so. Of particular concern, Reed notes, "is when people in an organization become disaffected and miserable, yet stay." There may be a variety of reasons they choose not to leave, but in each case this lack of commitment can spread a toxic culture by becoming "an insidious, slow-acting poison."[12]

The poison is often fatal. Mary Dowling, partner at For Purpose Law Group, said in her experience, "Board disputes related to founders syndrome is a leading cause to the demise of a nonprofit, often leading to dissolution."[13]

Let that sink in for a moment. A primary reason nonprofits go under isn't a lack of funding, or an unsuccessful program, or a bad economy. It's *toxic leadership*.

We've seen the symptoms of toxic leadership; now what's the cure? As tempting as it may appear at first simply to axe toxic leaders, that potential solution—however expedient—is often shortsighted. Many of these people still have valuable skills, connections, and abilities. "Most founders are dedicated to the mission and vision of the organization," George Mason's Schmidt said. "After all, they conceived of the idea and found a way to implement it in an ongoing venture. A board that focuses on this mission will realize that one way to further it is to determine how best to use the founder's visionary skills."[14]

Ultimately, the key to avoiding (or dealing with) toxic leadership starts from the top, and that's the board of directors. "Fish rot from the head," said Tom Fetter, San Diego businessman and veteran of numerous local boards, including the august San Diego Zoo.[15] Board members must take as gospel their duties of *obedience*, *loyalty*, and *care*. They also must work to ensure their organization is not overly dependent on any one person, and the founder recognizes his or her identity must be separate from the organization's. And, after some reasonable period of time, founders who serve on the board need to step off.

Executive succession planning is another key activity of highly function-ing boards, and it's often harder to do with the incumbent looking on.

Take a Sabbatical

While we're discussing professional development and toxic leadership, here's an example of a practice that can help with both. No, we're not suggesting that you send your CEO off for six months to conduct aca-demic research like some university professor. But getting them out of the office to refresh and renew offers significant benefits to the CEO, the team, and the organization as a whole. The good news is there are foundations that recognize these benefits and—apart from making grants to defer the cost—can help guide the process to make sure the wheels don't come off the bus.

Here's one: The Fieldstone Leadership Network San Diego (FLNSD). The organization, which was founded by the Fieldstone Company—a major real estate development firm, "has served over 1,200 nonprofit leaders and 645 organizations throughout Southern California . . . (with a) continuum of programs and networking opportu-nities that enrich the skills and relationships of leaders to become ex-ceptional and effective."[16] FLNSD provides executive coaching, learn-ing groups, retreats, team building, and numerous education resources to its "network" of over one thousand senior-level nonprofit executives. But our favorite is their sabbatical program, which, in conjunction with the Clare Rose Foundation, provides funding (up to about $50,000 each) and hands-on training to four nonprofit leaders each year in the planning and execution of three-month sabbaticals. Although the recipi-ent of the sabbatical commits to really "drop out" and spend the time on pursuits unrelated to work (and disconnect from email and social me-dia), the program is not about taking a vacation. As Janine Mason, FLNSD's founder and executive director told us: "I love the word sab-batical, but ours is actually capacity building. We build the capacity building of the leader because we're giving him/her a sabbatical and the time to rejuvenate, to rest and to come back with a refreshed perspec-tive and energy level. This prolongs their time in their role and in the sector. But we're also investing in the organization as one of the condi-tions of the sabbatical is you can't bring in an interim—while the execu-tive is away, the organization has to be led by either a person from within the organization or a team of people. Generally, we work for a year with an organization, to get them ready for the opportunity, and provide access to a consultant for the preplanning, during, and post-sabbatical stages. Believe it or not, the planning is important, but the return phase is the most important—and the hardest."[17] Some of the program's many benefits—apart from rest, renewal, and burnout prevention of the leader, include:

- The staff is able to grow by assuming new responsibilities, broadening individual and institutional knowledge, developing bench strength, and increasing awareness of the leader's role and responsibility.
- The executive's daily job duties shift, allowing more time and space for higher-level leadership work on a continuous basis.
- Time away serves as preventive medicine for "toxic leadership" and "Founders Syndrome."
- Staff development acts as insurance against the leader being hit by the proverbial bus (FLNSD prefers "winning the lottery") and assists in succession planning.
- The board and staff deepen their relationship and cultivate mutual appreciation.

Mason summarized these benefits: "As leaders we are often taught to never give up and to go the extra mile at all times. But an essential part of leadership is developing the discipline to take care of yourself so you are able to continue to take care of others and meet your organizational goals for the long run. Everything needs time to re-fuel or it stops working. The Clare Rose Sabbatical experience is powerful on multiple levels, but none is more important than developing an organization that has the capacity to withstand the absence of a member of its leadership team while continuing to deliver on mission."

Put another way, programs like this can be a great component in building what Peter Senge calls "the learning organization" in his book *The Fifth Discipline*.[18]

Working Together in the Cockpit

Most modern aircraft carry at least two pilots, each with a unique set of responsibilities. Sometimes they work together; sometimes they operate independently. Okay, sometimes one sleeps. We know it's not a perfect analogy. But, like copilots, a nonprofit's executives and board members must complement the work the other is doing for the organization to achieve peak performance. "I think there is a common belief that executive directors are sort of magical unicorns who can do everything," said *FutureGood* author Trista Harris. Spoiler alert: They can't. And trying to do so ultimately leads to burnout and costly turnover. "Really strong nonprofits have figured out ways to spread leadership throughout the organization," Harris added. "You must have boards with clear governance roles and responsibilities, as well as visionary leaders to bring your organization into the future. And you also need to have somebody who's working on the operations side to make sure the right system policies, practices, and tools are in place to operationalize that vision."[19]

It's easy to criticize what Pat Libby, founder of the University of San Diego's venerable Nonprofit Leadership and Management program, calls "Bobblehead Boards." That is to say, those that aren't contributing much to truly advance the mission. But, in many cases, board members would welcome the opportunity to play a leadership role; they just need to be encouraged and empowered to do so. Now working directly with nonprofit industry leaders through her consulting firm, Libby sees this a lot. "Board chairs and CEOs need to think strategically about recruiting board members and effectively deploying them in the interest of the corporation,"[20] she said.

What does a standard deployment look like today? Typically, board members are given assignments through appointment to various "standing committees." These are often formed for *fiduciary* work—think finance and audit—as well as for special projects (the dreaded annual gala). Nothing wrong with this approach. In fact, using committee membership as a recruiting tool for prospective board members is a terrific way to deepen the pool of people vested in the mission's success. What's much less common, however, is forming committees to tackle the *strategic* and *generative* modes of board governance. So, far from arguing for the abolishment of standing committees, we're actually saying there should be more! Now, we can envision the hue and cry—if not outright revolt—of many board members at the mere suggestion of this idea. If you're one of them, just consider what comes next before concluding we're nuts.

Sustainability Committee

At first glance, some might say, "We already have this. It's called the finance committee." To which we'd (respectfully) reply, "Emphatically not!" Sustainability goes well beyond the balance sheet, statement of activities, and cash reserves. Yes, these are all important—and there's certainly nothing wrong with having a bean counter from finance on your sustainability committee (as long as there's only one!). But this new committee should be a cross-functional enterprise that's tasked with continuously exploring existential risks, funding model alternatives, and strategic restructuring options. In our rapidly changing world, no organization can be too sustainable. And therefore issues affecting sustainability have to be constantly investigated and debated.

Impact Committee

Let's be clear: Your organization can be sustainable and ineffectual. Sustainable and unproductive. Sustainable and . . . dull. *Impact* is what ignites passion and inspires people! Just because you've ensured your nonprofit will be around for the foreseeable future doesn't mean anyone's better off if it is. Sorry to sound so harsh, but *sustainability* and *impact* are mutually exclusive. Great organizations have both, and that's where the impact committee comes in. This committee independently reviews such weighty questions as: "Should we exist?" "Are we meeting the mission?" "How can we do it better?" Its members are obsessed not with *what* their organization is doing, but *why* it matters.

Leadership and Risk

Close your eyes for a moment. Ah, almost got you, didn't we? Okay, squint, so you can still read the rest of this paragraph. But try to imagine our world without the benefits of technological and scientific breakthroughs brought about by people who were encouraged to take risks. If we only go back a few decades, ours was a world where we had to walk all the way across the room just to make a phone call or change channels on the TV. It was the Dark Ages, kids. But where did the encouragement (and funding) to change things come from? In a word: *leadership*. Risk-taking activities at any organization start at the top. Unfortunately, they can also end there—without ever getting off the ground. And that scenario is too often the case with today's nonprofits. In short, the sector has a risk-aversion problem.

We've already talked about this in the context of mergers and acquisitions, strategic restructuring, and other "Wall Street" ventures. But the issue goes far beyond this—to the elemental and cultural levels of many organizations—and can affect everything from how (or *if*) money is invested to whether new programs are launched. One nonprofit CEO put it this way: "There is very little incentive for nonprofits to embark on a risky project, and few organizations have the resources to cover a failure." Ah, yes. Along with *fundraising*, there's another "F-word" that sends chills down the spine of many a nonprofit CEO and board member: *failure*. In fact, if you combine the two you might well ask whether some nonprofits shy away from pursuing risky ventures because (1) those ventures may fail or (2) they may succeed, requiring leadership to do additional fundraising to support the new programs. In other words, damned if you do, damned if you don't.

What if instead we reframed the question by asking what extra good these organizations could do—what additional *impact* they could have—with some more money? The CEO we just mentioned is right, though. Most smaller nonprofits simply don't have the financial wherewithal to comfortably pursue riskier projects. The NFF's Antony Bugg-Levine says fewer than half of nonprofits have even enough cash on hand to cover three months of operations. The end result is that the organizations we rely on to solve some of society's most serious and swampy problems often can't experiment with brave new solutions.

So what to do? One idea is for nonprofit leaders to begin rethinking how they view risk and failure in their organizations. Opportunity International, one of the largest micro-financing organizations in the world, showcased what it called "Our Wall of Failures" in a report a few years ago. Its leadership does this to highlight a critical element of long-term success: learning from what doesn't work. Trista Harris mentions another way to acknowledge ventures that don't succeed: "The Heath

Foundation hosted a happy hour some years ago where they had an open microphone and asked people to publicly talk about their greatest mistakes."[21] There's something very cathartic about owning an outcome—good or bad—and nonprofits (and their funders) should embrace—indeed celebrate—failure. This celebration needs to take place at the highest leadership level, so all employees throughout the organization know it's okay to fail. Only by bringing failure out into the open can it serve to teach organizations not to repeat the mistakes of the past. Almost everyone we interviewed agrees that the need for leadership to encourage risk-taking in their organizations is paramount. This is particularly true at the board level. "CEOs need permission to fail from their boards," said one nonprofit expert. We agree, and we would add that both boards and executives are responsible for providing leadership that supports activities that may fail.

Philanthropist Malin Burnham provides a great example of the importance of risk-taking and why he's always encouraged it in his organizations: "Thomas Edison failed a thousand times to invent the light bulb. What if he'd stopped at 999?" The point, Burnham added, is "don't be ashamed of failure. You're one step closer to success and you learn from it."[22]

We've already mentioned the lack of financial incentives as one reason nonprofits are risk-averse. Why else? "I think one of the things that happens with nonprofits is they feel like their mission is too important for them to fail, and so they don't believe they can make mistakes," Harris said. The upshot, she continued, is that many organizations "sit in this space of carefulness, and that doesn't allow you to innovate or try new things." Harris believes this overly cautious approach stymies organizations and prevents them from having the impact they otherwise could if they'd just experiment a little more. "For our sector in particular, it's actually really important for us to fail fast and move on,"[23] she added.

We know that's easier said than done. The calculus of risk-taking differs between the social sector and Silicon Valley. Through their fiduciary lens, nonprofit directors worry about the improper use of public funds and forfeiting their board seats. Executives, for their part, worry about losing their jobs and tarnishing their reputations.

So what's the right balance between innovation and imprudence? The ADL's Jonathan Greenblatt thinks there should be more risk-taking in the nonprofit sector, but acknowledges the incentives often don't support this behavior. "The absence of pressure [from owners or investors] or the promise of a liquidity event, coupled with an environment where there's been ample giving year after year, makes it easy for nonprofits to just keep doing what they've always done," he said. But Greenblatt is optimistic and sees change on the horizon. This, he believes, will be driven in part by the development of new technologies to measure impact, which in turn will attract additional sources of capital to the nonprofit sector. "When we can understand with precision what really works," Greenblatt said, "money will flow toward those solutions." He predicts the continuing rise of Big Data as well as an "outcomes mentality" will spur this trend. "It's not if," he said. "It's only a matter of when."[24]

There's yet another cog in the leadership gear that needs mentioning: funders. A big reason many nonprofits play it conservative and avoid risks is they fear backlash from funders. But is this fear warranted? "One of the more sobering findings we see repeatedly is that there is a disconnect between how nonprofits view the work they're doing and how that performance is perceived by the foundations funding the work," said the Center for Effective Philanthropy's Phil Buchanan. He believes this disconnect often starts early in the relationship, when nonprofits fail to ask funders for what they really need to move the needle. Instead, they only ask for what they think funders are willing to give them. And then, if programs don't work out, he said, "Many nonprofits sweep failure under the rug because they mistakenly believe it will hurt their reputations." In Buchanan's experience, however, the opposite is true. "Celebration, or at least acknowledgement, of failure actually burnishes an organization's reputation," he said, "because it creates an image of transparency."[25]

The Rhode Island Foundation's Jessica David is one of many foundation leaders who echoes this view. How does her organization look at failure? "It's a combination of something that's celebrated and held up as an example to learn from," she said. "We recognize that if we only make a bunch of really safe investments, we're not doing our job." David is quick to mention that only if there's open and honest communication between her foundation and the nonprofits it supports can everyone learn from investments that don't work out and become better. "What really frustrates me," she added, "is when things don't go the way you think they will, and yet the organization tries to convince you everything's great. In any relationship, you want your partner to be honest." Unlike fine wine, problems don't age well. Early identification of potential issues is key to addressing them. "If we know sooner than later," David said, "we might be able to help by providing additional resources, bringing in someone with technical expertise, or linking [an organization] with another that's gone through something similar."[26]

Still feeling a little skittish about being brutally honest with your funders? Like anything you say can and will be used against you? Just know you're not the only one out there who makes mistakes.

"Let's Stop Reinventing Potholes"

Back in 2007, the *Chronicle of Philanthropy* published a refreshingly open opinion piece written by two titans of the nonprofit sector. At the time, Paul Brest was president of the William and Flora Hewlett Foundation. His coauthor, James E. Canales, was head of the James Irvine Foundation, both based in the San Francisco Bay Area. The men candidly discussed lessons learned from major grants their respective foundations made—with disappointing results—and offered suggestions on how other organizations could avoid similar mistakes. The Hewlett Foundation had committed $20 million to a decade-long project that fell "far short of achieving the hoped-for [results]." For his part, Canales cited the difficulties that led the Irvine Foundation to "a significant midpoint redirection of a $60 million effort to improve educational achievement at low-performing schools." Not exactly things most prestigious foundations would even want to quietly mention. But Brest and Canales didn't just mention their mistakes; they shouted them from the rooftops! They publicly issued thick reports detailing why the mistakes occurred and what they learned from them.

Look up the definition of *leadership* in any dictionary and it sounds a lot like this. However, they were just doing what they felt had to be done, because hiding their projects' shortcomings would have come at too great a price. As Brest and Canales wrote in the *Chronicle of Philanthropy* article, "Such reluctance [to disclose failure] has real costs—it wastes time and money. Foundations cannot learn from their mistakes if nobody acknowledges making errors. We deprive ourselves of the enlightenment that comes from finding out why something didn't work.

And we miss the opportunity to help colleagues learn from their peers." They go on to argue for a different approach, one in which all stakeholders admit and share their mistakes—then move on. They want the nonprofit sector to take full advantage of one of its most abundant resources: *knowledge*. "We issued these reports because we believed they provided important lessons for grant makers and nonprofit groups about what it takes to bring about major changes in communities," Brest and Canales wrote. "The only thing philanthropy needs less than reinvented wheels is reinvented potholes."[27]

"Innovate or Die"

There's still some debate as to the precise provenance of this quote. Management guru Peter Drucker is often credited with its coinage, but others, too, certainly could have had a hand in bringing it into the modern lexicon. No matter who's responsible, the sentiment is clear: If you don't outrun the pace of change in your industry, you're done. The nonprofit sector may not immediately spring to mind when we think of innovative industries, but perhaps it should. The Maritime Museum's Ray Ashley described nonprofits like his that depend on a steady stream of visitors for survival by saying, "We're not like shade plants. We need to live in the sunshine and constantly reinvent ourselves to continue garnering support from our patrons." In 2012, Ashley had a big opportunity to put his museum's money—and that of its supporters—where his mouth was.

That year, the Maritime Museum began construction on *San Salvador*, a full-scale historical replica of the first European vessel ever to reach the West Coast of America. (If you're interested, the original *San Salvador*—captained by Juan Rodriguez Cabrillo—landed at what's now known as San Diego on September 28, 1542.) Like Cabrillo's voyage, Ashley's undertaking involved a lot of risk. The six-year project would ultimately cost more than twice the museum's annual revenues. In the end, however, *San Salvador* was a success, and today the museum's newest flagship is credited with drawing many of the 130,000 people who visit the Maritime Museum each year. (Full disclosure: one of us served on the museum's finance committee during construction, while the other worked for a commercial bank that helped fund the project.) Now with the benefit of hindsight, Ashley smiled as he reflected on those early days. "If you come to the conclusion that there is no way you can survive by just staying where you are, then the less risky path is to actually do something and try and change the equation," he said. "Sometimes the safest measures are the boldest."[28]

Information Technology

As in most industries, technology has a big role to play in helping non-profits innovate and stay ahead of the curve. With the pace of change today, that role is more important than ever. Amit Patel is a managing director in Accenture's Nonprofit Group, a specialized arm of the consulting giant whose objective is to "help domestic and international nonprofit organizations and foundations define strategic objectives and then design and implement successful projects that drive value."[29] The author of numerous articles and blog posts on the subject of emerging technologies and their applications to nonprofits, Patel cites technology as an area where boards should take a particularly active leadership role—especially in keeping current on how technology could impact mission effectiveness, or, in some cases, change the organization's mission altogether. "Nonprofits should look closely at who their competitors are. And not just for resources, but also other organizations that are working in the same issue area," he said. Patel groups the competition into two camps, which he calls "experiential and perceptual competitors."[30] To make his point, he gives an example of the market disruption precipitated by advancing technologies used by firms from Amazon to Uber. This change, Patel said, not only created new competition, but also fundamentally altered "what people's perceptions [of a service] are, what their expectations are, and what they demand from you as a provider."

Patel views technology as a powerful enabler of stakeholder engagement and believes board members should have a leadership role in determining how technology can be used to further an organization's mission. He cautions against leaving technology adoption to "back office" staff to manage. Rather, he said, it can be seen as a generative process that can engage everyone throughout the organization. "There are many examples of cutting-edge applications of technology," Patel noted, "from educational organizations using artificial intelligence to predict and change dropout rates, to the Anti-Defamation League scanning social media via AI to expose and combat hate speech."

So whether we're talking about organizations innovating through new programs, experiences, or technologies, where can boards and executives turn to develop the leadership chutzpah necessary to turn audacious dreams into actions? Think most leaders are just born that way? Think again. They're developed over time, through hard work and training. But most people working in the nonprofit sector don't exactly have a lot of spare time on their hands. And outside training costs loads of money. Doesn't it?

Do just a little digging, as we've done (hey, we never claimed to be investigative reporters), and you're sure to find a raft of resources for leadership development—from online seminars, podcasts, and research to in-person training, coaching, and consulting. All free or relatively inexpensive. We've already mentioned one of the top providers of these tools: The Bridgespan Group. But we haven't yet introduced you to Preeta Nayak, Bridgespan partner and coauthor of the book, *Nonprofit Leadership Development: What's Your "Plan A" for Growing Future Leaders?* Nayak heads up the consulting firm's Leading for Impact® program, an intensive two-year experience designed to help teams of nonprofit executives tackle a specific strategic challenge while at the same time develop a leadership pipeline for the organization. The first six months of the program include several rigorous daylong workshops with a cohort of local organizations, where teams learn and start to apply critical skills. It's here they also work on a customized project under the auspices of Bridgespan's coordinators.

Following this initial period, the team then works on another project, again with coaching from Bridgespan consultants. Designed primarily for nonprofits with average annual budgets in the $3–$30 million range, these programs are available in select cities across the United States. According to Nayak, Bridgespan works with roughly fifty organizations per city, in cohorts of eight to ten to provide collective support. The cost for each organization is $80,000–$100,000 for the two years. However, Nayak says, when Bridgespan introduces the program to a new city, it works with local sponsors who recognize its value and subsidize 80 percent of the program cost, making the actual price tag for nonprofits closer to $20,000.[31] Not bad for what's tantamount to a master's degree in organizational leadership.

All well and good if you're operating in one of the locations where Bridgespan has set up shop. But what if you're not? In response to high demand for its programs from organizations in other cities (and countries), Bridgespan created two online curricula for leadership teams focused on organization-specific projects. Designed to be completed in three to four months, they cover leadership development (*Investing in Future Leaders*) and strategy for impact (*Achieving Strategic Clarity*). Structuring the experience around *teams* is deliberate. Doing so mitigates the risk of individual turnover and helps institutionalize the leadership knowledge learned. "Most digital tools we see tend to be focused on individual learning," Nayak explained. "Like Leading for Impact, our digital programs are focused on executive team engagement and learning. We also wanted to make sure people had a chance to apply the concepts and that it wasn't just about talking about things theoretically."[32] And so Bridgespan built these *Leadership Accelerator* programs, as they're known, to give teams of up to eight members an opportunity to make meaningful headway on a salient issue during the program, when resources and support are at their peak. Each team pays $5,500. Bridgespan ran the initial pilot in 2018, and within the first year or so, more than one hundred teams have completed a project within the Accelerator series.

FLY

All right, enough with the hypothetical. Let's take a real organization that went through one of Bridgespan's accelerator programs and look at the results. But before we do, please take us at our word that we didn't choose the organization just to fit the airplane analogy we've used throughout this chapter. The nonprofit is called Fresh Lifelines for Youth. That's right: FLY. Following a tremendously successful, ahem, pilot program, the organization formally incorporated in 2000 with a mission to "prevent juvenile crime and incarceration through legal education, leadership training and one-on-one mentoring."[33] With revenues of about $5 million, FLY is one of many nonprofits punching above its weight by doing impactful work without a great deal of extra money or time to devote to formal leadership training for its staff. Yet after some deep strategic planning with its board (*generative thinking!*), FLY's executives charted a future course for the organization and recognized that talent development would be critical to achieving their goals. So with the full support of the board and executive team, FLY enrolled in Bridgespan's Investing in Future Leaders program.

Over a period of five months, the entire four-member executive team, plus the organization's director of talent, immersed themselves in the training. Their curriculum included online lessons with guided team meetings, where the group walked through a series of steps, or "milestones," to create and put into place solid talent development practices. Each milestone carried with it a set of "pre-work" for members to complete using an interactive online platform and a guided "Team Summit," where the collective group came together to discuss individual learnings from the pre-work and make critical decisions. FLY's director of talent served as the "project lead," and had access to a set of project management tools provided by Bridgespan. Among those were timelines to help the team assess its progress, as well as meeting facilitation guides—all supplemented by regular calls with a Bridgespan coach (a senior Bridgespan manager), who provided individualized guidance.

It was a lot of work. And a big commitment, both from the organization and its leadership team. But the end results—which included a customized strategic plan for FLY and enhanced, transferrable skills for its leaders—were game-changing. As FLY's founder and CEO, Christa Gannon, later reflected: "One thing that we'll be doing differently as a result of this program is we will be very strategic about the talent that we're developing internally, and very intentional about how we as leaders give them experiential opportunities within the organization to develop critical skills."[34] Gannon believes her team's shared experience in the program provided the blueprint for how best to achieve this. "When we talked about it as a team," she said, "we realized, 'how can we not do this?' We have to do this work because everything else, like our theory of change strategy, isn't going to be effective if we don't have the talent in place to make it happen." In other words, the success of any program, strategy, or mission hinges on the skills and abilities of those charged with carrying it out. An *A-level* team with a *B-level* plan beats an *A-level* plan with a *B-level* team every time. "It never feels like the right time to take on big projects like this," Gannon added, "but we knew it was critical to our success."[35]

Critical, indeed. For her 2018 book, *Social Startup Success*, author and Stanford lecturer Katherine Kelly Janus surveyed more than two hundred nonprofit leaders in the fields of philanthropy and social entrepreneurship to determine how the best organizations achieve sustainability. One of her key findings: *leadership*. "Senior leadership is critical to the path to scale," Janus said. Her research concluded, "one of the strongest findings was that the organizations that tended to scale more quickly said that a catalyst for growth was hiring a chief operating officer, or a director of programs, or a head of development. And that makes sense because [nonprofit executives and leaders] say that hiring their senior team was what allowed them to focus their time on the strategic planning and fundraising that helped their organization grow."[36]

Unquestionably, leadership is an important catalyst for growth and sustainability. But we must also bear in mind that it can show itself in many guises. Character counts. "Too many leaders are hired for their technical or strategic skills," said Ashoka's Bill Drayton. "Too few have adequate people skills." It's these "soft skills" Drayton believes are increasingly important. Particularly *empathy*. "Without this," he said, "you can't effectively work with others in today's interconnected world."[37]

The best-selling author and acclaimed research professor at the University of Houston, Brenè Brown, thinks there's at least one more indispensable soft skill: *courage*. "Courage is a prerequisite for all leadership," she said. The good news is, like leadership, courage can be taught. The main thing that's required is a willingness to be vulnerable, and that means being comfortable knowing there's a risk you may fail. Not all risks are created equal, though. "One of the things that we learned in the research," Brown said, "is that people who have the skills to get back up from a fall will engage in smarter risks and more courageous behaviors than people who don't."[38]

Ready for more good news? Resilience and persistence can be taught, too. That means a nonprofit can soar to new heights when those traits are present, plus board members and CEOs who fly the plane together, with three pairs of goggles—fiduciary, strategic, and generative—each with a different lens. Continuous review and training will also lead to a smoother flight, along with not tolerating bobblehead members and maybe even adding a few new committees. Then, strap in for takeoff.

6

A BRIDGE TO SUSTAINABILITY

Trust-Based Philanthropy

We hope by this point you're more than a little convinced that one of the paramount pillars of sustainability among nonprofits is cultivating rock-solid relationships with donors, staff, board members, and other key stakeholders. Yes? Good. Now, for extra credit: What's the foundation upon which these relationships are built? What's the glue that bonds *all* good relationships? Two questions, one answer: trust. Period. Without it, you have nothing.

The Scottish author and poet George MacDonald is credited with the proclamation, "To be trusted is a greater compliment than being loved." And while both sound really awesome to us, trust has to be feeling pretty good about itself even to be mentioned in the same breath as *love*! Yeah, it's that important. Okay, now a warning: This chapter is going to get a little . . . well, squishy. (Don't worry, quants, we'll hit you with some hard numbers later.) We're going to talk about relationships and trust, and look at a number of funders that are at the vanguard of nothing less than a sea change in the nonprofit sector.

Nancy Jamison, the long-serving former CEO of San Diego Grantmakers, is impressed by the work of the Whitman Institute, which built a framework for a set of practices called "trust-based philanthropy." It's a monumental departure from the Golden Rule that has traditionally governed most grantor/grantee relationships, from a "those who have the gold, rule" to a "we're in this together" approach. Whatever name you choose to give it, trust-based philanthropy is a reset of the power dynamics that have defined the nonprofit sector since time immemorial.[1]

To be clear, the old ways still exist. But many of the leaders and experts we spoke with are deeply committed to helping transform and enhance the flow of capital to the third sector. Notice the word *capital*—because the concept of trust-based philanthropy provides that money and other resources can be used for operations, capacity building, infrastructure, program creation, asset acquisition . . . in short, anything! You know the term for this: *unrestricted funding*. The old model funnels (restricted) resources to programs, while trust-based philanthropy directs resources to organizations to *implement* programs, deliver social value, and solve problems. There's nothing particularly unique about how money gets sent. The magic is in the mindset. It's in the trusting!

Nonprofits fortunate enough to be working with funders who embrace these more enlightened grantmaking practices have the opportunity to use capital as a "bridge" to develop sustainable organizations rather than as a "pier," which by its nature leaves you stranded at a certain point. If you're willing to forgive us our dubious analogies, let's continue and meet some truly progressive funders.

THE WHITMAN INSTITUTE

Though we first heard the term trust-based philanthropy from Jamison, she didn't coin the term. That honor likely goes to the Whitman Institute (TWI), a relatively small foundation based in San Francisco. In 1985, at an age when many are busy charting a course through their golden years, Frederick Crocker Whitman founded TWI as an organization to study how people could improve their thinking and decision-making skills. The great-grandson of one of San Francisco's founding fathers, railroad baron Charles Crocker, Whitman created his eponymous institute as a way to reconcile issues of mental illness that had been present in his family throughout his life.[2]

In 2005, the year following Whitman's death, TWI changed its focus from an operating institution to a grantmaking foundation in an effort to attract more organizations that could help foster dialogue around a common mission. Today, TWI's core philanthropic principle "offers a new way of looking at traditional funder-grantee relationships [by recognizing] the unique—yet equally valuable—contributions of grantmakers and grantseekers."[3] In other words, it's based on trust, and a partnership approach to solving societal problems. For its part, TWI's goal is "lifting barriers that prevent nonprofits from focusing their time and talents on the work that matters." Central to achieving this goal is an unwavering trust that the foundation's grantees—those doing the work—know best how to spend grant money. This belief is so important that TWI's leaders have codified it around six "pillars" that represent the foundation's core philanthropic approach:[4]

- Multiyear, Unrestricted Funding; Main Idea: Unrestricted funding over time is essential for creating healthy, adaptive, effective organizations.
- Do the Homework; Main Idea: Before entering into a grantmaking relationship, the onus of due diligence should be on the grantmaker, not the grantseeker.
- Simplify and Streamline Paperwork; Main Idea: Nonprofit staffs spend an inordinate amount of time on funder-driven paperwork; they will be more effective if they're freed up to concentrate on the mission.
- Transparent and Responsive Communication; Main Idea: Open, honest, and transparent communication minimizes power imbalances and helps move the work forward.
- Solicit and Act on Feedback; Main Idea: Grantees provide valuable perspective that can help inform a funder's support and services.
- Support Beyond the Check; Main Idea: Responsive, adaptive nonmonetary support can help foster healthier organizations by bolstering leadership and capacity.

WORK ON MISSION, NOT ON FUNDRAISING

We think that last pillar is particularly cool. Not only is TWI writing checks, but it's also doubling down on its investment by asking grantees, "What else can we do? What other resources do you need to succeed?"

Just the humility inherent in those questions is so wonderfully refreshing. And, collectively, TWI's pillars positively ooze trust. Think about all the benefits this type of relationship paradigm accrues to nonprofits. Organizations redirect the time, money, and other resources previously devoted to fundraising toward working on the mission. Plus, multiyear grants allow organizations to budget better and make longer-term investments in capacity-building, upgrade systems and technology, hire and pay top talent, and evaluate programs to see what works and what doesn't. Then on top of all this, TWI offers to leverage its own expertise and multi-industry relationships to open doors and help its grantees thrive. Wow!

Vu Le, executive director of Seattle-based Rainier Valley Corps and author of the deliciously cheeky blog *Nonprofit AF*, sees other indirect yet equally important benefits of this approach for grantees. Le believes strong partnerships based on respect make the entire sector more effective. And, in a nice bit of positive reinforcement, he said this mutual trust actually makes nonprofits more honest, since they know their transparency won't be met with disapproval or (worse!) loss of funding. "It's much easier to be honest if there is trust," he wrote. Ultimately, Le believes, trust improves morale, which is unquestionably good for business. Few things can sink an organization like employee detachment and apathy, and "nothing destroys morale faster or more assuredly than feeling like people you work with don't trust you."[5]

Power imbalances—real or perceived—between funders and nonprofits can also cause grantees to morph into organizations they were never meant to be in an attempt to mollify benefactors by working to comply with their often-conflicting demands. Trista Harris has a name for this phenomenon, noting, "I think foundations help to create these things called Franken-Nonprofits—organizations that had a core mission at one point, before they bent and twisted so much to meet foundation guidelines that suddenly they have twenty different programs that are all doing something a little bit different. It really weakens their effectiveness."[6] And when funding is tight, as it was for years after the 2008 financial crisis, grants directed to particular programs restrict organizations' ability to perform triage on these donor-specific activities and redeploy resources to maintain core services. "We have created these amazing bureaucracies," Harris said, "which make it really difficult to be flexible."

So how do you avoid turning your organization into a Franken-Nonprofit? Trite as it sounds, those inspirational shopping mall kiosk posters had it right: "Stay True to Your Core Values and Beliefs." "Chart a Course and Stick to It." "Never Let Others Define You." Or, if we're staying with 1980s lore, maybe Nancy Reagan offered the best advice: "Just Say No." We get it—this can be really tough to do when overbearing Megafoundation comes calling with a big blank check in hand. Ali Malekzadeh, president of Roosevelt University in Chicago, believes, however, that "sometimes you just have to turn down certain offers." Especially when they come with too many strings attached. "You cannot give donors all the control," he said. Not every donor is one you want. Some simply aren't good for your brand. Others demand you move away from your mission or just make you jump through too many hoops. "Give me a maximum of two or three requirements or criteria, and then let us do our jobs," Malekzadeh said.[7]

Fine, but his university isn't wholly dependent on grants and donations to survive. Sticking to principle is much harder if you're a Main Street nonprofit struggling to keep the lights on or deliver services to those in need without the luxury of consistent tuition payments and a committed alumni base. Which is why trust-based philanthropy can be such a positive change for these organizations and their funders.

SURFING FOR GRANTMAKERS

The fact that we live in Southern California almost necessitates at least one surfing analogy. (For the record, neither of us surfs. One prefers the relative dryness of boating; the other is a landlubber afraid of being consumed by a large carnivorous fish.) As Kristi Kimball and Malka Kopell proclaimed in their 2011 article, "Letting Go," "We would probably be better off as a society if the decision-makers in the nation's large private foundations took up surfing. Why? Because surfing is about letting go, and that's what foundations must do to achieve higher impact."[8]

The authors describe how historical power imbalances can impede program effectiveness, citing examples of grantmakers insisting on haphazard methodologies and measurements or unrealistic goals without the benefit of "on the ground" experience. Many foundations, they say, operate with "tunnel vision"—that is, believing there is only one work-able solution to a given problem. "The more that foundations dictate to grantees how they should solve social problems," Kimball and Kopell maintained, "the more they constrain the grantee's leadership, exper-tise, and ability to innovate—and the more bureaucratic work they create for them."

This burden of bureaucracy is only compounded when a nonprofit is dependent on funding from multiple sources and thus has to juggle different or competing requirements. (Franken-Nonprofit: *It's alive!*) And therefore, funders would be doing an enormous service to their sector and to society at large if they'd stop trying to micromanage so much and *just let go*. "Surfing is incredibly humbling, an encounter with the enormous power, beauty, and unpredictability of the ocean," Kim-ball and Kopell wrote. "No surfer would attempt to change the shape of the waves or the schedule of the tides, because these forces are far beyond any one person's control."[9]

"A ROSE BY ANY OTHER NAME..."

If we were in the development department—heck, any department!—of a Main Street nonprofit, we'd likely be reading this, exclaiming, "Yes! Yes! A thousand times yes! Where can my organization get on this bridge to sustainability?" It turns out the answer, fortunately, is *lots of places*. Just under a number of different names. "Feedback led us to name and frame our approach as trust-based philanthropy," explained John Esterle, co-executive director of TWI. "We hold the name lightly since we recognize that many other funders employ similar practices, but may not use that term."[10]

One such funder is the Robert Sterling Clark Foundation (RSC). RSC's eponym and founder was the son of Edward Clark and a member of one of New York's most distinguished families. The elder Clark achieved prominence by developing a worldwide market for Singer sewing machines in the late nineteenth century. Incorporated in 1952, the foundation today focuses on "helping create and sustain a vibrant New York City . . . by investing in leaders, the organizations that devel-op them, and the networks of which they are a part."[11] With over $80 million in assets, RSC refers to itself as "More than a check writer—a collaborator" and espouses philanthropic practices that are very similar to TWI's. It calls its approach *grantee-centric philanthropy*, and the foundation's leaders "firmly believe that our grant recipients are best equipped—better than we are—to make decisions about how their grant awards should be spent." Like other foundations that have seen the value in ceding some control to their grantees, RSC is apt to fund multiyear unrestricted grants for general operating support, professional development, and other needs not directly tied to any particular program. It passionately believes "[grantees] are the mission-driven, field-expert professionals," and works diligently to give the organizations it works with "time and space to invest [their] grants wisely and make long-term decisions."[12]

Not content simply to keep this wisdom confined within the philanthropic illuminati, RSC is collaborating with TWI and other funders, such as the Headwaters Foundation, to help foster better relationships and communication with nonprofits they support. The goal is nothing short of creating a seismic shift in the traditional model and spreading the practice of trust-based philanthropy throughout the sector. The group takes this mission seriously and employs a variety of strategies to reach as broad an audience as possible. One arrow in their quiver includes a series of blog posts that—in tones ranging from playful to urgent—explore the precepts of trust-based philanthropy. All should be required reading (especially for obstinate foundations that haven't yet learned the lessons of surfing), but here's an excerpt from one we particularly liked because its message is direct and dire:

> General operating funds allow us nonprofits to be most effective at helping people, including saving lives. By restricting funds you are impeding our work; therefore, your philosophies and policies are causing people to get hurt and die. And that is unethical.[13]

Pretty much cuts right through the haze, doesn't it? For trust-based philanthropy to really work, it has to involve a holistic mindset shift that affects every step in the grantmaking process. Take the quotidian task of applying for funding. RSC encourages potential grantees to submit applications prepared for *other funders*—without asking them to make any changes! (The collective "ooh" you heard was the sound made by every grant writer who just read that sentence.) "We were all too familiar with the wide range of specialized RFPs, individualized budget formats, and many, many different attachments that funders request," RSC said. "The proposals [prospective grantees] have written for other funders work just fine for us."[14] In RSC's estimation, the information it can glean from other proposals is perfectly sufficient to get the foundation started on its due diligence. From there, they can pull applicants' 990 data, conduct interviews, and, "most importantly, meet with them and observe their programs." Sound refreshing? Like ice-cold lemonade on a summer day, folks.

LESSONS FROM FOUR FOUNDATIONS

In 2017, Rockefeller Philanthropy Advisors (RPA) and a "steering group" of four prominent foundations completed a yearlong study on how to improve their grantmaking practices to achieve greater impact. The four—Draper Richards Kaplan, Porticus, Ford, and Skoll—together with RPA, collectively advise or directly distribute hundreds of millions of dollars annually across the globe. In other words, these are pretty important and influential people in the grantmaking world. Okay, we won't bury the lede. Their recommendations based on the survey are for funders to:

- **Empower:** Consciously and intentionally shift the power dynamics between grantees and funders.
- **Accelerate:** Hold active and honest discussions with grantees about strategic non-monetary support.
- **Learn:** Develop more knowledge on shifting systems, and when and how to support grantees in that effort.
- **Collaborate:** Share information more effectively with other stakeholders.
- **Streamline:** Redesign the grantmaking process, including applications and reporting.[15]

Hmmm . . . sounds a lot like Whitman's pillars, doesn't it? (If not, you've clearly dozed off at some point. It's okay. We don't judge. Just get some sleep and then please reread the first half of this chapter.) And as with those pillars, RPA's study findings are a clarion call to funders for less restrictive, multiyear funding—with the specific recommendation being to perhaps *double* or *triple* the duration of a typical grant, arguing that doing so saves valuable time for grantees and funders. The authors also advocate for "providing funding tranches by milestones achieved rather than by individual line items (that require grantee staff time to juggle between line items rather than working at the strategic level)."

Now, if you'd kindly indulge us our wanderlust for a bit, we're going to zip from one side of the country to the other and meet a few more funders that are doing some wildly innovative things to help improve philanthropy. Kinda like speed dating, but without the awkward conversation. We'll start on the East Coast, in the Commonwealth of Massachusetts. Ready? Let's go!

Cummings Foundation—Sustaining Grants

Originally named the Cummings Properties Foundation when it was founded in 1986, today this private foundation is one of the largest in New England, with some $2 billion in assets. The Cummings Foundation takes a slightly different approach to deploying its formidable largesse to help build sustainability among grantees with its *$100K for 100 Program*. How's it work? Each year, hundreds of organizations vie for invitations to apply for one of the one hundred unrestricted grants of $100,000 each awarded locally.[16] But it gets even better: After receiving the initial $100,000, recipients are then eligible to apply for a portion of a second round of ongoing funding, totaling $15 million each year. Individual grants typically range from $20,000 to $50,000 annually per participant—for up to ten years! As the foundation states, "The long-term support is intended to alleviate the burden of continuous fundraising, allowing the staff to focus more of their time and energy on delivering and enhancing their important services."

Weingart Foundation—Unrestricted Operating Support

Let's pop on over to the other side of the country—Los Angeles, in particular. There, that was easy. It's here we find the Weingart Foundation, an $800 million heavyweight providing grants that are very similar in purpose and function to those funded by the Cummings Foundation. Weingart dubs the program Unrestricted Operating Support (UOS), a term that represents no less than the foundation's "primary vehicle for supporting and building the long-term capacity and effectiveness of nonprofits, collaboratives, and coalitions."[17] Flexible funding options? Check. Unrestricted multiyear grants? You bet—to the tune of some $60 million over the last ten years.

In 2017 and 2018, Weingart partnered with Harder+Company Community Research to gain insight into how UOS helped strengthen sustainability at four of the foundation's grantees. The results of these case profiles showed unequivocally "that our unrestricted support allowed organizations to invest in mission-critical infrastructure needs on a variety of levels," said Joyce Ybarra, director of learning at Weingart. (An aside: How cool is that job title? Shouldn't *every* foundation have a director of learning?! It just screams "We're committed to getting better!") What's more, "It is evident that there is strong value in the support we provide beyond the grant," Ybarra said. In the case of each of the four grantees it looked at, "we were able to provide additional tools and resources that offered tailored supports to the grantees (targeted capacity building, PRI funding, rapid response grants, strategic restructuring, etc.)." Win. Win. Win. Win.

Sobrato Family Foundation—General Operating Support

Silicon Valley isn't exactly known for egalitarianism and equal opportunity these days. But some five hundred miles up the coast from LA, there's a foundation working hard to change this. Formed as the philanthropic arm of the Sobrato Organization—which traces its roots to the acquisition and development of Silicon Valley real estate—the Sobrato Family Foundation strives to remove barriers to opportunity and create lasting economic change in at-risk communities throughout the Bay Area. It does this by concentrating its philanthropy on a core value of General Operating Support (GOS), which is consistent with the foundation's belief that these grants "help fund critical internal organizational needs, while also introducing the idea that providing unrestricted funding promotes candid conversations between nonprofits and funders about the real cost of managing projects and providing services."[18] The result has been over $55 million awarded to nearly two hundred community organizations across the region over the past decade. Of course, like any good funder, the Sobrato Foundation commissioned a report to examine the impact of its work on grantees and see what lessons could be learned. We'll list the report's key takeaways here. Stop us when they start to sound familiar.

- Nonprofits need GOS for organizational and programmatic expenses.
- GOS is an investment of confidence, not only resources, in the organization.
- Funders' expectations for GOS vary, and they should be clearly defined and periodically reviewed.
- GOS grantmaking often requires additional time and care.
- GOS can help promote candid conversations between nonprofits and funders.[19]

The California Endowment—Democratizing Philanthropy

Back in Los Angeles is where we find the California Endowment (CalEndow), the largest private healthcare foundation in the state, with more than $3 billion in assets. Though it's headquartered in LA, CalEndow actually promotes a variety of health and human services initiatives in fourteen communities throughout California. And the foundation has been practicing trust-based philanthropy for nearly a decade as part of its strategy of investing to create healthy communities. Steve Eldred, CalEndow's senior program manager, explained this strategy exists within a broader framework whereby the *community* establishes the priorities, and then CalEndow selects key anchor organizations to fund (on a multiyear basis, of course). "Rather than make specific and inflexible grants with line item budgets and detailed work plans," Eldred said, "we provide program support grants with complete budget flexibility, or unrestricted grants for general operating support."[20] He and his team gather relevant information by actively communicating with many community stakeholders—nonprofits, residents, private businesses, governments—in a kind of virtuous feedback loop that ensures all voices have a chance to be heard. And that's key. For this approach to work, funders must spend a lot of time in the communities grantees serve. In Eldred's view, it's all part of a larger industry trend away from what he calls "responsive grantmaking"—when funders take unsolicited applications from myriad nonprofits that may or may not be mission-aligned with their priorities. This practice takes way too much time for foundations to administer, Eldred said, and in the end only roughly 10 percent of applications are successful.

CalEndow is now poised to help take trust-based philanthropy to the next level. "Today, we're going further in this approach by bringing community members in to help design how funds will be spent," Eldred said. He adds that these residents represent the majority of a steering committee that reviews proposals and then makes the ultimate funding decisions. "We're basically putting money into a pool and letting the community go through the process of setting up the evaluation criteria, making the grants, and developing relationships with the grantees."

Eldred has another term for this approach: *democratizing philanthropy*. The goal is putting power into the hands of those in positions to best recognize areas of need, and then making sure the funding runway is long enough to ensure those needs are properly addressed. "By working with a ten-year timeframe, even if we're slowly making two- to three-year grants," Eldred explained, "the expectation is that there's going to be a continuation of funding for the next logical evolution of the project we started."

This "stakeholder-centric" model practiced by CalEndow and others goes by several different names, the most widely adopted of which is *participatory grantmaking*. As GrantCraft (a service of Candid) points out, while there is no formal definition of participatory grantmaking, there's near universal agreement among those engaged in the practice that it must have several elements:

- Emphasizes "nothing about us without us."
- Shifts power about grantmaking decisions by involving—or giving all power to—the people most affected by the issues or problems.
- Empowers and gives agency to people who benefit from funding to determine the priorities of their lives.[21]

Jamison views all of this—trust-based philanthropy, multiyear and unrestricted funding, withering of the overhead myth, and the tectonic shifting of historical power dynamics—as a continuum of contemporary best practices in the nonprofit sector. "If you're a philanthropist, you need to pay attention to those with lived experience and on-the-ground knowledge of what communities need," she said, "and not think that just because you have money that you know better."[22]

Increasingly, others are coming around to this perspective. Recognition by funders of the benefits of changing the balance of power from historical "suspicion-based" philanthropy to trust-based philanthropy is spreading, though considerable effort still needs to be made to increase its adoption. In a 2017 report on funder/nonprofit relationships, Exponent Philanthropy found fully half of funders always try to use others' experiences and perspectives to become more knowledgeable. However, the same report found barely a third of funders (35 percent) "often acknowledge the existence of [unequal power dynamics] and actively work to minimize it."[23]

The James Irvine Foundation

With $2.3 billion in assets, the James Irvine Foundation grants some $100 million per year in California following practices analogous to trust-based and participatory philanthropy. No big surprise. After all, Irvine's CEO Don Howard is the coauthor of "The Nonprofit Starvation Cycle," the seminal work explaining the negative impacts of funders not supporting the true costs—including overhead!—nonprofits incur in fulfilling their missions.[24] "What we've been trying to do at Irvine is respect the knowledge of our nonprofit grantees in how to solve problems in their communities," Howard explained, "and give them the resources to do it on their terms without micromanaging the process or being overly prescriptive."[25]

True to this mantra, Irvine has shifted a lot of its grantmaking to more flexible forms—including funding for general operating support—which gives grantees dominion over how best to deploy the money. The work starts with Irvine and its nonprofit partner investing considerable time up front to define the specific outcomes both want to achieve. This process has the added benefit of engendering mutual trust, which Howard sees as the sine qua non of any productive relationship. With a foundation of trust firmly in place, Irvine makes the grant and then lets the organization figure out how to turn goals into realities. "What I'm hoping we're doing at Irvine is pioneering a bit of a different approach," Howard said, "which has at its core a good deal more trust in nonprofit leaders' wisdom and ability to solve problems."

The William and Flora Hewlett Foundation—Strategic Philanthropy

Ready for some more moniker madness? Another way to label trust-based grantmaking practices is *strategic philanthropy*, a term preferred by the Bay Area's venerable Hewlett Foundation. In a 2017 essay published in the *Stanford Social Innovation Review*, Hewlett's president, Paul Brest, commented that almost 50 percent of the foundation's $400 million in annual grants is designated for general operating support because, he said, "we think of ourselves as strategic and results-oriented."[26] But wait a minute. Wouldn't the word "strategic" imply a more focused, program-based approach to grantmaking? Brest acknowledges that point of view, though he argued, "a strategic funder can often have the most significant and sustainable impact through general operating support grants."

As an example, he cites a museum's need for unrestricted funding simply to maintain the quality and viewability of its collection. Indeed, it would be much more difficult for museums to put out compelling exhibits for the viewing public featuring excessively decrepit artifacts and antiquities. The Maritime Museum's Ashley agrees. "As cultural institutions, museums are really more like zoos," he said. "Both spend a large portion of their annual budget on the care and feeding of their assets."[27] Brest does draw an important distinction, however, between simply writing checks without the expectation of having any influence over how the money is spent—think: the crinkly bills you drop in that Salvation Army kettle—and what he calls "negotiated general operating support." The latter arrangement—the type practiced at Hewlett—involves supporting an organization's "operations as a whole," but only after substantial due diligence and dialogue with the grantee about what outcomes will be achieved, how the work will get done, and how progress will be measured.

The San Diego Symphony

So far, we've looked at the practice of trust-based philanthropy only from the standpoint of foundations and other institutional funders. What about individual philanthropists? Well, there are a lot of them—each with unique methods and motivations—so it's hard to draw many conclusions without painting with too broad a brush. That said, we didn't even have to travel outside our hometown of San Diego to find at least one powerful example of a couple that thoughtfully structured a mega gift to ensure its recipient had both the resources and flexibility it needed to thrive. That beneficiary was the San Diego Symphony. Established in 1910, the century-old institution has endured a series of financial troubles over its long history—culminating with it (and several predecessor organizations) suspending operations or declaring bankruptcy on at least four occasions. And issues like these are not unique to San Diego's symphony. Way back in 2003, a half-decade before the Great Recession, the *New York Times* reported, "Nearly a dozen orchestras across the country have either closed or are in danger of doing so."[28] The situation hasn't improved much. Regardless of critical acclaim, many of the nation's symphonies, operas, and theater companies are still financially vulnerable from funding models that fail to provide adequate resources and flexibility.

Enter Joan and Irwin Jacobs. They are internationally known philanthropists who, in 2002, pledged what was at the time the largest gift ever made to a symphony orchestra—a giant bequest to the San Diego Symphony to the, ahem, *tune* of $120 million! Almost as remarkable, the symphony had only emerged from bankruptcy several years beforehand and, despite this, the Jacobs still made their gift with relatively few . . . *strings* . . . attached. Okay, okay, we'll stop. But talk about trust! Unlike many sizable donations to arts and culture institutions, the funds pledged to the San Diego Symphony weren't all designated to the organization's endowment. Rather, the Jacobs structured their bequest in several phases. "It wasn't a lump sum," the *Voice of San Diego* wrote in an article published ten years after the couple's original announcement. "The gift comes in three parts: $20 million in $2 million installments over ten years, directly into the day-to-day budget; $50 million in $5 million installments over ten years into the symphony's endowment, from which it can only withdraw a small percentage every year; and $50 million when the couple passes away."[29]

Why do it this way? Reflecting on what motivated them, Joan Jacobs described what she and her husband had been doing to support the symphony in the years leading up to their transformative gift. "We'd been giving [the San Diego Symphony] one or two million a year and they were just limping along," she said from a tastefully appointed office in the couple's sunlit La Jolla home. "And finally we said, 'This is silly. They're not going to go anyplace with it. We need to make a significant gift or we are going to have to stop.'" (Amusing sidebar: Mrs. Jacobs told us they informed the symphony about their gift by leaving a voice-mail. Can you imagine being the one to take that message!?)

The Jacobs also knew many other organizations that received large upfront gifts spent the money and didn't improve their long-term sustainability. Or, perversely, the windfalls actually reduced donations from others because of a belief that the institution no longer needed funding.

As chair of the symphony's foundation board, Jacobs understood well that, donations or not, consistently putting out a quality product was the only way to ensure the organization's survival. "Ultimately," she said, "any nonprofit—especially a cultural nonprofit—has to create an experience or provide a service that is valued by the stakeholders in their community. Otherwise—whether it's next year, five years, twenty years from now—they're going to be back in a position where they need donations just to continue operating." By structuring their gift to provide annuity-style operating capital for at least a decade, the Jacobs gave the symphony's leadership ample time to make improvements to the music, staff, and programs. Indeed, part of the money was spent to increase musicians' salaries to attract top talent. This, management hoped, would lead to a better product that the public was willing to pay for.

Did it work? Well, the symphony has maintained a balanced budget every year since the gift was made. "[It] was regarded as a good regional orchestra when [former symphony CEO Ward Gill] arrived in San Diego in 2003," the *Voice of San Diego* wrote in 2011. "Now the orchestra is a top-tier, world-class ensemble . . . attracting some of the world's top talents like pianist Lang Lang and cellist Yo-Yo Ma as guest artists."[30] And, after news of the Jacobs' largesse broke, the *New York Times* declared the San Diego Symphony Orchestra was "placed firmly on the nation's musical landscape."[31]

Today, the symphony is helmed by industry veteran Martha Gilmer. After a thirty-five-year career at the venerable Chicago Symphony Orchestra, Gilmer took the position of CEO of the San Diego Symphony in the fall of 2014. Speaking about the Jacobs' gift, she said, "It was a pivotal moment in the life of the symphony, because often arts organizations are so focused on what is urgent that they can't look long term."[32] Gilmer believes the decision to include money for operational expenses, staff salaries, and program expansion, as well as seed an endowment that can be drawn on over time, sent a clear message to all stakeholders that the symphony's sustainability was paramount.

The effect was contagious. Gilmer explained the structure of the donation helped raise operating dollars from other funders, because they were confident the symphony would be around for future generations. And since some donors like to gift into endowments, while others prefer more immediate funding, the structure established a mechanism for both. Staff and musician retention also benefited. "People need to know that they're going to come here and have a viable place to work and make a difference, and that it's sustainable," Gilmer said.

Just as the Jacobs envisioned, their gift was leveraged in many ways. It allowed the symphony to invest in talent, infrastructure, new programs, and new facilities. It provided a solid foundation upon which could be built a funding model with multiple streams of revenue. It also enabled the symphony to expand its donor base and cultivate a broader, more diverse audience. The latter has been accomplished through development of new performances, such as outdoor bayfront jazz concerts, as well as the creation of educational programs designed to appeal to all ages and cultures.

The symphony shows no signs of resting on its laurels. New facilities in different locations are in the works, including an ambitious plan to build a permanent waterfront amphitheater that will accommodate up to ten thousand people, and feature state-of-the-art sound, lighting, public amenities, and food and beverage services. "It's all designed not only to bring great artists and great music to a wider public audience," Gilmer said, "but also to help the symphony make San Diego an even greater destination."

None of this progress happened overnight. The Jacobs' gift represented *patient capital* that enabled the symphony to transition from a funding model reliant on finding enough donor support each year to keep the doors open, to one that is diversified and balanced. As Gilmer put it, "we're a third, a third, a third in terms of the mix between earned revenue, contributed revenue, and endowment revenue."

As for the Jacobs, Gilmer said: "When Joan and Irwin walk up the stairs after a concert and are proud of how the orchestra's played, that's their reward. Because I know that they, like so many other donors, derive tremendous satisfaction from making something important possible. And that's the great joy of philanthropy."[33]

IS GRANTMAKING GETTING SMARTER?

It might be tempting to interpret what's been written in this chapter as the heralding of a new Age of Philanthropic Enlightenment. And if that's your take, you wouldn't necessarily be wrong. Something exciting certainly seems to be afoot, and it's not limited to the relative few examples we've highlighted. A 2017 report on a national study of funders conducted by Grantmakers for Effective Organizations (GEO)—a nonprofit industry organization with more than seven thousand members—illustrates the growing importance of trust-based philanthropy and similar practices. In fact, themes that by now you should be able to recite in your sleep also managed to pop up in the GEO report's recommendations that "actually make a difference for [members'] grantees":[34]

- Strengthening funder/grantee relationships (including changing power dynamics)
- Providing flexible, reliable funding (unrestricted and multiyear)
- Including grants for capacity-building (infrastructure, professional development, etc.)

Again, there's still ample room for improvement. The report points out that while nearly 90 percent of grantmakers offer some kind of capacity-building support, less than a quarter of members say they include funds for general operating support in their grants. The good news is members also seem to recognize the deficiency. Only a handful of GEO survey respondents think their organization's culture is currently set up to maximize funding effectiveness, a sentiment that, hopefully, augurs a strong desire for change.

Alphabet Soup

Whether called unrestricted operating support, participatory grantmaking, or any other of the alphabetic permutations that have come to signify the practice of trust-based philanthropy, it would be nice if the nonprofit sector could agree on a single term so we all have a common frame of reference. But that's probably wishful thinking. Plus, it's really beside the point, which is that exciting shifts in historical paradigms are changing philanthropy dogma for the better. "It's pretty simple," said Howard, from the Irvine Foundation. "[T]he message is really about funders and grantees knowing one other and recognizing the best way to approach partners based on their unique priorities and styles." Sometimes, one of the shortest words in the English language—"no"—is the hardest to say, and Howard, too, stresses that not all available funding is money you should take. "Don't accept resources from an organization that's going to encourage you to do things that aren't what you think are the right things to do," he said, adding that nonprofits also need to make sure to ask funders to include all indirect expenses so they can cover the full cost of implementing a project.

Those with the gold may still rule, but the philanthropic plutocracy is definitely under strain. With any luck, today's and future generations may well witness a shift to that other, more familiar, *Golden Rule*. You know, the one about respectful reciprocity and treating others the way you'd like them to treat you. It's happening, and the organizations we've talked about are proving it every day. So, Main Streets, do your homework and seek out funders that are embracing these new models of giving. Have meaningful discussions with current and prospective donors about how they're practicing trust-based philanthropy. Before too long, you just might find you're replacing piers by building bridges.

7

SHOW ME THE NUMBERS!

Impact Assessment and Evaluation

In God We Trust; All Others Must Bring Data. These well-known words—or at least their sentiment—are generally attributed to twentieth-century engineer and statistician William Edwards Deming. They provide an apt segue from our previous chapter.

Apocryphal or not, the quote certainly seems like something Deming would have said. After all, he's widely considered a pioneer in the pursuit of modern Total Quality Management (TQM).[1] You know TQM. It's that system of well-integrated business operations made famous by Toyota. And for it to work—or more accurately, for a company's leadership to *know* if it's working—data, lots of it, must be rigorously measured and meticulously analyzed. We just finished talking about the (admittedly) touchy-feely topic of trust and how critical it is to high-functioning relationships. Well, guess what? Data are the fertile soil in which the trust tree grows. If that's too oblique a reference for you, try this: Trust is a *lot* easier to build—especially between funders and their grantees—if you bring data to back up the impact you say your programs have.

Publicly traded for-profits certainly get this. Measuring and reporting results have become their own art form on Wall Street, thanks to stringent SEC regulations. Think quarterly earnings reports, annual reports, analyst guidance calls, and so on. The government sector, too, has its own raft of reporting agencies, and in 1993, the U.S. Congress created the Government Performance Results Act (GPRA) "to ensure that [the federal government and its departments] . . . assess the effectiveness of their programs."[2]

In previous chapters, we've highlighted how nonprofits are different from their counterparts in other sectors. And mostly this is a good thing—except when we consider how many nonprofit organizations report results to their stakeholders. Or rather, how many don't. Sure, organizations publish a few perfunctory financial and regulatory reports (like IRS Form 990), but too often those lack readily quantifiable and understandable *impact* data. (And don't even get us started on the situation with internationally based NGOs. Seriously—it's the unregulated Wild West when it comes to their mandated reporting.)

So if rigorous results reporting is required for other sectors, why not for nonprofits? Think about it: How many sophisticated investors would buy stock in a company that didn't report timely, actionable data? Yeah, yeah, there are those who buy based on emotion, a "hot stock tip," or some other form of limited information. But these people aren't investors; they're gamblers. As one of our economics professors used to say, if you're going to "invest" this way, it's better just to spend your money at the craps table in Vegas. At least there you've got good buffets and entertainment.

As in the for-profit sector, today's nonprofits need to work to attract a growing number of stakeholders motivated by data-driven results. Their *investors*—foundations, donors, even employees—are demanding ever greater accountability and assessment of mission impact. Fortunately, new tools and technologies are being developed to satisfy this demand, which at its core stems from a singular goal: a desire to deploy financial and human resources where they can do the most good. Stakeholders are no longer forced to rely on specious anecdotes about program effectiveness. But neither do they have to require time-consuming and costly studies—like double-blind or randomized controlled trials—that may be out of date before they're published. A healthy and attainable middle ground exists.

To borrow a metaphor from *The X-Files* (remember Scully and Mulder?), making decisions based on viewing hand-picked photos of smiling revelers at the annual gala is using "I Want to Believe" as a measurement criterion. Mulder abidingly accepted that aliens exist—despite the lack of concrete evidence. Scully, on the other hand, was skeptical about the existence of visitors from other planets unless "sightings" were supported by scientific data. But, as the show's tagline reminds us, *The Truth Is Out There*. Actionable and accurate impact information exists. Increasingly, nonprofits and their funders want this information, and they're willing to pay to get it.

In this chapter, we'll discuss some of the contemporary developments in evaluation and impact assessment. We'll also explore how nonprofits—and their funders—are adapting and prospering in this new environment by using these developments to improve sustainability. Don't worry—we promise not to delve into the somewhat arcane world of Theory of Change diagrams or logic models. It's well beyond our level of expertise; plus we want you to stay awake.

In his 2013 annual letter titled "Measuring Progress," Bill Gates reviewed how much had been achieved since the signing of the United Nations (UN) Millennium Declaration in September 2000. From this declaration, 191 UN member countries agreed on a set of eight interdependent Millennium Development Goals (MDGs) for improving the lives of the world's poorest and most at-risk people. Key among the requirements from UN agencies, developed countries, and developing countries alike was a demand for specific impact targets and "more rigorous evaluation to measure effectiveness."[3] Frankly, it's hard to envision a more ambitious plan, or a more complex undertaking, than a group of nearly two hundred diverse countries that don't even share a common language working together on issues like eradicating extreme poverty and hunger and achieving universal primary education.

Gates points out that while not all MDGs had been achieved, "we've made amazing progress," and the 2015 target of cutting extreme poverty in half around the world "has been reached ahead of the deadline, as has the goal of halving the proportion of people who lack access to safe drinking water."

Impressive results—especially considering their audacity and the relatively short amount of time it took to achieve them. How did it happen? According to Gates, "setting clear goals, picking the right approach, and then measuring results to get feedback and refine the approach continually helps us to deliver tools and services to everybody who will benefit." How encouraging is this?! Shouldn't the achievement of so many magnanimous objectives—ahead of schedule, no less—give every Main Street nonprofit in the world a great big ol' shot of hope and excitement that they, too, can make meaningful progress toward clear-set goals?

But to do so, Gates mentioned, you need to have a system in place for evaluating results. A policy brief by the European Commission described the key ingredients necessary for measuring social impact.[4] It says you must:

- Identify objectives
- Identify stakeholders
- Set relevant measurements
- Measure, validate, and value
- Export, learn, and improve

Pretty simple and straightforward, right? Simple, yes. Easy, no. As always, the devil is in the details. Does your nonprofit have the resources—human and financial—to fully commit to the evaluation process? Is a culture of impact measurement already baked into the DNA of your organization? If not, implementing the previous steps might seem a bit like building your airplane while flying it.

WHY IS EVALUATION IMPORTANT?

We get it. This stuff is hard for many—okay, most—nonprofits. Let's face facts: it's tough to find people who started a social venture because they love harvesting and analyzing reams of data. They created their organizations because they wanted to change the world! That passion certainly is critical in helping get an idea off the ground. And it's difficult, if not impossible, to test a concept you've only just developed. There simply isn't enough information to work with. So it's completely understandable that nonprofits operate on hope during this initial start-up phase.

From the get-go, "social organizations are faith-based enterprises," said Silicon Valley entrepreneur and startup guru Steve Blank.[5] "You're actually the head of a religious organization on Day One, whether you know so or not." The mistake many nonprofits make, he believes, is to continue this way indefinitely, without ever testing to see if their assumptions are correct and their programs actually work. Rather, according to Blank, they should pilot, fail, learn, and then move on—all the while collecting valuable data. "What you really want to do," Blank said, "is replace the faith with facts as rapidly as you can."

To be sure, some nonprofits get along just fine for quite a while using hoped-for or perceived results to attract donors. Authors William Foster, Peter Kim, and Barbara Christiansen write that one type of organization, dubbed "The Heartfelt Connector," can sustain itself "by focusing on causes that resonate with the existing concerns of large numbers of people at all income levels, and by creating a structured way for these people to connect where none had previously existed."[6] They cite the Make-a-Wish Foundation and the Susan G. Komen Foundation as examples.

Another general classification of nonprofits that have grown large without necessarily submitting to rigorous program evaluation is what Foster, Kim, and Christiansen call the "Local Nationalizer." Think Big Brothers, Big Sisters or Teach for America. These nonprofits, the authors say, have succeeded in "creating a national network of locally based operations." Organizations that employ a Local Nationalizer funding model "focus on issues . . . that are important to local communities across the country, where government alone can't solve the problem." To be clear, many large, internationally known organizations like those mentioned no doubt recognize the importance of program evaluation and expend major efforts and resources measuring results. However, it's also true that many organizations with similar models—particularly Main Street nonprofits—do not. Well-intentioned though they are, they continue on as faith-based organizations in perpetuity.

Just because a select few nonprofits operate without testing or evaluation doesn't mean that strategy should be widely adopted. After all, change is constant, and even those organizations that have managed to skate by with a dearth of data might not be able to do so forever. As Foster and his team point out, funding markets are dynamic and can shift on a whim, leaving certain organizations vulnerable. They note, "The first Earth Day in 1970 coincided with a major expansion in giving to environmental causes; the Ethiopian famine of 1984–85 led to a dramatic increase in support for international relief; and awareness of the U.S. educational crisis in the late 1980s laid the groundwork for charter school funding."

The point the authors make is that there's an element of randomness to what opens people's hearts and wallets. As Americans, we are charitable and generous. But we're also a nation of dabblers, susceptible to the latest cause du jour. "Changes cannot be foreseen," Foster, Kim, and Christiansen write, "and, hence, cannot be depended on as a source of funding."

LESSONS FROM CORAL

Earlier, we discussed the reports generated by two large foundations concerning significant programs that failed to meet their funders' expectations. One of these programs, launched by the James Irvine Foundation in 1999, was called Communities Organizing Resources to Advance Learning (CORAL). At the time the largest program initiative in the foundation's history, CORAL was "an eight-year, $58 million effort to improve the educational performance of low-achieving students in five California cities."[7] When it was clear the ambitious initiative wasn't producing the hoped-for results, James E. Canales, then Irvine's president, helped commence a major mid-course correction. Among the many lessons learned from this endeavor, Canales offered the following suggestions apropos of evaluation:

- "Do not commit to a major effort without well-vetted goals and rationale as well as clear means to measure results along the way and an information system that has been tested in the real world.
- At the start of a project, commit to enlisting an outsider to conduct a midpoint review."[8]

These lessons were expensive but valuable, and lend credence to Bruce Hoyt's pyramid analogy for nonprofit success. In it, you'll recall, evidence-based outcomes form the foundation upon which everything else—scalability, revenue, funding, and ultimately, sustainability—is built.

THE DEMISE OF THE OVERHEAD MYTH

We've alluded to the demise of the overhead myth, and now we must concede—with apologies to Mark Twain—reports of its death have been greatly exaggerated. But make no mistake, the myth is withering on the vine. Swelling ranks of influential funders armed with (of course) data on the many benefits that accrue from eliminating misleading measurements of performance—like indirect cost ratios or overhead—are shining an unflattering light on numerous nonprofits that have been flying under the impact-detection radar for a long time. Put bluntly, "The overhead ratio has been giving cover to wasteful organizations for decades," said *Uncharitable*'s Dan Pallotta, "because all that organization had to show you was that they had low overhead, which they could do with any variety of accounting tricks, and never answer the question about whether they were having an impact."[9]

It certainly makes sense that both funders and grantees would welcome replacing nonsensical metrics with those rooted in meaningful data. But beware: this transition won't be kind to everyone. "More data and clarity around what produces relevant, measurable impact could actually lead to a smaller number of nonprofits, as those that don't measure up fail, and fewer organizations start up," said Dr. Nelli Garton.[10]

Garton is founder and chief impact officer at Tablecloth, a data analytics company that offers nonprofits a dashboard of real-time performance metrics. Besides being useful for crafting compelling narratives around the effect programs are having, tools like Tablecloth help organizations that implement a system of social impact measurement derive a host of other benefits. The consultancy firm inFocus Enterprises summarized five such perks in a December 2016 report:

- You could report back to funders on time with quality reports (accountability).
- You can use the strength of your impact measurement, and results, to attract new funders (fundraising).
- You can use findings from your impact measurement to improve your activities, leading to better results for your participants (learning and improving).

- You have powerful data/stories to use to promote your organisation (marketing and communication).
- You can use findings from your impact measurement to share with other organisations in the sector and collaborate (collaboration). [11]

YOU GET WHAT YOU PAY FOR

Some folks of a certain age may remember those words from entrepreneur John Arbuckle in a coffee commercial. (Others, like one of us, heard that name and thought it was Garfield's dad. Turns out he spelled his name "Jon." We digress.) The sentiment described is similar to what we heard over and over from industry leaders during the course of our interviews: Some things are just worth the extra expense. Impact data collection is one of them, and it starts with funders. "If funders are going to ask organizations to collect data," said Stanford's Kathleen Kelly Janus, "they have to pay for it." [12] Not enough do. According to Janus's research, only 40 percent of the funding directed at nonprofits in the United States is unrestricted. "That's crazy," she said. It's tantamount to "going into a restaurant and saying I'm going to pay for the food, but I'm not going to pay for the plate. And I'm not going to pay for the chef's time to prepare it, or the menu preparation. But we do that in philanthropy all the time."

Nonprofits have a responsibility, too. They, Janus said, have to work to create a data-driven culture and meticulously collect information. Good or bad, the data have to be authentic. She adds that organizations also must be honest with their data and with their funders about what's working and what isn't. Doing so pays off. Organizations, said Janus, "that were able to create better transparency with their donors ultimately had better outcomes, because they were able to show that they were rigorously attacking the problem and develop their programs accordingly."

In return for accurate information about the efficacy of programs their dollars support, funders also need to be willing to look through a longer lens. That way, nonprofits don't have to worry about losing funding in the middle of collecting data, and they can take a long-term view of their projects to assess impact. Like the "virtuous ecosystems" we've already described, let's call this the "virtuous cycle of evaluation."

Sometimes, though, perceptions of this virtuous cycle can vary based on who's doing the beholding. "Foundation leaders overwhelmingly say that nonprofits should be held to higher standards of evidence,"[13] said Phil Buchanan of the Center for Effective Philanthropy. He added that leaders also think their foundations should help grantees achieve these standards, and most believe they are in fact providing the financial and other support necessary to do so. But, Buchanan said, the majority of nonprofits are receiving no such support—an argument bolstered by Janus's statistic on the percentage of funding that's truly unrestricted. "In other words," according to Buchanan, "foundation CEOs believe they are helping nonprofits improve their performance assessment capacity, but that's not what their grantees are experiencing."

There are exceptions, of course. Many funders do back up their words with dollars to help organizations with program assessment and impact measurement. In the aggregate, though, "there are some important disconnects," Buchanan said. As an aside, he added that in his experience, the majority of nonprofit leaders welcome thoughtful evaluations of their organization's programs. "What they're opposed to is having funders dictate measurements that really aren't relevant or indicative of impact or success," he said.

Mario Morino, co-founder and chairman of Venture Philanthropy Partners, strikes a similar chord in his book, *Leap of Reason*. "To make the leap to managing to outcomes," he asserts, "nonprofits need creative funders willing to think big with them—not just pester them for more information on results."[14]

Ultimately, though, evaluation is most effective when it originates from within the organization that's doing the work. According to the Denver Foundation's Dace West, many of the most successful nonprofits—and those that consistently get funded—use data collection and impact assessment as a means to improve their programs and processes rather than simply as an accountability tool. In other words, evaluation is part of their DNA. West also cautioned against ignoring potentially valuable input from frontline staff when organizations perform a self-evaluation. Those closest to the mission, programs, and clients, she said, often have the best information on what's actually working.[15]

NOT A PANACEA

There's a mountain of evidence supporting the use of data collection and impact assessment within organizations. But what happens when even the best-laid plans don't produce meaningful results? Investing finite resources in program evaluation can be fraught; the process can be exceedingly complex and costly, and the results it produces are not always clear, timely, or—most important—actionable. Even randomized controlled trials—to most, the "gold standard" of evidence gathering—sometimes suffer from these limitations.

In their 2018 article, "Ten Reasons Not to Measure Impact—and What to Do Instead," authors Mary Kay Gugerty and Dean Karlan describe how the research nonprofit Innovations for Poverty Action (IPA)—an organization working to promote impact evaluations—"has conducted more than 650 randomized controlled trials (RCTs) since its inception in 2002." The results were decidedly mixed. "These studies have sometimes provided evidence about how best to use scarce resources," Gugerty and Karlan wrote. "But the vast majority of studies did not paint a clear picture that led to immediate policy changes." No doubt a bit deflating for IPA as well as for the myriad organizations working to solve global poverty. The authors do offer a flicker of hope, though, writing, "Developing an evidence base is more like building a mosaic: Each individual piece does not make the picture, but bit by bit a picture becomes clearer and clearer."[16]

EVALUATION HACKS

Given the surfeit of responsibility and paucity of resources Main Street nonprofits have to balance every day, it's no wonder such a large number of them never get around to effectively measuring outcomes. And among those intrepid few that do, "far too many are missing the forest for the trees,"[17] wrote Morino. "They focus more heavily on the mechanics of measurement than on understanding what the data reveal." It doesn't have to be this way. A recurring theme in our discussions with industry leaders was their recognition of the value of less elaborate, less costly, yet equally effective methods of assessing impact as compared with more complex programs of data collection and analysis. In keeping with today's zeitgeist, we'll call these "evaluation hacks."

What follows is a brief anecdote we heard during our research that illustrates this concept. A social services nonprofit wanted to track the success of participants in its programs to determine if the organization's curriculum led to better life outcomes. Rather than reinvent the wheel and create a wholly new system of data collection, it turned to a tool that already exists: LinkedIn. It used the site to gather information on people who had gone through their programs: colleges attended, jobs held, promotions earned, honors bestowed. All for free. The organization followed participants' careers online and used people's progress as a proxy for program efficacy. Was it the ideal indicator? No. But that's rarely required. "Don't get too hung up on crafting the perfect measurement tool," advised Third Sector Capital's John Grossman. Rather, he said, "measure the 'good enough,' as long as it's indicative and compelling."[18]

Kim Ammann Howard, director of Impact Assessment and Learning at the James Irvine Foundation, agreed. "I think a lot of the time the challenge with evaluation is that people want it to be great, and so they don't do anything because it won't be great," she said. Her message, to turn an old phrase, is not to let the perfect be the enemy of the good. "It's most useful to have information that's going to inform and speak to the work," she said, "and if it has to start with proxy data that indicate progress towards desired impacts, that's okay."[19]

One final point on this: Don't try to measure everything! This is advice from Dr. Laura Deitrick, associate director of the Nonprofit Institute at the University of San Diego. Part of Deitrick's work at the university is teaching research methods, program design, and evaluation techniques to students and nonprofit leaders. She's been doing it for years, and one of the key messages she tries to impart through her course is to "select a few relevant things that are indicative of your mission and lend themselves to quantification and storytelling, and measure them."[20]

And be strategic for goodness' sake! If your decision will be the same no matter what the data say, pick something else to assess and move on. Otherwise, you're just engaging in an academic exercise, not a practical pursuit.

THE CULTURE OF EVALUATION AND LEARNING

The Irvine Foundation's Ammann Howard described how her team approaches planning and implementing an evaluation of its grants—many of which are part of multiyear initiatives. Hint: It starts at the *beginning*. Unlike many nonprofit evaluation practices that occur only with hindsight—often because a funder requested it ex post facto—"the evaluation umbrella at Irvine happens at the start," Ammann Howard said. "It's imperative that people are clear on the impact they want to have and that they figure out how they're going to know if they're successful in getting there." In other words, it's not only about determining *whether* goals were met, but also putting in the time up front to figure out *what* the best goals are and *how* to achieve them.

Consistent processes like those at Irvine don't just happen. They're deliberately created as part of a culture where evaluation and continuous improvement is valued, encouraged, prioritized, and funded. This last one is key. If you're not putting a regular line item in the budget for evaluation, you're saying it's not important. Period. Full stop.

It's all part of developing what the Center for Nonprofit Excellence (CNE) calls a "learning culture."[21] In it, knowledge has to be institutionalized and spread throughout an organization by rote. "Reflection," "feedback," and information sharing must exist in concert to "take organizations beyond an emphasis on program-focused outcomes to more systemic and organization wide focus on sustainability and effectiveness."

Along with this holistic change in perspective, according to the CNE, "learning cultures are poised to respond quicker, be more adaptable, be more collaborative and more successful." If done right, these assets don't have to stay contained within a single organization, either. Lessons gleaned through a learning culture can and should be spread far and wide to others within the sector, so everyone can benefit from this collective wisdom.

DON'T FLY BLIND; USE YOUR DASHBOARD

If you'll kindly indulge our sense of nostalgia, we'll revisit for a moment an analogy drawn earlier in the book: that of nonprofit boards and their

CEO as the twin engines of an airplane. We think we've just about exhausted that comparison, but first we'd like to add another piece of equipment: the dashboard. This one serves not only an organization's leadership, but also its clients, collaborators, employees, volunteers, and funders. In short, *all* stakeholders.

If you've flown anywhere in the last decade or two, you've likely noticed tiny computer screens attached to the seatbacks. (PSA: Try not to touch them very much; they're some of the dirtiest parts on the plane! You're welcome.) In addition to offering movies, games, and a host of other in-flight entertainment, these little gadgets also let you choose a channel that shows selected bits of the airplane's telemetry: altitude, airspeed, wind velocity, and so on. From first class back to steerage, the rank and file now has access to some of the same information the pilots use. Wouldn't it be nice if the same were true with nonprofits? Dashboards that report key performance indicators (KPIs) to board members are becoming de rigueur in many organizations. So why not extend this information to all stakeholders and provide them with real-time reporting on mission effectiveness and program impact?

As author Lawrence Butler writes in *The Nonprofit Dashboard: Using Metrics to Drive Mission Success*, dashboards should "present a quick, comprehensible overview of an organization's status and overall direction."[22] Ideally, they would provide indicative and actionable data stakeholders can use to "readily spot changes and trends in these measurements." Sound a little scary? Sure. After all, transparency means you offer the good, the bad, and the ugly for the whole world to see. But imagine the benefits: increased credibility, improved stakeholder engagement, and continuous improvement, to name a few!

It gets back to the *learning culture*. However, just as the passengers on the plane don't see *all* data available to the pilots, some discretion is required in creating "evaluation dashboards" for the masses. Caveats about choosing the right things to measure apply here, too. Make sure you're reporting *outcomes*, rather than *outputs* (more on this in a bit). Finally, it's worth bearing in mind the timeless "KISS" principle (Keep It Simple . . . ahem, Silly). If the information isn't relevant, succinct, and displayed in a way that positively pops off the screen, your dashboard won't be used to its fullest potential, if at all.

ONE MISSION, TWO METHODS

To compare two different methods of evaluation, let's look back at a couple of PFS projects we discussed in chapter 2. Both, you'll recall, operated with the objective of reducing rates of recidivism among incarcerated populations. In the earlier (and larger) program, Roca sought to measure the effectiveness of its intervention via a multiyear randomized controlled trial. By contrast, TLM determined impact (and, by extension, how much money investors earned) by using a simple, straightforward calculation on the cumulative number of hours inmates work. Is one method better than the other? It's still early days and therefore hard to say definitively. Plus, there's an implicit assumption that the number of hours inmates work is indicative of the long-term outcomes TLM wants to achieve. What's clearly not in doubt, however, is that the proxy for impact used by TLM was way easier and much cheaper to implement. Yes, its project was also smaller ($800,000 versus $30 million), a fact that only underscores the importance of trying to extract the maximum amount of useful data with the minimum outlay of resources. These are critical considerations for most Main Street nonprofits. Had TLM opted for a costly scientific trial to prove its program's efficacy, that decision may well have killed funding for the project before it ever got off the ground.

To further illustrate the utility of "indicators" rather than voluminous reams of data, let's look at a potential PFS-type project we're working with. The project involves an intervention for all students in a public high school, beginning in their freshman year and lasting until they graduate, with the objective of substantially reducing dropout rates and increasing college enrollment upon graduation. It's modeled after an identical program at a similar school in a comparable community that's been in process for two years and is demonstrating highly favorable results. These are primarily disadvantaged youths, and it clearly would be unfortunate to deny incoming freshman the opportunity for a better education while waiting two years for the now-junior class students at the first school to graduate. The solution: develop indicators of program efficacy that will reasonably predict success, such as results of standardized tests and number of advanced placement classes attended.

Like the proverbial tip of the iceberg, even seemingly simple evaluation measurements often have a lot more to them than first meets the eye. Carrie Stokes Holst is a senior manager of impact and borrower services at Mission Driven Finance, an impact investment firm working to provide underserved businesses (including a number of nonprofits) and communities access to affordable capital. When we spoke with Holst about her firm's process of choosing and validating performance indicators, she described a deal that used the number of jobs created as evidence of impact in a local workforce training program. Easy to track? Check. But, Holst continued, "a lot more is embedded in that single number."[23] She stressed that validating even straightforward measurements requires a great deal of due diligence to truly demonstrate effectiveness. In this example, for instance, Holst and her team had to ask questions such as, "Did the person keep the job, and for how long? Did they scrape by on minimum wage, or earn enough to comfortably sustain themselves and their families? Was the job a springboard to a fulfilling career that improved their quality of life?"

Impact assessment is a delicate dance balance between quantitative and qualitative factors, with the aim of answering, "Why do we want this data, and what's the story we're trying to tell," Holst said. Ultimately, she noted, "The eternal point of contention in these deals is balancing, synthesizing, and condensing that data into something that is meaningful."

OUTPUTS VERSUS OUTCOMES

Earlier in the book, we introduced Antony Bugg-Levine, CEO of the Nonprofit Finance Fund, a leader in providing social-sector funding and consulting services. During our conversation, he told us about a book co-produced by his firm and the Federal Reserve Bank of San Francisco, titled *What Matters: Investing in Results to Build Strong, Vibrant Communities.*[24] In it, Bugg-Levine wrote, "We know that the deepest aspirations of the people who work in and run [nonprofit] organizations, and the government officials and private donors who fund them, is to make long-term and sustained positive impact on the clients and communities they serve." However, he added, "that's not the way the social sector works." Rather, he describes a system that frustrates many nonprofit leaders by rewarding activities rather than results.

Take the shelter that receives financial support for providing beds to the homeless. That's a noble activity, right? Yes, but who cares if it does nothing to address the lack of permanent housing these people face? After all, the root problem we're seeking to solve is chronic homelessness, isn't it? Kathleen Kelly Janus speaks of a complete reorientation of our perspective—one in which we "fall in love with solving the problem, not with a particular solution."[25] Then, she said, we must rigorously test our concepts for impact on that specific problem.

We'd be willing to bet you've run into another instance of misaligned incentives, perhaps recently. Just ask yourself how your health care team gets paid. The answer is for providing treatments, running tests, performing procedures—you get the point. Doctors are compensated for *activities*, not for keeping you well enough to avoid treatment in the first place. The healthcare sector, like so many others, is oriented around *outputs*. And outputs are not impact! Outcomes are.

A distinction without a difference? Hardly. This is far more than an exercise in semantics, though it's certainly understandable why non-profits tend to evaluate activities as a means of determining effectiveness. Activities are observable, easy to summarize, and can make for compelling storytelling. And so, argue the authors of a recent article on measurement and evaluation published in the *Stanford Social Innovation Review*, "faced with the methodological difficulties of measuring impact, many organizations simply give up or stop at the output—versus outcome level—and thus fail to measure any impact at all."[26]

Ultimately, the bottom line is simply this: Outcome measurement tells you whether your organization is achieving its mission. A guidebook developed by the National Resource Center suggests answering the following three questions to determine if you're really looking at outcomes rather than outputs:

- What has changed in the lives of individuals, families, organizations, or the community as a result of this program?
- Has this program made a difference?
- How are the lives of program participants better as a result of the program?[27]

Seem a little woo-woo? We totally understand; we've been talking a lot in generalities. So let's choose a specific sector of the nonprofit community to illustrate the point: arts and culture organizations. Just to add another degree of difficulty, how about *museums*? Not exactly an industry that would appear to lend itself to impact evaluation, is it? Outputs are easy to track, though: the number of warm bodies through the turnstile, a tally of class field trips, the amount of merchandise sold at the gift shop. And on and on. While measurements like ticket sales certainly are helpful for budgeting (not an insignificant endeavor, we concede), they're completely useless for determining impact. Remember, impact is directly linked to mission. Do you think most museums' mission statements read something along the lines of: "To Attract 100,000 Visitors Each Year"? Doubt it. As one museum leader explains, "[Museums] really have a responsibility to define who do you serve, how are you going to serve them, what resources are you willing to dedicate, and then to measure that work so you can put in place a process of continual improvement."[28]

Okay then, let's drill down a little farther to look at a couple of examples where museums have cracked this code, and what it's done for them.

USS *Midway* Museum

We return to this grande dame of the seas, first introduced in our opening chapter on funding models. Given the *Midway*'s success as a revenue generating powerhouse, it would be pretty easy for the museum's leadership simply to rest on its laurels, count its cash (delivered by outputs, mind you), and call it a day. After all, plenty of money is coming in, so anything else is just gravy. Isn't it? Not for the *Midway*, whose stated vision and mission is "to become America's living symbol of freedom," and "to preserve the historic USS *Midway* and the legacy of those who serve, inspire and educate future generations, and entertain our museum guests."[29]

Preserve the museum and entertain guests? Those are the easy ones—accomplished with outputs like ticket sales sufficient to produce the cash flow necessary to keep the *Midway* shipshape. (C'mon, you're used to it by now.) On the other hand, educating future generations, preserving legacies, and becoming a living symbol of freedom? Yeah, those are a bit more esoteric and don't quite lend themselves as easily to impact assessment. The museum needs more information to assess its progress toward those goals. Sure, the *Midway*'s leadership rigorously collects qualitative data through visitor surveys, but even that doesn't paint a complete picture. For instance, visitors may have a terrific time and then promptly forget everything they learned. Or, they may not remember the *Midway* as a symbol of anything other than a fun place to see some cool airplanes. So, how can leadership really tick the "educate future generations" and "become America's living symbol of freedom" boxes on its scorecard? Let's keep looking.

Like many museums, the *Midway* puts on numerous pedagogical programs designed to enrich the overall guest experience. Two of these programs in particular serve as the backbone of the *Midway*'s education initiatives:

- *Midway Institute for Teachers* (MIT) provides professional programs and presentations designed to help history and social studies teachers learn about World War II, the conflicts in Korea and Vietnam, and the Cold War. The aim is for educators to bring knowledge, stories, and history—taught from a variety of perspectives—into their classrooms.
- *Midway University* offers a host of unique hands-on learning experiences for students, all presented onboard in the ship's top-notch facilities. Kids and their families can also spend the night on the *Midway*, sleeping in actual crew berths and dining in the mess hall—all meant to bring history alive.

In the course of setting up its own learning culture, the *Midway*'s leadership did at least two really smart things. One, it actively sought feedback from the end users of its services—the customers! For-profit businesses regularly do this. Really, nowadays you can't even buy a pack of gum at the local 7-Eleven without receiving an invitation to complete a three-page survey about your experience. Too often, however, non-profits fail to collect data from those in a unique position to offer useful information about the programs and services they're using.

Two, the *Midway* recognized that its routine surveys and follow-ups with visitors and participants alone were not adequate to properly assess progress toward the organization's stated goals. So, it partnered with a local university to conduct an in-depth research study of the museum's programs to determine how much of the knowledge gleaned by participants actually was retained. For example, the *Midway*'s leadership wanted data on how the MIT program impacts teachers' ability to incorporate stories and information into their classroom lessons. And it wanted specific recommendations on how to better its programs in the future.

For an investment (yes, *investment*) of $20,000, the *Midway*'s staff, board members, funders, and other stakeholders were able to independently verify that efforts in pursuit of their mission were effective and worthwhile. They also received valuable, actionable data that can be used for continuous improvement.[30]

But $20,000! Who's got that kind of money lying around? Well, consider this: The museum's fifty-page report—created in concert with a respected university using rigorous research methodologies—was key to the *Midway* securing a $10 million donation for program expansion and collaboration with another academic institution. In the world of finance, this would be known as a high *return on investment* (ROI). If that's not your bailiwick, no worries. Just remember this simple formula: Evaluation = Funding.

New Bedford Whaling Museum

A cross-country flight from San Diego, and an hour's drive (okay, without traffic) south of Boston is where you'll find another maritime-themed institution, the New Bedford Whaling Museum. (What can we say, when you live near an ocean you like nautical stuff.) Separated from storied Martha's Vineyard by a scant twenty miles of ocean and a phalange-shaped archipelago, the city of New Bedford could hardly contrast more with its tony island neighbor. High levels of poverty and unemployment abound in this bayside enclave of some ninety-five thousand residents. But over the last twenty years, New Bedford's century-old whaling museum has worked to change this reality for many of its locals.

If you visit the museum, you'll certainly get your fill of ships, scrimshaw, and, of course, skeletal remains of the hulking cetaceans evocative of the region's maritime history and economy. What you may not notice, however, is the museum's high school apprenticeship program, which "provides low-income, academically motivated students with access to resources and experiences that deepen community engagement, promote personal and professional development, and cultivate college and career success."[31] Now, if all that seems somewhat beyond the pale for a mere whaling museum, consider that part of its mission is to educate the public about people's historical interaction with whales. This includes the lore of America's whaling industry and the culture of immigrant populations from Cape Verde and the Azores, among many other places.

The museum accomplishes this in part through its three-year apprenticeship program, which aims to develop youth to serve as ambassadors while also preparing them for their futures beyond high school. Participants visit college campuses, get career advice from professionals, and have the opportunity to job-shadow at companies in the area. The museum even facilitates "support through the college application and financial aid process." And, student apprentices become "brand ambassadors" who assist in reaching communities that traditionally had little reason to connect with the museum and its programs.

All good stuff, right? But how do we know if it really works? At the time we spoke with her, Sarah Rose was the museum's vice president of education and programs. Under her leadership, the apprenticeship program became one of twelve winners of the prestigious National Arts and Humanities Youth Program Award in 2017. Celebrated as "the nation's highest honor for after-school and out-of-school-time arts and humanities programs,"[32] the award was created to recognize curricula that demonstrated effectiveness in "[opening] new pathways to learning, self-discovery, and achievement" for America's youth—especially those representing disadvantaged communities.

Rose told us that shortly after she arrived at New Bedford in 2014, she remembers excitedly explaining to a board member (an educator, as was Rose for nearly ten years prior to joining the museum) that fully 100 percent of the apprenticeship program's graduates went on to college. Imagine her surprise, then, when that member unexpectedly responded, "So what? How do you know your program's true impact?" Though a little deflated, Rose understood the genesis of the member's skepticism. She knew that, particularly among the underserved, young people gaining admission to college was only one indication of mission success. And a potentially ephemeral one at that. "When I think about individual students, it's never a straight path," Rose said. "There's always some life circumstance that's tripping them up, such as financial factors, mental health, family issues, drugs."[33]

So how did she make sure she was evaluating the right outcomes (long-term achievement) as opposed to more convenient outputs (college matriculation rates)? "We brought in a consultant to help us think through what we believed students should be getting out of the program, and how we were going to measure it," Rose explained.

The $12,000 cost (covered by a grant) resulted in a strategic road map, replete with objectives that went far beyond just "admission to college." These included well-defined education and career readiness standards, as well as a logic model of student performance benchmarks that themselves are regularly tested for relevance, and modified if found to be ineffective. Under this new impact assessment process, individual student advancement toward mastery of twelve specific skills is evaluated three times each year. Along with the results of these tests come recommended remedial actions if students are found to be falling short of expected proficiency levels. Bottom line: the museum's apprenticeship program is thoughtfully engineered to relevant standards that are germane to participants' long-term success. And the desired outcomes are clearly articulated, well understood, and consistently measured to ensure continuous improvement.

What's more, Rose and her former colleagues believe recognition of the program's impact resulted in existing donors increasing their support. They're also confident this recognition helped attract new funding from first time donors, following completion of a $10 million capital campaign that included construction of a new building that quadrupled the museum's educational facilities. A final benefit: that board member no longer gets to ask, "So what?"

NICE TO HAVE, BUT . . .

"How am I supposed to afford fancy consultants for an impact assessment?" Fair question. The answer, you might well have deduced, is you don't have to. As we've heard, meaningful measurement doesn't require perfect data. It requires "good enough" data, which often are easier to obtain than you might think. We're absolutely awash in information. Corporations, governments, and nonprofits are all sitting on heaps of valuable data. They just need to do a better job of sharing. Credit card giant Mastercard, for example, recently opened its massive trove of payments information through a "data philanthropy program" designed to "allow [Mastercard's] proprietary insights to be put toward furthering research and programs advancing social good."[34] What is critical, however, is integrating and operationalizing the data you collect into clear *outcomes* that are consistent with your mission.

Also, as we've discussed, funders are increasingly recognizing the accretive value that springs from proper impact assessment, and embracing their shared responsibility to provide resources in support of evaluation. The 2017 study by Grantmakers for Effective Organizations found that 71 percent of respondents reported they provide support for evaluation and learning, areas that were also identified as key ways to help grantmaking "get smarter." The study reported that, "Continuous improvement is at the heart of effective evaluation. Collecting the right information—including both quantitative and qualitative data—we can learn from what's working and what isn't." It concluded, "Grantmakers are in a unique position to create conditions for learning in our organizations and in our communities."[35]

Though reports like the GEO study show funders are willing to kick in to defray the costs of evaluation, they can't be expected to foot the bill alone. So, just how much should nonprofits budget for impact assessment? According to a detailed guide published by the W. K. Kellogg Foundation (yes, the breakfast cereal guy), "A general guideline is to allocate five to ten percent of your total program cost for performance monitoring and/or a process or formative evaluation."[36]

Certainly not insignificant figures, especially given many nonprofits are busy trying to make a dollar out of fifteen cents. But again, think of this money as an investment that will pay handsome dividends down the road. The *Midway* Museum parlayed an impact assessment report into a $10 million donation, an amount equal to the capital campaign the New Bedford Whaling Museum was able to pull off due to incontrovertible evidence of its signature program's efficacy. Think these are just isolated examples cherry-picked to make a specious argument? Think again. Evaluation = Funding, folks.

One word of caution before we close this chapter: The prevalence of so much data and information can have a downside. For one, it makes it a lot harder to separate the signal from the noise. Overreliance on external information can also gradually erode leadership's willingness to make intuitive decisions. Absent empirical data, some executives may begin to lose confidence in their innate ability to deftly guide their organizations to successful outcomes. Yes, data are important. But so is trusting your gut. Nonprofits need both Moneyball and management. Perhaps, then, we should revise our nonprofit success formula to read something like this: Leadership + Planning + Implementation + Evaluation = Funding. There, that's better.

Mulder, we can't operate on blind faith. Like Scully, you need facts and proof. So let's augment those glossy photos in the annual report with real, actionable, and timely data! You, your funders, and your stakeholders will know what you're truly accomplishing, and how you can continue to improve it.

8

TELL ME A STORY

The Tip of the Sustainability Spear

At this point, we've discussed funding models, raising capital, paying your people what they're worth, collaborating, evaluating your impact, leadership and board governance, finding the right funders, and measuring your sustainability. Whew! If you're still with us, you're probably thinking, enough already!

But, all your great work in those areas won't do much for you if people don't know about it. So, in this chapter we're going to talk about the final step, the one that must be *incorporated* with everything already discussed to build sustainability: telling your story.

To begin, we'll practice what we preach, and tell a story.

INVISIBLE CHILDREN

Invisible Children was founded with a mission to raise awareness of kids conscripted as soldiers to fight bloody civil wars in central Africa. In 2012, the organization created a video (*Kony 2012*) to bring attention to the abuse of these children by the Lord's Resistance Army (LRA) and its leader, Joseph Kony, in one of Africa's longest-running armed conflicts. As was reported in 2014, "the group's 30-minute documentary about Kony's horrific war crimes and abuse of child soldiers garnered more than 100 million views in six days, making it the most viral video in history." The result? Invisible Children raised $5 million in two days. It should be added that such a rapid and unanticipated inflow of donations was a contributing factor to the organization's later restructuring and downsizing—a fact that only underscores the importance of integrating a comprehensive marketing plan into your overall strategy.[1]

The idea we want to emphasize here is that Invisible Children didn't just mention a problem and then ask us to help them solve it. Instead, they effectively used a story to tie their subject (Joseph Kony) to a specific request (donations to bring Kony and the LRA to justice).

What's our point? It's simply to get your attention about the power of telling your story *when it's integrated* with what we've covered in earlier chapters—and what can happen when it's not. We're not trying to sell the virtues of advertising, like Don Draper and the Madison Avenue types depicted in *Mad Men*. But why go to all the effort of putting the other building blocks in place if you don't continually communicate your message—and the results you can be proud of—to clients, funders, employees, community thought leaders, and other stakeholders in a meaningful, memorable way?

So why tell stories? Because words matter. Carefully chosen and artfully arranged, they provide a singular view into the human condition. They create emotional resonance, and serve as the connective sinew that binds us all together in a shared experience. "Stories can shape people," Bridgespan writes in *Why Nonprofits Need to Be Storytellers*. "[They] can inspire them to think and act differently. Stories are what can connect your nonprofit's community, funders, beneficiaries, and employees with your cause and vision."[2] Stories ignite passions!

We spent an entire chapter on the importance of gathering data to measure impact. But stories are how you bring those data to life and imbue them with a sense of humanity that inspires people to act. Information and storytelling are part of a virtuous cycle: The more insight you have into the impact of your programs, the more effective you'll be at communicating that impact to stakeholders—which in turn can lead to greater and more diverse funding streams for your organization. And the result of this? That's right, more powerful programs.

"It's that in the one-two punch of persuasion," said nationally recognized author Andy Goodman, "the 'one' is the story that gets people to pay attention to you for a second. And then you come in with a number two punch, which is the data that says, 'And I've got more than one story to tell you. This one story I told you is illustrative of hundreds of stories, thousands of stories. Here are the numbers that back up what I'm saying.'"[3]

And you're not just telling your story to a single person. Ideally, you want to reach as broad an audience as possible, so the story should be crafted in such a way to resonate with the "numbers person" and the "bleeding heart." In other words, data and statistics should be tempered with humanity. Put a face on the figures. To dig up an old saw: Data tell. Stories sell.

Blah, blah, blah. Let's move on already, we hear some of you saying. This is supposed to be a book about strategies for sustainability, isn't it? You may be thinking that since you run a nonprofit, you're not selling anything. Wrong. You are selling something—in fact, a very important thing. You're selling social change. You're selling your vision of how the world should operate to make people's lives better.

Now, neither of us was an English major, and we certainly aren't claiming to be master storytellers. Plus, so much has already been written on how to create compelling prose that we won't spend a lot of time on what ingredients make for a good story. But a few quick tips may provide some helpful framing. According to Goodman, you should:

- Name your protagonist.
- Fix him or her in time and space.
- Create an inciting incident, something that throws his or her world out of balance.
- Describe the barriers the protagonist runs into on the way to achieving the goal.
- Celebrate achieving the goal. Or if the goal wasn't met, share lessons learned along the way.[4]

SYLVESTER'S STORY

Let's look at an example of Goodman's rules in action. We recently attended a "friendraiser" for the nonprofit Freedom for Immigrants (FFI), an organization focused on abolishing immigrant detention and addressing human rights abuses against those in custody. FFI believes so strongly in the power of a compelling narrative that it has created an award-winning platform for immigrants held in detention "to challenge injustice through the oldest art form"—storytelling.[5] Peruse FFI's website and you'll find plenty of additional insight into the motivation behind these narrative projects. "Storytelling," the organization believes, "allows us to experience the similarities between ourselves and others. It allows us to link present struggles for justice to similar struggles of the past. And it allows us to create an archive of the present for future generations to learn about subaltern histories that are often forgotten."

One of those histories nearly forgotten is that of Sylvester Owino, a Kenyan immigrant who in 2003 was convicted of second-degree robbery in San Diego. He spent nearly a decade in immigrant detention, awaiting the results of an asylum petition. Like many immigrants, Owino feared for his safety should he be deported back to his native country. Here's how this story was told at FFI's event—filtered through Goodman's structural prism:

- Protagonist: Sylvester, a detained immigrant fighting for his freedom
- Fix him in time and space: Fled persecution in Kenya in 1998; arrived in the United States
- Inciting incident: Beaten and abused at the hands of the Kenyan government; convicted of second-degree robbery in the United States in 2003; incarcerated in numerous detention centers/county jails for many years after seeking asylum
- Barriers faced: No access to legal representation; denied bail on multiple occasions; asylum petition dragged on
- Celebrate achieving the goal: FFI arranged for counseling, advocacy, and legal services (including a $1,500 bail bond), which led to Sylvester's release from incarceration; today, he's married with a young daughter and runs his own successful catering business, which—to further bring Sylvester's story to life—provided the food at FFI's event

Our aim is simply to draw your attention to the potential power of storytelling to engender action—especially *when it is integrated* with the other key building blocks of sustainability we've discussed. Really, why undertake all the effort of hiring eminently capable leaders, assembling a top-notch board of directors, and skillfully measuring the impact your organization has without also telling your amazing story to clients, funders, employees, community leaders, and other stakeholders? Seriously, people, you're doing great work. Now sing it from the rooftops to anyone who will listen!

THE OVERHEAD MYTH, REDUX

Yes, we know singing can cost money, and contribute to—gasp!—overhead. Throughout this book, we've tried to disabuse skeptics of the fanciful notion that measuring effectiveness by using shortcuts (like the ratio of overhead to direct program spending) is unhelpful at best and catastrophic to an organization's survival at worst. So, true to form, we're going to take another whack at that overhead myth piñata. Grab your stick and blindfold.

How big a third rail issue is the notion of sales and marketing expenses in the nonprofit sector? In *Uncharitable*, Dan Pallotta argues, in effect, that nonprofits should be permitted to spend freely on overhead—including (perhaps especially) marketing—provided they create impact. For years, this view guided Pallotta TeamWorks, the for-profit company he established to raise money for myriad charities fighting everything from AIDS and breast cancer to suicide. In under a decade, the fundraising events created by Pallotta's company "grossed $556 million in donor contributions and netted $305 million for charity after all expenses."[6] Then the company folded. According to Anthony Filipovitch in his 2010 review of *Uncharitable*, "The business collapsed when criticism of the high administrative ratio (45%) and high executive compensation [from $200,000 annually to nearly $450,000] led clients to withdraw their support."[7] In other words, blowback from the perception that Pallotta and his company were enriching themselves at the expense of charities caused many—including those directly benefitting from Pallotta TeamWorks' efforts—to head for the hills. The feeling was that charitable organizations shouldn't have to pay such a high price to market their causes—not even if that marketing raises over a quarter of a billion dollars.

How much should nonprofits spend on marketing? Let's first look at what their for-profit cousins are doing. According to a recent industry study conducted in part by Deloitte, marketing expenses account for, on average, 11 percent of total company budgets. At almost a quarter of their annual budgets, consumer packaged goods companies (think General Mills, Kellogg, etc.) spend by far the most on marketing, "followed by consumer services, tech software/biotech, communications/media, and mining/construction."[8] (If you're curious, transportation, manufacturing, and energy companies—at 4 percent of budget—spent the least.) For comparison, *The Chronicle of Philanthropy* cited a recommendation by marketing and communications consultant Nancy E. Schwartz that nonprofits "spend between 10 and 20 percent of their budgets on marketing."[9]

Seems pretty consistent thus far, right? Well, what's the percentage spent on marketing at your organization? The 2017 Nonprofit Communications Trends Report found that though a mere "7% of nonprofits spend little to nothing" on communications (including marketing), nearly one in five "find money for communications only as needed."[10] Translation: They're not budgeting for it. And—repeat it with us this time—*if you're not budgeting for something, you're saying it's not important!*

Let's be clear: Marketing differentiates your organization. It helps you compete for talented humans and philanthropic dollars—both scarce resources. It's an investment in future growth, not simply overhead. And marketing—for nonprofits especially—is storytelling. Think just because you're busy saving the world you don't need to stand out from the pack? Well, guess what? GuideStar lists 2,921 organizations that are focused on providing shelter for the homeless. Why should someone support yours?

WHAT'S A MARKETING EXPENSE?

Of course, "marketing" in the nonprofit realm can assume many guises, making comparisons in spending levels among organizations difficult if not impossible. Some nonprofits maintain a separate line-item budget for marketing; others integrate communications spending into specific program budgets. Sector-wide, though, nonprofits are required by generally accepted accounting principles and IRS regulations to report expenses in buckets based upon "function," for example, program, management, and the dreaded "fundraising expenses." And when employ-

ees wear many hats—as they certainly do at most Main Street nonprofits—this calls for an often subjective allocation of organization costs.

Given the tempestuous nature of the overhead debate, it's understandable that many nonprofits skew toward keeping (or at least reporting) their fundraising allocations—along with any expenses not directly
spent on programs—on the low side. Because of this, as well as the
myriad methods organizations use to apportion their expenditures, it's
tough to make many meaningful inferences based on published data. As
one report stated, financial metrics such as nonprofits' program spending and fundraising efficiency ratios "are only as good as the numbers
used to calculate them. Unfortunately, research shows that in many
cases the numbers are not good at all, and that practices vary so widely
that comparisons among organizations may lead to flawed conclusions."[11]

RETURN ON (MARKETING) INVESTMENT

Whatever the reported numbers are, impact created by marketing dollars shouldn't be taken as a fait accompli. That's right—not only does
program effectiveness need to be evaluated, but similar rigor should
also be applied to measuring the return on your marketing investment.
"The key," said Steve Bellach, co-founder of BottomLine Marketing, a
consultancy that designs branding and marketing programs for businesses—including many nonprofits, "is to create a system of relevant
metrics to determine the impact of dollars invested in a marketing and
strategy initiative."[12] Before measurement can even start, though, Bellach and his team work with organizations to help them determine what
they're going to say and how they're going to say it, starting with asking
what tone is desired.

The answer to that question depends heavily on the audience you're
trying to reach. Thus, Bellach's firm conducts a holistic 360-degree
interview system wherein all stakeholders—internal and external—are
polled to establish a baseline of how an organization is perceived in the
marketplace. Once who's being targeted has been figured out and with
what message, testing the effectiveness of a given marketing campaign
can begin. The goal, Bellach likes to say, is to focus on the *aim* in *ready,
aim, fire.* "If you can say we spent $10,000 on this communications

effort, and it generated a million and half dollars in new funds, you've demonstrated the return on that investment," he explained. What's more, "you show you're extremely responsible with how the money is being spent."

Sometimes this sort of calculation is easy to do, but often it isn't so straightforward. Many benefits of a particular marketing effort are difficult to quantify—such as enhancing an organization's image or reputation in its community. For example, a nonprofit we work with is currently engaged in helping immigrants who are seeking asylum in the United States. At the time of this writing, press coverage of the issue— particularly along the U.S. southern border with Mexico—is constant and intense. Hardly a day passes without news agencies reporting on the immigrants' plight and the attendant need for human services— many of which are provided by nonprofits. Against this backdrop, the organization's leadership determined that both the scale of need and groundswell of public interest justified a significant investment in telling its story. The return on this marketing and communications effort? It's uncertain now and may never be fully known. But the potential to increase awareness of the organization and its cause, attract new funders, and bolster mission impact was too compelling to pass up. The CEO and board decided to take a calculated risk (read those statement disclosures, folks: *all investing involves risk*) and commit precious resources based on the organization's mission-driven values, rather than on anticipated financial returns.

SUSTAINABILITY AND STORIES

In her widely read book, *Social Startup Success*, Kathleen Kelly Janus concludes that "telling compelling stories" is of the five keys to achieving sustainability in the nonprofit sector.[13] Financial sustainability, as Janus defines it, is the capacity to consistently reach $2 million in annual revenue, and whether you agree with her yardstick or not, there's little doubt that great storytelling is strongly correlated with organizational longevity. According to Network for Good, the maker of fundraising and donor management software for nonprofits, "Storytelling is the single most powerful communications tool you have available, bar none."[14] In a guide published to help organizations craft cogent narratives, the company identifies three factors that make the medium particularly effective:

1. **Stories help us remember.** When you have facts you want people to remember, it's much more likely they'll be remembered if you contain those facts within a story.
2. **Stories influence how we decide.** In 1990, a study was done on how people on juries came to conclusions. According to it, most construct a story based on the facts offered in the case. Then they compared the stories they constructed with the stories the lawyers presented. Jurists would side with whoever's story matched their own the closest.
3. **Stories link us to our sense of generosity.** Studies also show that donors tend to give twice as much when presented with a story about an affected individual as opposed to reading huge abstract numbers of the overall scope of a problem.

Types of Stories

Just as nonprofits have to work to reach a diverse audience that includes donors and clients, as well as leadership and staff within the organization itself, their message, too, must be customized for maximum effect. Though seemingly simple and consistent, a single story (think the much ballyhooed *elevator pitch*) just won't cut it. Indeed, *The Nonprofit Storytelling Field Guide and Journal* describes three basic story formats targeted at funders alone:

Donor Stories are stories you can collect from your donors. These stories illustrate why your donors give to your cause. A donor story is a way for potential donors to see your organization through the eyes of one of their peers. This kind of story works very well when placed on your website, included in your newsletter, or when you bring a donor along with you to make an ask of another donor.

Impact Stories are the stories that focus on the effect you are having in the life of one of your clients. Or, in the case of an environmental or animal organization, it's the effect you are having in the community. These stories are the stories you would typically tell at a gala, or when talking with a potential donor as you lead up to asking them for a gift.

Thank You Stories are really just impact stories you tell a donor as you are thanking them for their gift. The impact you share with them should be directly tied to the gift they gave. This way, the donor can see the difference they personally made with their gift. [15]

Beware the Single Story

Prevailing wisdom holds that your story should encapsulate a consistent message. We agree. Nonprofits are well served by creating a cohesive and consistent brand across multiple platforms, including social media, according to Accenture's Amit Patel. [16] But be careful not to conflate this notion with the idea of telling a single story. Your audience is diverse; your narratives should be, too. Simply regurgitating the same information over and over is, in a word, boring—for the storyteller and the listener. Perhaps more insidious, it risks creating stereotypes—of your organization, your mission, and your stakeholders. In her 2009 TED talk, *The Danger of a Single Story*, novelist Chimamanda Ngozi Adichie provided an example of this risk: "If I had not grown up in Nigeria, and if all I knew about Africa were from popular images," she said, "I, too, would think that Africa was a place of beautiful landscapes, beautiful animals, and incomprehensible people, fighting senseless wars, dying of poverty and AIDS, unable to speak for themselves and waiting to be saved by a kind, white foreigner." [17]

Stateside, we don't have to look any further than to our own political system for evidence of this reductive form of narration at work. Columnist David Brooks observed as much in a *New York Times* op-ed piece. "American politics," he wrote, "has always been prone to single story-ism—candidates reducing complex issues to simple fables." [18]

The Sacred Bundle

Goodman, the author and storytelling specialist, is another who thinks nonprofits should carry multiple narrative arrows in their quiver. "I'm not a big believer that an organization can be represented by a single story," he said. "And I'm not a big believer in the elevator story. I've seen too many examples where organizations do so many different things and deliver so many different benefits that one story often doesn't capture it all." Rather, Goodman recommends every organization have at least one of the following types of stories—what he refers to as the "sacred bundle":

- The nature-of-our-challenge story illuminates the people behind the problem you're trying to address.
- The creation story, generally for audiences that already care about your issue, shares who started your organization, why, and when.
- The emblematic-success story affirms that your organization is doing unique good in the world.
- The values story illustrates your organization's core values and how it lives them.
- The striving-to-improve story helps create a culture of empathy and growth within an organization by reflecting on mistakes and what was learned from them.
- The where-we-are-going story answers the question: If your organization does its job, what will we see in five to ten years?[19]

Another KISS

No matter which story you're telling, you'll want to make sure your message is concise and cogent. This has never been more important than it is today. Smartphones, social media, and their technological ilk have supplanted the flowery missives of yesteryear with a miasma of microblogging. (Okay, that sentence notwithstanding.) We've become increasingly impatient with lengthy presentations, speeches, and advertisements. The key is to create an emotional hook—quickly—to catch people's interest before their smartphone-addled brains move on. Once captivated, they'll be apt to invest the time to learn more.

With that in mind, here's another "KISS" principle: Keep It Short and Simple. According to Lori Jacobwith, the founder of Ignited Fundraising—a company that harnesses storytelling to raise money for nonprofits—your story should take between six words and two minutes to tell.[20] Anything longer and your audience is already mentally planning their weekends. Value your words and deploy them strategically.

Storytelling to Grantmakers

Just because you have limited time and space to convey the details and credibility of your organization doesn't mean your message has to be dull and dry. It shouldn't be excruciating to read, write, or listen to. Fortunately, many have caught wind of the trend toward storytelling in grant writing and make a concerted effort to showcase their nonprofit's narrative in a way that evokes a visceral response. The sweet spot is highlighting *the features and the benefits* of your programs—using the best of both to create a grant proposal that's genuinely engaging to read, while still providing funders with all the information they'll need to make an informed decision.

What's Your Brand?

If you were asked to name a few nonprofits—just off the top of your head—which would you choose? The Red Cross/Red Crescent? Special Olympics? The Humane Society? Habitat for Humanity? Why do these organizations and others like them spring to mind? Sure, they've been around awhile, achieved a certain scale, and are trusted to do important work. But each has also worked to integrate storytelling into its culture as part of a strategy to curate an effective brand. In fact, they've done this so well that we need only mention a few words to evoke their names. Disaster relief: The Red Cross/Red Crescent. Athletic achievement for people with disabilities: Special Olympics. Animal welfare: The Humane Society. Affordable housing: Habitat for Humanity. Now that's branding! If we played *The $100,000 Pyramid* using those organizations, we'd crush it!

Careful, though. It takes more than a catchy name and fancy logo to secure lasting recognition by the masses. "A brand is a psychological construct held in the minds of all those aware of the branded product, person, organization, or movement," writes Nathalie Kylander and Christopher Stone in their article, "The Role of Brand in the Nonprofit Sector."[21] Having a strong brand also creates trust among stakeholders, which "provides organizations with the authority and credibility to deploy [financial and human resources] more efficiently and flexibly than can organizations with weaker brands."

Marketing and storytelling are tools to create this brand awareness in the minds of multiple audiences—within and outside an organization. Good brands elicit a positive association with just a short visual or verbal cue, and often share the following elements:

- **Uniqueness.** Find the heart of your organization, the very essence at its core. Think about the reason why you're passionate about what you do and what you stand for.
- **Authenticity.** Take a long look at your strengths and the history of your organization, and then reflect those back upon the community. Donors must feel absolutely certain that you're an organization that keeps promises and stays true to its core values.
- **Consistency.** Every message you put out should relate to the one that came before it and add to it. Consistency is reflected not only in your words and actions, but in the look and feel associated with your organization. This leaves people with a solid, strong, and singular impression of who you are and what you stand for.[22]

Who Are Your Storytellers?

When organizations think about crafting their messages, many immediately jump to donors as their default audience. Understandable. After all, to borrow Willie Sutton's response when asked why he robbed banks, "that's where the money is."[23] But as we've said, there's a much wider audience out there that needs to hear your story, and each one may require a unique narrative expressed in a particular way. Describing how his firm helps nonprofits identify and target specific recipients of their stories, Bellach said he starts "with market segmentation, target audience identification, and then determines what is the message that's going to attract them and resonate with them to engage with your organization."[24]

Creating a general outline—a model that's consistent with your core message and values, but leaves room to customize your story depending on who's telling it—is a smart strategy. The goal is to reach as many people as possible and foster a legion of *brand ambassadors* who can spread your message to the four corners. All stakeholders should be prepared to talk about your mission, brand, and impact by telling stories. Done right, this army of ambassadors complements your development department and becomes another effective fundraising tool.

It's worth bearing in mind that storytelling is as much for a nonprofit's internal staff as it is for external stakeholders, though employees are often overlooked as brand ambassadors. They shouldn't be. They're the ones in the trenches day in and day out—closest to both programs and their beneficiaries. Leverage that proximity and let workers herald their organizations' triumphs—provided their lips are loaded with a consistent message.

Ultimately, you want to create what Julie Dixon, former research director at the National Journal's Communications Council, described as a "vibrant storytelling culture."[25] Doing so, she wrote, "means the difference between whether your organization has a living, breathing portfolio of different stories, from different perspectives, that share its impact—or just a single, somewhat stagnant story. It's the difference between having one person in the organization dedicated to storytelling . . . and everyone in the organization having compelling stories at their fingertips."

Through research conducted with the Center for Social Impact Communication at Georgetown University, Dixon identified two primary drivers behind the creation of successful storytelling cultures: "a mindset and appreciation for stories, and capacity." This mindset, she discovered, begins with leadership serving as exemplars of good storytelling. By embracing stories as the powerful narrative tools they are, and modeling this appreciation for others within the organization, the CEO and leadership help staff "understand the story planning process, as well as how stories add value to their own work and the organization's work as a whole," she wrote.

Of course, as we know by now, saying you value something and actually investing in it are two very different things. Thus, the capacity Dixon cites refers to organizations' willingness to budget for "the systems, talent, and resources" necessary to nurture a storytelling culture. Oh boy, you're thinking. Another expense item we can't afford. How is my nonprofit supposed to find the money to hire professional marketers to shape our story? First, there are many grantors that will fund the development of a marketing and branding strategy. Just make sure you look for one whose values and vision are aligned with your mission. Second, you don't have to search outside your organization for help.

Many nonprofits, especially smaller ones, can "focus on building internal capacity—training individuals, hiring staff with existing storytelling interests and skills, or spreading training opportunities across teams," Dixon said. And don't forget those board members! If you can't hire or train a communications director, recruit a communications expert for your board.

Remember, too, that many times clients—the end-users of your services—can be the most effective storytellers. They're the ones whose lives have been most affected by the programs and services organizations want people to support, and therefore are in the unique position to inspire action through their first-person narratives. We saw this earlier with Mary Catherine Swanson's AVID. She didn't have to market much to school districts to have her programs included in their curricula, because the kids—the beneficiaries of those programs—told such compelling stories. They were AVID's brand ambassadors.

And finally, there's the media. No, we're not talking about social media here (though it's also an important marketing channel). The media we're referring to are those professional outlets—radio, podcasts, print, television—that get paid to tell stories. Why not make one of them tell yours? A lot of times, organizations just sit back and wait for reporters to drop down from the heavens and sing their praises. That's a passive approach, and one that relies on hope. Hope, dear reader, is not a strategy.

Rather, according to Peter Panepento and Antionette Kerr, authors of *Modern Media Relations for Nonprofits*, nonprofits should actively seek to work with specific media outlets that will be receptive to covering their organization and help tell their story. Yes, this strategy requires much more effort and upfront research to determine which reporters, writers, and editors you should build relationships with. But the payoff from an investment in relationship building can be invaluable—especially if, as the authors note, your organization or leadership finds itself caught up in some kind of controversy or scandal.

We suggest a great place to start is with those ubiquitous galas. Representatives from the media often are there, and many times that's because they have a particular affinity for who you are and what you do. Sound promising? Make sure, as Bruce Hoyt from Gary Community Investments stresses, your board and leadership view these events as the relationship builders they are, and not simply as venues for fund-raising.[26]

With the wellspring of good that stems from effective storytelling, we're tempted to suggest yet another standing committee for your board of directors—one focused on creating a powerful organizational brand through diverse stories. These narratives don't all have to come at once. If you're just beginning, try to get one compelling story out into the world and then build on it. Keep in mind, though, that just as a single death is a tragedy, while a million is a statistic, a single, targeted tale that strikes a sympathetic chord in enough people can move the needle much more than a million sporadic press releases.

There's an important difference between simply conveying information like you'd read words on a page, and truly *telling a story*, as you would if you got into character, put on voices, and really drew in your audience. The latter is so much more engaging! (One of us has four-year-old twins who would happily attest to this.)

The Maritime Museum's Ray Ashley understands this distinction well. After all, there are a lot of places people can go to see floating hunks of wood and metal without paying for it. Out of context they may be momentarily interesting, but the feeling is ephemeral. It's the stories and the history you hear while sailing on the world's oldest active merchant ship—a vessel that has circumnavigated the globe twenty-one times, as the museum's *Star of India* has—that permeate your soul and create the visceral experiences you'll remember. Ashley used an apt metaphor to illustrate the point: "From our visitors' perspective, it's the difference between just watching the play, and actually being in the play," he said.[27]

What's your story? You know you have one—or several—that are darn compelling and deserve to be heard. Make sure they are! Remember that donors may be impressed with your numbers, but they will be moved to action as a result of the stories you're able to share.

9

CREDIT AND SUSTAINABILITY

Lending to Nonprofits

"The desire of gold is not for gold. It is for the means of freedom and benefit."[1] Given some thought, these words by the transcendentalist poet Ralph Waldo Emerson speak to the underlying motivation for why we—individuals, businesses, even nonprofits—seek wealth. Really. Why take all the time and trouble to amass piles of green paper rectangles? Generally, most of us would agree, it's not for the innate pleasure of counting the money itself. Rather, for workers, income affords them the ability to provide for their families. For businesses, wealth enables the creation of value for shareholders. For nonprofits, the "desire of gold" is to allow them to continue executing on their missions. Money, asserted Emerson, is freedom.

Oh boy, you're saying. So now you guys are philosophers, too. No, no. Far from it. In fact, if we're being honest, one of us thought Nietzsche played football for the Green Bay Packers in the 1960s. Philosophers we're not. But we do know a thing or two about finance, and this notion of access to capital as a liberating force got us thinking. (Emerson would be proud.) *Debt* gets such a bad rap, but used properly, *credit* can unlock the "means of freedom and benefit" for many nonprofits. It really is an underused—and often misunderstood—tool, and that's true for a number of reasons. Boards often view indebting their organizations as anathema to good fiscal stewardship. Certain nonprofits themselves may not be creditworthy. And worse, their leadership may not even know *why* they aren't. So in this chapter we're going to demystify credit for you. We'll explore the types of loans available and the benefits of using them responsibly, and provide a glimpse into what lenders look for when evaluating nonprofits.

THE LOAN UNIVERSE

We'll start with some good news: You're probably already more familiar with the landscape of credit products available to nonprofits than you might think. Indeed, the standard types of loans don't vary much from those offered in the for-profit sector, or, for that matter, to individuals. Let's take a look at what's out there.

Lines of Credit

Lines of credit provide access to liquidity and working capital to help organizations ensure they have enough cash on hand to cover unexpected expenses and meet their short-term needs. Often in the course of a nonprofit's business cycle, there are timing differences between when cash has to go out to pay for various expenses and when it comes back in. Lines of credit are designed to help bridge those funding gaps.

Let's say, for example, your organization has secured a grant to fund certain programs. Great, right? But what if (as is common), the terms of the contract state you first have to pay for the costs associated with getting these programs off the ground before the grant proceeds will reimburse you? Sure, you have enough cash on hand (we hope), but do you really want to burn through a big chunk of your liquid assets while waiting to collect the grant money? You're also likely not too keen on the idea of selling some of your investments (if that's even an option) to cover the upfront program costs. In cases like this, a line of credit may offer a way to bridge the short-term gaps in funding many nonprofits experience. And by *short-term*, we're almost always talking about a period of time less than one year between when operating receivables are created and when they're collected. As such, most lines of credit offered by lenders will be up for renewal on an annual basis, and may also require a "cleanup period" during which the outstanding balance on the line must be zero. This is done to ensure the line is truly revolving and isn't being used as a source of permanent working capital.

Term Loans

For longer-term projects, such as capital improvements or "one-time" purchases of durable assets like real estate or equipment, a term loan may offer a suitable solution. With these facilities, money is funded by a lender up front, and the balance is then paid back in installments of principal and interest over a fixed period of time. Generally, lenders will want to match the repayment period to the useful life of the asset being financed. For example, you may be able to pay back a loan to purchase real estate over a period of twenty years or more, whereas a loan to buy equipment—especially equipment that may soon be technologically obsolete—may come with a repayment term that's much shorter. And though many lines of credit carry a variable (or "floating") rate that's tied to an underlying index (such as Prime, LIBOR, or SOFR), and are repayable in monthly installments of interest-only based on the amount outstanding on the line, most term loans are available at fixed interest rates that stay the same over the life of the loan.

A rule of thumb that's handy in distinguishing between these two types of credit is that short-term loans (think lines of credit) should be used to finance short-term assets or projects (such as receivables collections or capital campaigns), while longer-term loans should be used to finance more permanent assets.

There are exceptions, of course, and hybrid line/loan approaches also exist. For instance, let's say a nonprofit wants to construct a new office building on a piece of land given by a wealthy donor. In this case, the organization may choose to take out what's commonly referred to as a *construction-to-perm* loan. Essentially, this means the nonprofit is approved to borrow up to a maximum amount (generally a percentage of the overall cost of the construction project), that will then be termed out over a set period of time after the construction is complete. While the project is ongoing, the organization can take advances on its line of credit to pay the costs of construction as they come due. Multiple advances can be made, and typically the organization is only required to pay interest on the amount that's been borrowed during this period (known as the *draw phase*). Afterward, the outstanding balance will start to *amortize*, meaning monthly payments of principal as well as interest will be due. Loan structures like this exist so borrowers have the flexibility to advance money only as necessary, rather than taking the entire lump sum up front and paying interest on the funds before they're actually needed.

Direct Purchase Bonds

Without getting too far into the weeds, we did at least want to mention another type of credit that, from the nonprofit's standpoint, functions a lot like a term loan. Direct purchase bonds (DPBs) carry advantages and disadvantages relative to more garden-variety term loans. For one thing, DPBs must be issued by *conduits*, which are governmental entities established to issue and sell tax-exempt debt. Whoa! *Tax-exempt?* That's right. Many DBPs are issued on a tax-exempt basis, meaning buyers of these bonds, such as banks, may not pay taxes on the interest earned. And while this perk doesn't directly benefit the nonprofit, it does mean lenders can offer rates that are lower than those commanded by taxable debt. The upshot is that organizations can often borrow less expensively by working with a conduit to issue a tax-exempt bond.

We mentioned there are disadvantages, and they can be significant. Among them is the fact that hiring outside professionals, such as attorneys and other advisors, to help set up the tax-exempt deal can be quite expensive (think six figures). For this reason, it may not make financial sense to issue tax-exempt bonds for smaller projects (less than a few million dollars), because the difference between taxable and tax-exempt rates might not be great enough to justify the added expense. Bottom line: Make sure you do the math. And then there's the time involved. Setting up and closing a DPB transaction can take months, so plan well ahead. As we've made clear by now, we're not lawyers or tax professionals. If you're considering a DPB to finance your project, you'll want to consult with both.

Commercial Cards

It's been said that paperwork wouldn't be so bad if it weren't for all the paper. And the work. Why then, in an increasingly digital world, do we still write so darn many checks? And then often manually reconcile each transaction! Cue the collective sigh of every nonprofit accounting department. But wait, hasn't check use been in decline for decades? Yes, it has. However, according to the U.S. Federal Reserve, we still cut nearly five *billion* of the stinking things in 2018 alone![2] And that's just commercial checks, to say nothing of the billions more we write to that stubborn friend who maddeningly refuses to get a Venmo account.

We went off on this little rant because it brings up an often over-looked source of credit for nonprofits: commercial cards. In fact, whether issued to businesses, organizations, government entities, or individuals, credit cards are one of the most common forms of lending around the world. (You probably have a card or two on you right now.) In our experience, however, many nonprofits fail to take full advantage of the potential benefits offered by commercial card programs. These include better management of an organization's cash through use of the float period (you know, buy now and pay later), robust reporting tools that can integrate with many accounting software programs, and a revenue share or rebate component through which nonprofits can earn cash back on routine purchases.

In addition to generating revenue by using cards for purchasing, accounts payable, and corporate travel and entertainment, organizations can significantly lower their cost per transaction. According to a recent industry survey, "The average administrative cost (sourcing, purchasing, and payment activities) of a traditional purchase order was reported to be $89.99. In comparison, the cost to procure and pay for goods and services with a [corporate card] was $20.14."[3]

Ah, then there's the *F word*: fraud. We'd be willing to bet that if you deal with your organization's money and you've been at your job for a fair stretch, you've probably had to contend with the fallout from fraud at some point. If so, then you know the drill: restricting your account (or closing it altogether and opening a new one), communicating the updated information to vendors, and generally just throwing a big ol' monkey wrench in your whole operation. You're not alone. In fact, nearly three-quarters of finance professionals said their companies were victims of fraud in 2016.[4] How can this happen so easily? Well, remember those billions of checks we issue every year? Each one has all the information a fraudster needs to gain access to your account: name, address, full account number, bank routing number. Check. Check. Check. Check. Enough checks already!

Judicious management of a commercial card program dramatically lowers the risk of external fraud. It also cuts down on the possibility of fraud perpetrated by someone within your organization through intelligent (and digital!) reporting capabilities and controls that can limit cardholder use. And abuse.

One final thought on this. It should go without saying that any responsible adoption of a commercial card program means you don't pay a dime in interest. Nothing! Nada! The full balance gets retired every payment cycle. The nanosecond you start accruing interest, it begins to outweigh all the benefits we just talked about. So please don't do it. Make sure you have the systems, processes, and—most important—cash flow to properly manage a card program. If you do, the rewards will accrue quickly, and you'll take your organization from the least secure method of payment—checks—to one of the most secure.

THE FIVE Cs OF CREDIT

Now that we've seen some of the basic types of credit available to nonprofits, let's talk about how to make sure your organization is approved for the loan you want. Specifically, what do lenders look for? In a nutshell, just remember the *Five Cs of Credit*: capacity (or cash flow), capital, collateral, conditions, and character. Though all lenders are unique, and use their own criteria for evaluating the creditworthiness of a borrower, most will employ a system of underwriting that weighs these five factors in some combination.

A quick word before we examine each in turn. Depending on your lender, one or more of the Five Cs may be given a greater degree of importance than the others. And a strong showing in one area could very well offset weakness in another. In other words, don't feel as if you're doomed for rejection just because your organization isn't batting a thousand across the board.

That said, nonprofits do have one distinct disadvantage relative to their for-profit counterparts—namely, a lack of owners. Why does this matter? Well, individual owners of a closely held business can often make up for a material weakness in their company's financial position by offering to personally guarantee the debt. Yes, lenders may give this option to nonprofits, too, but how many executive directors or board members do you know who would happily co-sign for a loan to their organization? It's not common, but it does happen. Remember we mentioned parenthetically way back in the first chapter that the "founding fathers" of the USS *Midway* Museum—about ten of them—personally guaranteed loans during the startup phase (secured by liens on their personal residences, no less)? Nice financing if you can get it—and what a statement about commitment it makes! But, since nonprofits typically have to stand on their own two feet from a creditworthiness perspective, it's doubly important that their leadership pay heed to the Five Cs.

Capacity

If we were forced to single out a particular metric that demonstrates a borrower's financial wherewithal, it would be this one—because by definition, *capacity* refers to a nonprofit's ability to repay its obligations. Also known as *cash flow*, it's simply a measurement of whether the organization consistently takes in enough money relative to how much it spends. Depending on how large the loan under consideration is, and what repayment terms the borrower is requesting, that difference between revenues and expenses (you know it as *net income*, or—more germane to nonprofits—*change in net assets*) will need to be a certain amount to satisfy the lender's underwriting requirements.

Now lenders—smart ones at least—understand nonprofits measure success in terms of their service to stakeholders, not the surfeit of cash they generate each year. Additionally, surplus resources are generally invested in furtherance of the mission, rather than distributed to shareholders as they are in the for-profit world. But make no mistake, though they're often used interchangeably, the monikers *nonprofit* and *not-for-profit* carry an important distinction. Despite our overwhelming use of the former throughout this book (we did so because it's more common and, frankly, easier on the eyes without those hyphens), not-for-profit more accurately describes how organizations should be run: not *for*-profit, though still capable of producing consistent operating surpluses. The term nonprofit, on the other hand, sounds as if your CPA spends a lot of time staring at red ink.

Sorry, got off on a little sidebar there. Semantics aside, organizations should achieve better than breakeven results most years. Of course there may be exceptions—one-time expenses pop up, capital improvements need to be made, grants sometimes take longer to collect than anticipated. But as a general underwriting rule, net income should be positive over a given three- to five-year period. Yes, your organization may have a new source of revenue coming in. Expansion of a program could increase an existing source of income. Or you might be planning to reduce expenses. All these things stand to improve the bottom line— but they haven't happened yet. They're projections. And while lenders certainly will take this into consideration (good underwriting is as much art as science), most drive with the rearview mirror more than the windshield. Translation: It's *historical* cash flow that's more heavily weighted.

So, just how much of an operating surplus do lenders expect you to have? Again, underwriting standards vary, but in general your adjusted cash flow should be sufficient to cover your required annual payments of principal and interest by at least 1.1 times. (Many lenders require coverage—often called a *debt service coverage ratio*—of 1.2 or higher.) Wait, *adjusted* cash flow? Yep, lenders will start with the excess of revenue over expenses and then add or subtract certain items to come up with an amount of money that's available for debt service. For example, depreciation is an expense lenders usually will add back. Why? Because it's a non-cash expense and therefore doesn't affect an organization's ability to repay its obligations. Remember: Borrowers don't pay back their loans with net income. They use *cash*.

Adjustments will also likely be made for nonrecurring revenue or expenses, such as a one-time gain or loss on the sale of an asset. In addition, the interest an organization paid during the year will be added back to arrive at its cash flow figure. That's because interest is already accounted for in the organization's debt service (principal plus interest) calculation, and therefore shouldn't be double counted by also including it when computing net income.

There's one final important point to make about all this: Any evaluation of a nonprofit's net income or cash flow should only focus on *unrestricted* revenue. Restricted funding by its nature has already been designated for a specific purpose—and unless that purpose is the repayment of debt, this income will be excluded.

Capital

Let's turn now from the income statement to another repository of key financial information: the balance sheet. When we're talking about capital in the context of nonprofits, we're referring to how the organization is structured—namely its *assets*, *liabilities*, and *net assets* (what would be called *equity* in the for-profit world). The mix is of paramount importance, especially given the variability in funding many nonprofits experience. Revenues may be lumpy. Major grants may only come in once or twice a year. But you still have to pay the bills each month—and in the case of your staff, more frequently than that. "Fiscal sustainability is all about the balance sheet," says JPMorgan Chase's Tim May, who serves as the bank's national credit executive for government and nonprofit lending. "The income statement can vary from year to year, but the balance sheet is where you'll truly see good management, fiscal discipline, and planning."[5]

And perhaps no other measure better reflects a strong balance sheet than an organization's *liquidity*—in particular, its unrestricted cash and investments. Again, the "unrestricted" qualifier is key, as these funds can be used for any purpose, including ongoing operational expenses. It's hard to overstate how critical it is for a nonprofit to maintain an ample store of readily available cash. Not only, as May points out, does it demonstrate leadership's focus on generating consistent operating surpluses, but having adequate liquidity also can serve as a buffer in bad years. Look no further than to the tragically topical COVID-19 pandemic for evidence of the seriousness with which organizations should regard having enough liquidity to sustain themselves during a downturn in revenues. In addition, that liquidity—which can include an endowment or investments, provided they can quickly and easily be converted to cash—signals to prospective funders, underwriters, and anyone else who's interested that your organization has the resources to withstand unexpected challenges.

Just how much cash is enough? Well, that depends on a number of factors, including how smoothly you expect your revenue to come in and how reliable those sources of revenue are. In general, though, you'll want to shoot for having the equivalent of at least three months' worth of operating expenses in the form of cash on hand (excluding investments). It should also be said that many organizations find it good practice to maintain an untapped line of credit they can use as a temporary source of liquidity. As a matter of caution, however, this strategy should only be used to fund short-term timing differences between expenses and revenues.

Finally, since this is a chapter on credit, we'll mention that most lenders will look at a nonprofit's liquidity through two distinct lenses: the amount of debt (current and proposed) an organization carries and its total annual operating expenses. At the risk of overstating the obvious, the more liquidity you have relative to these two figures, the better. As a very general rule of thumb, however, many experts say you should aim for a ratio of unrestricted cash and investments to both total debt and annual operating expenses of at least 50 percent. Yes, you read that right—but remember this is a goal.

There's another important story the balance sheet will tell, and, like liquidity, this one also happens to start with the letter L: *leverage*. (Hey, we're all about ease of recall.) Leverage simply refers to how much debt an organization carries, particularly in relationship to its *total fund balance*, or *net assets*. Unrestricted, of course. The logic here is pretty straightforward: The more debt you're obligated to pay, the greater the percentage of your revenue you have to divert away from people and programs. You know when economists start to throw around terms like *national debt* in the context of countries that live beyond their means? It generally doesn't herald prosperous times for those nations. Well, nonprofits are no different. To put some numbers around this for you, if the ratio of your organization's funded debt (the debt you've actually used, as opposed to, say, an untapped line of credit) to unrestricted net assets is less than one, that's usually pretty good. But if that ratio starts to drift up to two or three times your unrestricted fund balance, it may be cause for some concern. As we've said, used responsibly, loans can be a valuable and important part of an organization's capital structure. Just be sure not to overdo it. Think of debt like saffron in a Spanish paella: A little goes a long way. Come to think of it, you may actually have to take out a loan just to buy a tiny bit of that stuff. Have you seen how much saffron costs? Sorry, it's dinnertime as we write this.

Collateral

Anyone who's ever had a mortgage is probably familiar with the concept of *collateral.* (Hint: It's your house.) Quite simply, collateral refers to the asset, or assets, a borrower pledges to a lender to help the lender get comfortable with the organization as a credit risk. Why does this help? Because in the event you can't—or won't—pay back your loan, the lender can legally sell your collateral to make itself whole.

As in the for-profit world, the assets generally accepted as collateral include real estate, equipment, and marketable securities (investments, such as stocks, bonds, or cash). Accounts receivable can be taken as collateral, too, though the unique nature of nonprofit receivables— often donor pledges, grants, and the like—may limit their use due to issues with lenders' ability to perfect their legal interest in them. As a way around this—particularly in the case of lines of credit—nonprofits may be asked to provide what's known as a *blanket lien,* which essentially grants the lender a general interest in the organization's business assets.

It should be said that the type of collateral pledged typically matches the purpose and term of the underlying loan it secures. Short-term assets (receivables, for example, or a blanket lien), therefore, secure short-term loans and lines of credit (typically those made for a year or less). More "permanent" assets (think equipment or real estate) usually secure longer-term credit. Part of this matching means that for purchases, whatever you're buying—a building, an automobile, and the like—will serve as at least part of the collateral securing the loan used to make the purchase. Just don't count on the lender extending credit on the full value of your collateral. They may with certain assets; 100 percent financing on the acquisition of equipment, for instance, is relatively common. But usually lenders will offer credit only up to a certain percentage of an asset's value. Often called an *advance rate,* this percentage will vary based on the type of collateral. Take commercial real estate. Here, the advance rate may be up to 75 or 80 percent for multipurpose properties (meaning for purchases you'll need to come up with the additional 20 to 25 percent), or as low as 50 percent or less for properties that are more specialized in nature. It all depends on how easily a lender believes it could sell the property if it needed to—and at what price.

Important as it is, collateral does have limitations in terms of its value to a prospective lender. We've already brought up the potential issue around receivables. Another one concerns IRS rules that may restrict or outright prohibit the pledging of certain assets as collateral. This is particularly germane to nonprofits that carry tax-exempt debt, such as the aforementioned direct purchase bonds. We'll say it again, though: We're not tax professionals, so you'll want to consult one if you have any questions about your organization's ability to pledge a specific asset.

Finally, we'd be remiss if we failed to mention that many lenders make loans to nonprofits without any collateral at all (called *unsecured lending*). Not to *all* nonprofits, mind you. If an organization isn't willing or able to pledge any of its assets to secure a loan, it had better be solid in the other four Cs. Reverse logic doesn't hold, however. In other words, stellar collateral by itself typically doesn't make a potential borrower creditworthy. It's a deal *sweetener*, not a deal*maker*. Strong collateral can improve the interest rate and terms on a loan, but the organization has to qualify for that loan in the first place. And especially with nonprofits, lenders are apt to be conscious of the risk to their reputations that comes with possibly repossessing or foreclosing on an organization's assets. We certainly can see why. After all, would you want your name in the local paper as the lender responsible for closing down a food bank or homeless shelter?

Conditions

Not all economic times are created equal. Remember late 2007 to mid-2009? Of course you do—albeit probably not fondly if you were anywhere near the financial services sector, or had money invested in . . . well, just about anything. Globally, the financial markets were in disarray, and if you'd tried to obtain a loan at that time, there was a fair to middling chance you found the credit well pretty much dry. At the very least, lenders subjected individuals and businesses to increased scrutiny. More recently, beyond obvious health implications, the ongoing COVID-19 pandemic has decimated businesses across all sectors of the economy. As we write, not even state and local governments have demonstrated immunity to the pandemic's deleterious effects, as municipalities everywhere struggle to balance budgets and a flagging tax base. Sadly then, organizations that depend on government grants to fund a significant percentage of their operations may well find themselves locked out of the credit markets at the precise moment access is needed. Thus, the Great Recession and coronavirus crisis serve as stark examples of how conditions beyond anyone's direct control can nonetheless affect their ability to borrow.

And it's not just macroeconomics that matter. Conditions in your state, city, or even your local neighborhood will also be viewed as part of your organization's credit application. This fact only serves to further underscore the importance of many of the sustainability metrics we've already discussed. Does your organization have diverse sources of revenue that can be counted on even during periods of economic uncertainty? Have you built a strong balance sheet—with ample liquidity and net assets—during good times that will gird your organization when things are less rosy? Does your organization fulfill a unique demand for its product or service? In short, does the world—or at least some small part of it—need your nonprofit?

The answers to these questions, of course, will vary depending on the nature of the nonprofit. For example, cultural institutions such as symphonies and museums may well take a big hit in an economic swoon if consumers feel less flush (or, as it is today, less safe being together), and therefore curtail their discretionary spending. Because of this risk, lenders will look at these organizations' positions in their particular markets. Do they have strong name recognition? How vulnerable are they to competition for scarce entertainment dollars? Do they benefit from a large percentage of their revenue coming from membership or subscription sales (e.g., season tickets or annual passes) as opposed to more volatile ad hoc gate admissions? Customer demographics, too, will be examined (so if you run a cultural nonprofit, make sure you're capturing this data). Organizations that attract patrons from a wide geographic area will likely be viewed more favorably from a credit standpoint than those whose customer base is more parochial.

On the other hand, many social service nonprofits may actually see a marked *increase* in demand if financial calamity hits. And for those organizations that depend heavily on government contracts or grants to fund operations, this can present a double whammy. Just as many of the economically afflicted line up to take advantage of your programs, the money necessary to keep those programs going—or indeed expand them—may be drying up. Welcome to the social service paradox, a potentially painful phenomenon all too familiar to many in the sector. And while no one can consistently predict when and where financial fault lines will produce economic earthquakes, there are ways organizations can prepare for this inevitability.

Paramount among them is focusing on providing programs and services your community and your funders see as *essential*. Doing so increases your ability to raise revenue even in rough economic periods, and gives lenders comfort that your operations won't cease when the economy hits the skids. Cultivating a diverse funding mix of individuals, corporations, and foundations to complement any government contracts is also a good idea. So, too, is maintaining an experienced, well-connected, and reputable leadership team and board of directors—a point that, conveniently, leads us to our fifth, and perhaps most important C.

Character

Martin Luther King Jr. once remarked that, "The ultimate measure of a man is not where he stands in moments of comfort and convenience, but where he stands at times of challenge and controversy."[6]

At first glance, this quote may appear a bit weighty for a simple chapter on borrowing money. Look closer, though, and you'll see it actually gets right at the heart of what credit and lending are all about. Why? Well, to take a little liberty with another well-known proclamation: Money doesn't pay back debt—*people* do. Character, therefore, is everything. And lenders know it. So, just how do they assess not an organization's capacity to pay, but its leadership's *willingness* to pay, even in "times of challenge and controversy"?

In the for-profit world, lenders typically secure this commitment with a full guarantee from the owners of the business. Exactly how valuable this guarantee is can be determined in a number of ways, such as analyzing owners' personal financial statements, bank and investment accounts, tax returns, and personal credit reports. However, as we've pointed out, lending to nonprofits is usually done *without recourse—*

which is to say in the absence of any personal guarantee. How, then, do lenders gain a window into the probable behavior of an organization's leadership when all the chips are down?

Look just about anywhere in the investment arena and you'll see some variation of the statement, "Past performance is no guarantee of future results." Think of it as the financial services sector equivalent of the surgeon general's warning that's plastered on packs of cigarettes. The upshot: Just because a stock or other investment did well yesterday doesn't mean you can expect the same tomorrow. And yet, when we're talking about character, it's precisely a person's past behavior lenders rely on as an indicator of what that person is likely to do in the future. Remember, we said underwriting is as much art as science. Well, if an organization's financial statements are the quantitative black and white, its leadership's character represents the much more qualitative shades of gray.

Though it may sound trite, there really is no substitute or shortcut for lenders taking the time to get to know the people behind the organization at the other end of a credit relationship. Do the CEO, CFO, and board have experience successfully managing through challenging economic periods? If the current leadership has only been with the organization during boom times, that may be a tougher argument to make. But if they've hit a roadblock or two and can demonstrate how their team navigated through it—perhaps by cutting expenses, temporarily scaling back certain programs, or securing additional funding through a well-connected board—that's going to provide a strong sense of comfort to any prospective lender. Ultimately, we're back to storytelling—stories told through personal interactions that help color the portrait of one's character. In this respect, lending—contrary to the automated, mechanized, impersonal nature by which many perceive it to be practiced—is actually among the most human of endeavors.

COMING FULL CIRCLE

An astute reader—which we know you are—will have noticed many of this chapter's themes related to well-functioning nonprofits are echoed throughout the book. Diverse revenue streams. Strong financial management. Personal relationships and storytelling. Quality leadership. All these are critical to sustainability. And, not coincidentally, they're also important factors lenders look at when considering an organization's creditworthiness. Because lenders want to get paid back, and sustainable organizations are more likely to do that. Sorry, just wanted to overstate the obvious there.

So, is credit the right solution for your nonprofit? That depends a lot on why you're thinking about borrowing money. If a loan would add long-term value to the organization by helping take advantage of an opportunity—say, to purchase real estate or expand a program—or smooth out uneven cash flow, it's probably an option worth considering, provided you're crystal clear on how you'll pay it back. According to Propel Nonprofits, an industry consultant, "The right time to consider seeking a loan is when you know how the funds will be used, have a plan for repayment that is based on reasonable assumptions for future income, and have the support of the board."[7] On the contrary, if borrowing only provides a temporary salve on an otherwise faulty business model, you'll want to seriously rethink submitting that credit application. "Adding debt on top of accumulating losses is a step toward bankruptcy," cautions Propel. "If you don't have any realistic idea of when or how the loan can be repaid, it's time to step back for a more in-depth financial assessment."

Used responsibly and with the wherewithal for repayment, credit can be a powerful weapon in a nonprofit's financial arsenal. Deployed strategically, loans can provide organizations the flexibility and—returning to Emerson—freedom to fulfill their noble missions. Far from being a harbinger of distress—a flashing red light warning something's amiss—borrowing, and as important, the *ability* to borrow, can actually have the opposite effect of signaling to others—especially funders—that your organization and its leadership are indeed worthy investments.

10

IT'S OUT THERE

Where to Get Help

We've thrown a lot at you over the last couple hundred pages, and you've intrepidly hung in there the whole way. Congratulations! And thank you. We know your time is valuable, and you probably aren't inclined to spend it sleuthing through this book in search of a specific resource you'd like to investigate, or spinning your wheels online. We get it—there's a *lot* of stuff out there! Do an internet search on "financing nonprofits" and you'll find roughly 2.9 *million* results! "Nonprofit sustainability?" 39.6 million hits. Where to begin? Well, let us cut through the haze and shepherd you to those founts of wisdom we found particularly helpful during the course of our research.

THE MAGNIFICENT SEVEN

The publications, organizations, and experts cited here were our information lodestars throughout this project. We recommend all of them as go-to sources containing a plethora of comprehensive material on the topics we've covered. Each is a unique resource apropos of the spectacularly diverse people and perspectives represented in our social sector. There are seven in total, so we call them—naturally—*The Magnificent Seven*, in an homage to the 1960 classic film. (Yes, we realize the movie was remade in 2016. But it doesn't have Yul Brynner or Steve

McQueen, so just trust us and stick with the original.) One other note before we begin: We chose to include these resources entirely of our own volition; no compensation was solicited or offered. Okay, here we go.

The Publishers

Nonprofit Quarterly (nonprofitquarterly.org) and *Stanford Social Innovation Review* (ssir.org)

As you may have deduced, based on the number of times we've mentioned these two, we think they're great and should be required reading for anyone remotely interested in the world of nonprofits.

Nonprofit Quarterly (NPQ) and the *Stanford Social Innovation Review* (SSIR) are subscription-based publications (though each offers some good free stuff, too) covering an enormously broad range of issues and developments in the social sector. They both employ a variety of media—online, magazines, newsletters, and more—to tackle topics that are interesting, innovative, and important. For you audiophiles, SSIR even puts out a delightfully informative podcast. It also hosts a number of conferences and seminars—including an annual assemblage of thought leaders: the Nonprofit Management Institute.

The Rainmakers

Nonprofit Finance Fund (nff.org) and SeaChange Capital Partners (seachangecap.org)

Like the investment and merchant banks you may be more familiar with, NFF and SeaChange Capital Partners design, broker, and service transactions—for the social sector. They use their own money, as well as outside capital, to direct funding where it can create the most social impact. NFF has facilitated nearly $900 million in financing through its work with thousands of organizations nationwide.[1]

For their part, the founders and funders who created SeaChange over a decade ago did so with the vision of promoting transactions among nonprofits through a combination of grants, loans, and investments. Today, the firm leverages its vast network of "foundations, individuals, nonprofits, and public entities"[2] to convene stakeholders around myriad issues of social impact.

These aren't just dealmakers, either. Both NFF and SeaChange offer consulting services, advocacy, and advice to their clients, in addition to conducting a variety of research and education initiatives. Even a quick glance at their websites reveals a rich trove of helpful resources germane to nearly any topic of interest to nonprofits.

The Advisors

The Bridgespan Group (bridgespan.org) and Candid (candid.org)

Calling The Bridgespan Group an advisor seems somewhat inadequate—kind of like calling Leonardo da Vinci just a painter. Whatever is the corporate equivalent to a polymath, Bridgespan is it. Sure, it advises nonprofits and others in the social sector. But it also parlays the vast knowledge and insights gleaned from this experience into an almost encyclopedic repository of research. There's even a jobs board on its website for careers within and outside of Bridgespan. And finally, let's not forget those terrific nonprofit leadership development programs designed to help teams tackle tough problems while strengthening executive cohesion. We interviewed three Bridgespan partners during the course of our research; their work and wisdom were invaluable and are featured throughout this book.

At first blush, Candid might appear to be a resource primarily for funders rather than Main Street nonprofits. Not so! While it does aggregate and analyze reams of information from foundations, its real value is created by sharing this knowledge through searchable databases accessible to nonprofits, grantmakers, and others in the sector. Organizations can use these data to bolster their requests for funding with specific statistics and information highlighting the need for their programs. Nonprofits can also gain helpful insight into what kinds of programs funders are supporting in their communities. That's just the beginning. As reported in *Fast Company*, Foundation Center and GuideStar merged in 2019 to form Candid. The combined powerhouse leverages Foundation Center's database of thirteen plus million grants by more than 150,000 funders, and GuideStar's trove of information on nearly three million active organizations—promising to create "more uniformity and context in how this information about nonprofits is presented," and help "funders and nonprofits trying to better understand opportunity within the sector."[3]

Candid facilitates courses and training on a wide variety of management and leadership topics. In addition, there's also a companion service—GrantSpace—whose mission is to "provide skills, insights, and
connections for a stronger social sector."[4] It offers tools and training
resources covering fundraising, sustainability, leadership, and more.
Nonprofits can access a library of sample proposals for reference, as
well as other documents, e-books, and blogs. (In our best infomercial
host voice) But wait, there's more! They can also tap the GuideStar
database and Foundation Directory Online (FDO) (access to all
150,000 plus funders and their grants) through Candid's global partnership consortium, the Funding Information Network. The latter boasts
more than four hundred locations at libraries and community centers
around the country where you can access FDO for free and get a
specialist librarian's help to find prospective funders. But the pièce de
résistance has to be the Collaboration Hub, a searchable compendium
containing more than 650 examples of successful collaborations, including "back-office consolidation, joint programming, mergers, and alliances."[5] Each thoroughly vetted case "provides information about the
collaboration's participants, methods, successes, challenges, and lessons
learned."

The Techie

TechSoup (techsoup.org)

Last but certainly not the least magnificent of our seven stellar resources is TechSoup. An embarrassing bit of disclosure here: We'd
never heard of this organization before beginning our research, despite
its having been around for more than thirty years. We wish we'd found
it sooner, though, because a number of our favorite nonprofits could
have benefited from its services.

TechSoup does a lot of cool stuff, but in a nutshell, it partners with
more than one hundred technology companies (including household
names like Cisco, Dell, Microsoft, and Oracle) to provide hardware and
software solutions to nonprofits—helping those organizations integrate
and operationalize their data (to measure outcomes!). By offering
much-needed technology, resources, and education to nonprofits for
free or at deeply discounted prices, TechSoup fills a common gap in
funding: most nonprofit grants don't cover technology purchases or

investments in tech (see our numerous rants against the overhead myth).

Consider yourself a Luddite? No worries. TechSoup provides skills-based training and consulting services to help organizations optimize their IT infrastructure. In addition to these fee-based services, nonprofits (worldwide) can access TechSoup's community—an online space where members can take courses, browse articles and webinars, and access gobs of useful discounted software, services, and more. Best of all, this is an organization tailor-made for Main Street nonprofits. According to CEO Rebecca Masisak, 80 percent of the more than one million organizations TechSoup has worked with have budgets under $2 million.[6]

Bonus Help!

But wait, there's more! (Sorry, last time, because . . . well, it's the end of the book.) Though space doesn't allow us to list all the remarkable organizations and people we found so helpful—many of whom were kind enough to participate in our research—we did want to mention a couple of other topic-rich resources we hope will contribute to your success.

Nonprofit Academic Centers Council (nonprofit-academic-centers-council.org), NACC, as it's known, is an association of member colleges and universities with academic departments or degree programs focused on bettering our world. Individuals at more than thirty accredited institutions from across the globe perform research, education, and service to strengthen their communities and the social sector at large. Here's how that may be helpful to you: Collectively, these institutions have a ton of knowledge, material, information, and best practices to share. Many have centers that assist nonprofits with research and program evaluation and offer free or low-cost seminars, speakers, certificate programs, and more. It also (hint, hint) has students who often are required to work in field-study programs or other practica as part of earning their degrees. Translation: FREE LABOR! We know from experience. In graduate school, both of us served on teams that consulted with local and international nonprofits on projects ranging from designing fundraising programs to researching a micro-insurance model. We've included a citation for a sample of the resulting reports and a "best practices" library.[7] The bottom line: Free labor is good. Use it whenever possible.

And finally, we give you the National Council of Nonprofits (NCN), a network of state nonprofit associations that collectively represents more than twenty-five members and serves as a resource and advocate for nonprofit organizations across the country. It works to connect "policy dots across all levels and branches of governments," and "identify emerging trends, share proven practices, and promote solutions that benefit charitable nonprofits and the communities they serve."[8] Many of NCN's member associations are themselves terrific resources—including two whose leadership participated in our research: CalNonprofits (calnonprofits.org) and the Minnesota Council on Foundations (mcf.org).

So there you go. We hope you found what you've just read helpful, because now more than ever the world needs smart, sustainable nonprofits to continue improving our lives and livelihoods. As this book goes to press, the world is turned upside down by a pandemic, with all organizations suffering great uncertainty and navigating epic challenges.

Innovative funding models, new sources of capital, fair pay, strategic partnerships and collaborations, leadership, trust-based philanthropy, impact assessment, storytelling, access to credit markets—all of these have important roles to play in creating a healthy and vibrant social sector. Not every tool is right for every organization. There are no panaceas. But by learning the many strategies, tactics, and resources that are becoming refreshingly abundant, we hope you'll at least discover a few that are worth exploring, worth putting into action. Worth repeating.

ACKNOWLEDGMENTS

THE EXPERTS

With so many people to thank for taking their valuable time to assist us with *Building Smart Nonprofits*, it's hard to know where to start. We've provided a complete list here, but want to recognize a few who were particularly helpful and insightful to our research:

- Antony Bugg-Levine, CEO, Nonprofit Finance Fund (NFF) and coauthor of *Impact Investing: Transforming How We Make Money While Making a Difference*: In addition to leading NFF's $350 million investment portfolio and consulting practice, Mr. Bugg-Levine is the founding chair of the Global Impact Investing Network and "convened the meeting that coined the phrase 'impact investing.'"[1] A glance at the number of times we quoted him or his work in *Building Smart Nonprofits* evidences his many contributions.
- Phil Buchanan, president of the Center for Effective Philanthropy, and author of the recently published *Giving Done Right: Effective Philanthropy and Making Every Dollar Count*: His writings and thoughts helped steer us away from sounding like the "suits" who think adopting "more business-like practices" will cure all the third sector's problems.
- Laura Deitrick, associate director, University of San Diego Nonprofit Institute: Apart from not flunking one of us in her Applied Leadership course, Laura helped us conceptualize the original

proposal for *Building Smart Nonprofits*, and provided many other suggestions, encouragements, and introductions along the way.

- Bill Drayton, founder and CEO of Ashoka, author of *Leading Social Entrepreneurs Changing the World*: Mr. Drayton is internationally lauded and recognized as a visionary and the pioneer of the field of social entrepreneurship. It was truly an honor to hear his thoughts.
- William Foster, partner and head of consulting, The Bridgespan Group: Recognized as a thought leader on issues of social change and philanthropy, his prolific writings and our discussions regarding funding models and the issues related to nonprofits seeking to improve sustainability through profitable ventures were invaluable.
- Jonathan Greenblatt, CEO of the Anti-Defamation League, former director of the White House Office of Social Innovation and founder of Ethos Water (also, one of our favorite business school professors): His remarkable experiences in all three sectors provided us a unique perspective.
- Don Howard, CEO of the James Irvine Foundation and formerly partner, The Bridgespan Group: Don literally "wrote the book" on a critical impediment to sustainability ("The Nonprofit Starvation Cycle") and now leads one of California's largest private foundations. Our conversations, his insights, and the many introductions he made for us were of enormous assistance.
- Joan Jacobs, internationally recognized philanthropist: Mrs. Jacobs and her husband, Irwin Jacobs, were early participants in the Giving Pledge, "a commitment by the world's wealthiest individuals and families to dedicate the majority of their wealth to giving back,"[2] and were awarded the Carnegie Medal of Philanthropy. Our discussions, including how the couple decide which of so many nonprofits to support, were an insightful glimpse into the world of inspired contemporary philanthropy.
- Eric Nee, editor in chief, the *Stanford Social Innovation Review* (SSIR): Founder and leader of one of our "Magnificent Seven" go-to resources (see chapter 10), Mr. Nee's abundant writings (and SSIR's informative content), our conversations, and his kind introductions to numerous third-sector thought leaders were a major contribution to *Building Smart Nonprofits*.

- And finally, Dr. Paula A. Cordeiro: (full disclosure, an author's wife). Apart from normal spousal support–like encouragement/draft reviewing (and rejecting), Paula's forty-plus-year career in the world of nonprofits as an educator, university dean, foundation/nonprofit/NGO board member, and author contributed amazing insights and referrals to *Building Smart Nonprofits*.

Yes, nonprofits are different—and the willingness of all the busy people who agreed to make time to assist others in the sector by contributing to our research proves this point. Many thanks to:

- Kim Ammann Howard, director of Impact Assessment and Learning at the James Irvine Foundation
- Dr. Ray Ashley, CEO, Maritime Museum of San Diego
- Lindsay Beck and Catarina Schwab, co-founders, IPX Advisors
- Steven Bellach, co-founder, BottomLine Marketing
- Mark Berger, former CEO and president, Partnerships with Industry
- Phil Buchanan, president, Center for Effective Philanthropy and author of *Giving Done Right*
- Antony Bugg-Levine, CEO, Nonprofit Finance Fund
- Malin Burnham, philanthropist and author of *Community before Self*
- Cecile Chalifour, West Division Manager, JPMorgan Chase
- Jose Cruz, former CEO, Barrio Logan College Institute
- Dr. Laura Deitrick, associate director of the Nonprofit Institute at the University of San Diego
- Mary Dowling, partner, For Purpose Law Group
- Bill Drayton, founder and CEO of Ashoka: Innovators for the Public, and author of *Leading Social Entrepreneurs Changing the World*
- Steve Eldred, senior program manager, CalEndow
- Tom Fetter, philanthropist
- Robert Foster, director of Impact Investing, San Diego Grantmakers
- William Foster, partner and head of consulting, The Bridgespan Group

- Dr. Nelli Garton, founder and chief impact officer, Tablecloth Inc.
- Martha Gilmer, CEO, San Diego Symphony
- Jonathan Greenblatt, CEO of the Anti-Defamation League, former director of the White House Office of Social Innovation and founder of Ethos Water
- John Grossman, senior fellow, Third Sector Capital Partners
- Vince Hall, CEO, Feeding San Diego
- Trista Harris, former president of the Minnesota Council on Foundations and author of *FutureGood*
- Carrie Hessler-Radelet, CEO, Project Concern International
- Don Howard, CEO of the James Irvine Foundation and coauthor of *The Nonprofit Starvation Cycle*
- Bruce Hoyt, formerly senior vice president of Philanthropic and Impact Investing, Gary Community Investments
- Inga Ingulfsen, research manager, Global Projects and Partnerships, Candid
- Joan Jacobs, internationally recognized philanthropist
- Nancy Jamison, former CEO, San Diego Grantmakers
- Amanda Keton, Head of People and Foundation, Tides Foundation
- Jack Landers, Teague Insurance
- Pat Libby, founder of the University of San Diego's Nonprofit Leadership and Management Program
- David Lynn, CEO, Mission Driven Finance
- RADM John "Mac" McLaughlin USN (ret.), CEO, and Scott McGaugh, director of marketing, *USS Midway* Museum
- Ali Malekzadeh, president, Roosevelt University
- John MacIntosh, partner, SeaChange Capital Partners
- Anne Marbarger, executive director, Padres Pedal the Cause
- Jan Masaoka, CEO, California Association of Nonprofits (Cal-Nonprofits)
- Rebecca Masisak, CEO, TechSoup
- Janine Mason, executive director, the Fieldstone Leadership Network San Diego
- Tim May, executive director, Government and Nonprofit Banking Business Loan Center, JPMorgan Chase
- Preeta Nayak, partner, The Bridgespan Group

- Eric Nee, editor in chief, the *Stanford Social Innovation Review*
- Amit Patel, managing director, Nonprofit Group, Accenture
- Alicia Quinn, vice president of New Business Development, United Way of San Diego County, and former Director of Programs, Mission Edge
- Dr. George Reed, Dean of the School of Public Affairs, University of Colorado, Colorado Springs
- Cameron Ripley, CEO, Community Boost Consulting
- Larry Rosenstock, founder and CEO, High Tech High
- Willa Seldon, partner, The Bridgespan Group
- Liz Sheer, former professor of Nonprofit Leadership, University of San Diego
- Beth Sirull, president and CEO, Jewish Community Foundation, San Diego
- Carrie Stokes Holst, senior manager of Impact and Borrower Services, Mission Driven Finance
- Mary Catherine Swanson, founder, AVID
- John Vasconcellos, CEO of the Community Foundation of Southeastern Massachusetts
- Dr. Gary Weitzman, president and CEO of the San Diego Humane Society
- Katrina Wert, director of the Center for Workforce Initiatives, Community College of Denver
- Dace West, vice president of Community Impact, Denver Foundation
- John Yokelson, founder and president of Building Engineering and Science Talent, member of the Council on Foreign Relations, and author of *Loving and Leaving Washington: Reflections on Public Service*
- Yotam Zeira, former director of strategy and external affairs, Roca

ON A PERSONAL NOTE, FROM DAVID

Building Smart Nonprofits: A Roadmap for Mission Success wouldn't have happened without the encouragement of my dear wife Paula Cordeiro, who got tired of hearing me grumble about my experiences in the nonprofit sector and suggested that I get a second master's degree in nonprofit leadership at the age of sixty-eight (I wonder if the fact that she was then the Dean of the School and co-founder of the program had anything to do with it?). Paula grew up in a tenement home in an immigrant community, which created her passion for the third sector and led to her many accomplishments in education and the nonprofit world. Some of this rubbed off on me, and her domain knowledge and experience was an invaluable contribution to me throughout the planning and writing of *Building Smart Nonprofits*.

ON A PERSONAL NOTE, FROM MATT

To all those I've leaned on in countless ways over the years—some for my entire life—I offer my most heartfelt and sincerest gratitude. Thank you. Without your support, encouragement, and love, quite simply, this thing doesn't happen.

To my former boss and dauntless team leader, Mikal Quarles, for your steadfast backing during my day job. You helped keep my plate just clean enough that I could write a book after hours—and maintain at least most of my sanity.

To our esteemed editor in chief Adrienne Moch of Adrienne Moch Writing & Editing, our deepest appreciation for agreeing to take a flyer on a couple of unpublished bankers. As always, you took rough hues of red and blue and made brilliant purple.

To super-nannies Vanessa Francischett and Nina Warth, for expanding our family across continents, and for your amazing ability to convincingly explain to two inquisitive toddlers why "Daddy has to work." You've shown us every day that kindness and generosity are universal, and happiness sounds the same in any language. You're ambassadors for the best of humanity, and no matter where your journey takes you in this big, beautiful world, you'll always have a home here. Eat your heart out, Mary Poppins.

To one of my oldest and most treasured friends, Nick Kittle, for opening the door to some of the best source material, and for having the keen knack for reaching out with the perfect words of encouragement at the perfect moments. You are a powerhouse of positivity, my friend!

To a few more of my closest chums: Jake Brinson, Josh Brown, Brian Potts, Paul McLaughlin, and Rob Eley, for always showing up when it mattered. In your own unique ways, you boys helped raise me—while we raised hell. And I wouldn't change a thing. I'm eternally grateful for your love and friendship through the years.

To my dear aunt Margie Farnsworth—Auntie Em!—for your unwavering optimism and sage advice to just "Write what you remember." Those words got me unstuck more times than I care to admit. Thank you for that.

To my little sis, Jennifer Weber (sorry, still can't call you J. C.), for sharing this crazy trip called life with me. From backyard roughhousing and adolescent shenanigans, to the rawest heartbreak and the purest love—we've been through it all together, Jen. You're the most fearless and fiery soul I know. I love you.

To my dad and main man, John Craig, for teaching me through your example that gentleness and true strength can coexist. For showing me how to get busy living, and to make no small plans along the way. And for giving me the most precious of gifts: roots and wings. Your place in my heart will always be top shelf, no dust. I love you, D.

To my mom, Nancy Craig, for being my first love and truest friend. Your selflessness, grace, and sacrifice defy description. Your compassion and equanimity in all weathers inspires me beyond words. I'm everything I am because of your courage to care. Though I could only hold your hand for a brief moment, you'll hold my heart forever.

To my daughter, Kerrigan Craig—my Baby Bear—for teaching me more about myself than I ever could have imagined. I mean, really. Who asks a four-year-old for life advice? You never disappoint, my love. Your boundless curiosity, composure, and confidence belie your years, and I can't wait to watch you put a dent in the universe.

To my son, Landry Craig, for living out loud and always wearing your tender heart on your sleeve. Your sincere sweetness and sensitivity reflects the very best in people, and your earnest charm will take you far. Keep loving without limits, treat kings and commoners alike, and the world is yours, my son.

And most importantly, to my wife and the world's best blind date, Courtney Craig, for being—just you. What can I say that hasn't already been said a million times over? You're a superhero. No, wait. That's not nearly big enough. Superheroes have posters of you in their bedrooms.

You're my lodestar, my map, my compass. My arbiter of truth. You're allergic to duplicity, and loyal to all without condition. Beauty radiates from your heart, soul, and visage in equal measure. For all of this and so much more, I love you, Sweetie.

WEBSITES

To assist you in discovering more information about the organizations mentioned throughout the book, we've provided their URLs for your convenience.

- Ashoka: https://www.ashoka.org/en-US
- AVID: https://www.avid.org/
- Ballmer Group: ballmergroup.org/
- Barrio Logan College Institute: https://www.blci.org/
- BoardSource: boardsource.org
- BottomLine Marketing: https://blmllc.com
- The Bridgespan Group: bridgespan.org/
- The California Endowment: https://www.calendow.org/
- The Center for Effective Philanthropy: https://cep.org/
- Center for Nonprofit Excellence: https://www.cfmco.org/nonprofits/center-for-nonprofit-excellence/
- Center for Social Impact Communication: http://csic.georgetown.edu/
- The Charitable Defense Council: charitydefensecouncil.org
- Community HousingWorks: chworks.org
- Cummings Foundation: https://www.cummingsfoundation.org/
- The Denver Foundation: www.denverfoundation.org
- The Economist: https://www.economist.com/economics-a-to-z/
- Feeding San Diego: https://feedingsandiego.org
- For Purpose Law Group: https://www.forpurposelaw.com
- Foundation Center: foundationcenter.org

- Freedom for Immigrants: https://www.freedomfor immigrants.org/
- Fresh Lifelines for Youth: https://flyprogram.org/
- Gary Community Investments: https://www.garycommunity.org/
- GrantCraft: https://grantcraft.org/
- Headwaters Foundation: https://headwatersfoundation.org/
- Ignited Fundraising: https://www.ignitedfundraising.com/
- inFocus Enterprises: https://impactinfocus.com/
- Innovations for Poverty Action: https://www.poverty-action.org/
- Invisible Children: https://invisiblechildren.com/
- James Irvine Foundation: www.irvine.org
- La Piana Consulting: lapiana.org
- The Last Mile: https://thelastmile.org
- The Lodestar Foundation: lodestarfoundation.org/
- Minnesota Council on Foundations: https://mcf.org/
- Mission Driven Finance: https://www.missiondrivenfinance.com/
- National Council of Nonprofits: https://www.councilof nonprofits.org
- Network for Good: https://www.networkforgood.com/
- New Bedford Whaling Museum: https://www.whaling museum.org/
- Nonprofit AF: https://nonprofitAF.com
- Nonprofit Finance Fund: nff.org/
- The Nonprofit Institute at the University of San Diego: https://www.sandiego.edu/soles/nonprofit/
- NPX Advisors: npxadvisors.com/
- Project Concern International: https://www.pciglobal.org/
- Rainier Valley Corps: https://rainiervalleycorps.org/
- The Rhode Island Foundation: https://www.rifoundation.org
- Rhode Island Public Radio: https://thepublicsradio.org
- Robert Sterling Clark Foundation: https://www.rsclark.org/
- Roca: rocainc.org/work/pay-for-success
- Rockefeller Philanthropy Advisors: https://www.rockpa.org/
- San Diego Grantmakers: https://sdgrantmakers.org/
- San Diego Humane Society: sdhumane.org
- Sanford Burnham Prebys Medical Discovery Institute: www.sbpdiscovery.org/
- SeaChange Capital Partners: seachangecap.org

- SeaChange-Lodestar Fund for Nonprofit Collaboration: seachangecap.org/funds
- Sobrato Family Foundation: www.sobrato.com/sobrato-philanthropies/sobrato-family-foundation/
- Tablecloth: https://www.tablecloth.io/
- Third Sector Capital Partners: www.thirdsectorcap.org/
- Urban Greens: www.urbangreens.com
- *USS Midway* Museum: https://www.midway.org/
- Venture Philanthropy Partners: www.vppartners.org/
- W. K. Kellogg Foundation: https://www.wkkf.org/
- Weingart Foundation: https://www.weingartfnd.org/
- The Whitman Institute: https://thewhitmaninstitute.org/
- The William and Flora Hewlett Foundation: https://hewlett.org/
- Yalla: yallasd.org/

NOTES

INTRODUCTION

1. Bruce Hoyt, interview, August 2018.
2. "Robin Hood Is Mum on Gala Haul but It's More Than 54.5 Million," Bloomberg.com. Accessed July 10, 2019. https://www.bloomberg.com/news/articles/2018-05-16/robin-hood-is-mum-on-gala-haul-but-it-s-more-than-54-5-million.
3. Simone Joyaux, "A Too-Sad Truth about the Nonprofit Sector," August 17, 2012. Retrieved November 8, 2015. http://nonprofitquarterly.org/2012/08/17/a-too-sad-truth-about-the-nonprofit-sector/.
4. Phil Buchanan, *Giving Done Right: Effective Philanthropy and Making Every Dollar Count* (New York: PublicAffairs, 2019).
5. Phil Buchanan, "Business Thing," June 6, 2012, blog post, https://cep.org/author/philb/.
6. nccs.urban.org. Accessed October 11, 2018.
7. Eric Nee, interview, August 2018.
8. R. Reich and C. Wimer, *Charitable Giving and the Great Recession* (Palo Alto, CA: Russell Sage Foundation and the Stanford Center on Poverty and Inequality, 2012).
9. "Council on Foundations Statement on Passage of the Tax Cuts and Jobs Act," Council on Foundations. December 21, 2017. Accessed July 19, 2019. https://www.cof.org/news/council-foundations-statement-passage-tax-cuts-and-jobs-act.
10. Leslie Albrecht, "Americans Slashed Their Charitable Deductions by $54 Billion after Republican Tax-Code Overhaul," MarketWatch. July 11, 2019. Accessed July 25, 2019. https://www.marketwatch.com/story/americans-

slashed-their-charitable-deductions-by-54-billion-after-trumps-tax-overhaul-2019-07-09.

11. Sarah O'Brien, "Advocates: Cost of GOP Tax Bill Puts Entitlement Programs at Risk of Cuts." CNBC. December 6, 2017. Accessed July 19, 2019. https://www.cnbc.com/2017/12/06/advocates-cost-of-gop-tax-bill-puts-entitlement-programs-at-risk-of-cuts.html.

12. Candid, "The Financial Health of the United States Nonprofit Sector." Accessed July 25, 2019. https://learn.guidestar.org/products/us-nonprofits-financial-health.

13. "Economic Impact." National Council of Nonprofits. October 18, 2017. Accessed October 2, 2018. https://www.councilofnonprofits.org/economic-impact.

14. "The Nonprofit Sector in Brief," National Center for Charitable Statistics, https://nccs.urban.org/project/nonprofit-sector-brief.

15. "The Charitable Sector," Independent Sector, https://independentsector.org/about/the-charitable-sector/.

16. "The Nonprofit Starvation Cycle (SSIR)," *Stanford Social Innovation Review*. Accessed July 25, 2019. https://ssir.org/articles/entry/the_nonprofit_starvation_cycle.

I. FUNDING MODELS AND SUSTAINABILITY

1. Scott McGaugh, interview, May 2018.

2. William Landes Foster, Peter Kim, and Barbara Christiansen, "Ten Nonprofit Funding Models." 2009. https://ssir.org/articles/entry/ten_nonprofit_funding_models#.

3. Jonathan Greenblatt, interview, August 2018.

4. Don Howard, interview, August 2018.

5. William Foster and Jeffrey Bradach, "Should Nonprofits Seek Profits?" *Harvard Business Review* 83, no. 2 (2005): 92–100.

6. Admiral John P. McLaughlin (USNR-Ret), interview, May 2018.

7. Scott McGaugh, interview, May 2018.

8. Media Kit, *USS Midway Museum*. October 25, 2018. www.midway.org/contact/media-kit/.

9. Malin Burnham, interview, June 2018.

10. Admiral John P. McLaughlin (USNR-Ret), interview, May 2018.

11. Foster, Kim, and Christiansen, "Ten Nonprofit Funding Models."

12. Mary Catherine Swanson, interview, June 2018.

13. William Foster and Gail Fine, "How Nonprofits Get Really Big." 2007. https://ssir.org/articles/entry/how_nonprofits_get_really_big#.

14. Mary Catherine Swanson, interview, June 2018.

15. Mary Catherine Swanson, interview, June 2018.

16. "Our History," Feeding America. Accessed November 20, 2018. https://www.feedingamerica.org/about-us/our-history.

17. Vince Hall, interview, September 2018.

18. Vince Hall, interview, September 2018.

19. Vince Hall, interview, September 2018.

20. Foster, Kim, and Christiansen, "Ten Nonprofit Funding Models."

21. Vince Hall, interview, September 2018.

22. Kerstin Frailey, "What Does the Nonprofit Sector Really Look Like?" GuideStar Blog. Accessed January 28, 2019. https://trust.guidestar.org/what-does-the-nonprofit-sector-really-look-like.

23. Trista Harris, interview, September 2018.

24. Jan Masaoka, interview, June 2018.

25. "The Need," Barrio Logan College Institute. Accessed December 2, 2018. https://www.blci.org/the-needforblci/.

26. Jose Cruz, interview, April 2018.

27. Jose Cruz, interview, April 2018.

28. "Bill Drayton on the Power of Collaborative Entrepreneurship in McKinsey's 'What Matters?'" Ashoka, Everyone a Changemaker. July 18, 2016. Accessed December 2, 2018. https://www.ashoka.org/en-US/node/3481.

29. "Bill Drayton on the Power of Collaborative Entrepreneurship in McKinsey's 'What Matters?'"

30. Phil Buchanan, interview, November 2018.

31. Robert I. Sutton and Huggy Rao, *Scaling up Excellence: Getting to More without Settling for Less* (London: Random House, 2014).

32. https://www.businessinsider.com/scaling-up-excellence-robert-sutton-huggy-rao-2014-1.

33. Alison Griswold, "Two Stanford Professors Have a Fascinating Theory of Why Businesses Succeed." *Business Insider*, February 4, 2014. Accessed January 28, 2019. https://www.businessinsider.com/scaling-up-excellence-robert-sutton-huggy-rao-2014-1.

34. "Intellectual Property," Merriam-Webster. Accessed December 5, 2018. https://www.merriam-webster.com/dictionary/intellectual property.

35. Bruce Hoyt, interview, August 2018.

36. Foster, Kim, and Christiansen, "Ten Nonprofit Funding Models."

37. John MacIntosh, interview, August 2018.

38. Dace West, interview, September 2018.

39. Carrie Hessler-Radelet, interview, November 2018.

40. Alvin Toffler, *Future Shock* (London: Pan Books, 1970).

41. Trista Harris, interview, September 2018.

42. Foster and Bradach, "Should Nonprofits Seek Profits?" 92–100.

43. Foster and Bradach, "Should Nonprofits Seek Profits?" 92–100.

44. Alliance for Children and Families, "Joining Forces to Strengthen Human Services in America." Authority and Institutions Challenged. Accessed January 28, 2019. http://www.alliance1.org/web/community/national-imperative-joining-forces-strengthen-human-services-america.aspx.

45. Antony Bugg-Levine, interview, November 2018.

46. Eric Nee, interview, August 2018.

47. Foster and Fine, "How Nonprofits Get Really Big."

48. Foster and Fine, "How Nonprofits Get Really Big."

49. William Foster, interview, November 2018.

50. Eric Nee, interview, August 2018.

51. Bruce Hoyt, interview, August 2018.

52. Carrie Hessler-Radelet, interview, November 2018.

2. WALL STREET FOR THE THIRD SECTOR

1. Kimberly Amadeo, "Greed Is Good . . . or Is It?" The Balance Small Business. Accessed January 08, 2019. https://www.thebalance.com/greed-is-good-or-is-it-quote-and-meaning-3306247.

2. Drew DeSilver, "For Most Americans, Real Wages Have Barely Budged for Decades." Pew Research Center. August 7, 2018. Accessed February 27, 2019. http://www.pewresearch.org/fact-tank/2018/08/07/for-most-us-workers-real-wages-have-barely-budged-for-decades/.

3. Patrick Santana, "Nonprofits and Tax-Exempt Bonds." Step by Step Guide for Starting a California Nonprofit—CalNonprofits. Accessed January 4, 2019. https://calnonprofits.org/resources/nonprofits-tax-exempt-bonds.

4. Terry Lane, "Can Nonprofit Corporations Issue Stock?" Small Business, Chron.com. November 21, 2017. Accessed January 5, 2019. https://smallbusiness.chron.com/can-non-profit-corporations-issue-stock-65592.html.

5. Dan Pallotta, *Uncharitable: How Restraints on Nonprofits Undermine Their Potential* (Medford, MA: Tufts University Press, 2010).

6. Written by Giving, "Giving USA 2018." Giving USA. Accessed February 27, 2019. https://givingusa.org/giving-usa-2018-americans-gave-410-02-billion-to-charity-in-2017-crossing-the-400-billion-mark-for-the-first-time/.

7. https://dealbook.nytimes.com/2013/11/11/plan-to-finance-philanthropy-shows-the-power-of-a-simple-question.

8. Eric Nee, interview, August 2018.

9. "The Rise of Socially Responsible Investing," ETFdb.com. Accessed January 21, 2019. https://etfdb.com/practice-management/rise-of-socially-responsible-investing/.

10. "Sustainable Investing: The Millennial Investor," Ernst & Young. https://www.ey.com/Publication/vwLUAssets/ey-sustainable-investing-the-millennial-investor-gl/$FILE/ey-sustainable-investing-the-millennial-investor.pdf.

11. "Impact Investing," The GIIN. Accessed January 16, 2019. https://thegiin.org/impact-investing/.

12. "Strengthening the Impact Investing Movement (SSIR)," *Stanford Social Innovation Review*. Accessed January 15, 2019. https://ssir.org/articles/entry/strengthening_the_impact_investing_movement.

13. "Annual Impact Investor Survey 2018," The GIIN. Accessed January 15, 2019. https://thegiin.org/research/publication/annualsurvey2018.

14. William Foster, interview, November 2018.

15. Zenobia Jeffries Warfield, Chris Winters, Tracy Matsue Loeffelholz, Ed Whitfield, Chuck Collins, Deonna Anderson, Ivy Brashear, Vicki Robin, New Economy Coalition, Working World, Southern Reparations Loan Fund, and Institute for Policy Studies, "The Good Money Issue." *YES! Magazine*. Accessed January 15, 2019. https://issues.yesmagazine.org/issue/good-money/theme.html#7thArticle.

16. "Steps to Catalyze Private Foundation Impact Investing," National Archives and Records Administration. Accessed January 15, 2019. https://obamawhitehouse.archives.gov/blog/2016/04/21/steps-catalyze-

17. Andrew R. Sorkin, "Blackrock Will Put Climate Change at Center of Investment Strategy," *New York Times*, January 4, 2020.

18. Clara Miller, "The World Has Changed and So Must We." Accessed January 15, 2019. http://www.frbsf.org/community-development/files/miller.pdf

19. Natasha Singer and Mike Isaac, "Mark Zuckerberg's Philanthropy Uses L.L.C. for More Control." *New York Times*. January 19, 2018. Accessed February 27, 2019. https://www.nytimes.com/2015/12/03/technology/zuckerbergs-philanthropy-uses-llc-for-more-control.html.

20. "Market Making for Mission (SSIR)," *Stanford Social Innovation Review*. Accessed January 15, 2019. https://ssir.org/articles/entry/market_making_for_mission.

21. Jessica David, interview, August 2018.

22. Jessica David, interview, August 2018.

23. "Report: Warehousing Wealth," Institute for Policy Studies. July 25, 2018. Accessed January 9, 2019. https://ips-dc.org/report-warehousing-wealth/.

24. Dace West, interview, December 2018.

25. Larry Kramer, "Hewlett Foundation's Leader Makes a Case against Impact Investing." *The Chronicle of Philanthropy* (January 2019): 8–11.

26. "Basics," Utah High Quality Preschool Program, Pay for Success. Accessed January 7, 2019. https://www.payforsuccess.org/learn/basics/#what-is-pay-for-success.

27. http://www.payforsuccess.org/sites/default/files/pay-for-success.pdf.

28. "The Payoff of Pay-for-Success (SSIR)." *Stanford Social Innovation Review*. Accessed January 7, 2019. https://ssir.org/up_for_debate/article/the_payoff_of_pay_for_success.

29. "Our Story," Roca. Accessed February 27, 2019. https://rocainc.org/about/our-story/.

30. "Pay for Success," Roca. Accessed January 5, 2019. https://rocainc.org/work/pay-for-success/.

31. "Pay for Success."

32. John Grossman, interview, 2018.

33. Yotam Zeira, interview, January 2019.

34. Bruce Hoyt, interview, August 2018.

35. Bruce Hoyt, interview, August 2018.

36. John Grossman, interview, 2018.

37. Bruce Hoyt, interview, August 2018.

38. "The Last Mile," The Last Mile. Accessed February 27, 2019. https://thelastmile.org/.

39. "The Last Mile," NPX. Accessed February 27, 2019. https://npxadvisors.com/impact-security/the-last-mile/.

40. "Making an Impact, Literally," Media2.Mofo.com/documents/npx-impact.pdf. Accessed February 27, 2019.

41. "Expanding the Playbook," NPX. Accessed April 2, 2019. https://npxadvisors.com/.

42. Lindsay Beck and Catarina Schwab, interview, August 2018.

43. Will Schupmann and Matthew Eldridge, "Impact Securities: A New Twist on Pay for Success." Urban Institute, Pay for Success Initiative. June 14, 2018. Accessed January 14, 2019. https://pfs.urban.org/pay-success/pfs-perspectives/impact-securities-new-twist-pay-success.

44. Bill Bradley, Paul Jansen, and Les Silverman, "The Nonprofit Sector's $100 Billion Opportunity." *Harvard Business Review*. August 1, 2014. Accessed January 14, 2019. https://hbr.org/2003/05/the-nonprofit-sectors-100-billion-opportunity.

45. John MacIntosh, interview, August 2018.

46. John MacIntosh, interview, August 2018; "Leveraged Opportunities," SeaChange Capital Partners. October 10, 1970. Accessed January 28, 2019. http://SeaChangecap.org/glossary/leveraged/.

47. Antony Bugg-Levine, interview, November 2018; Nancy Jamison, Interview, April 2018.

48. Antony Bugg-Levine, interview, November 2018.

49. Antony Bugg-Levine, interview, November 2018.

3. EQUAL PAY FOR EQUAL WORK?

1. Nancy Jamison, interview, May 2018.

2. "NFF's Annual Survey: 3,000 and Counting," Top Indicators of Nonprofit Financial Health, Nonprofit Finance Fund. July 18, 2017. Accessed December 26, 2018. https://nff.org/blog/nff's-annual-survey-3000-and-counting.

3. Quentin Fottrell, "Fortune 500 CEOs Are Paid from Double to 5,000 Times More Than Their Employees." MarketWatch. May 19, 2018. Accessed March 24, 2019. https://www.marketwatch.com/story/fortune-500-ceos-are-paid-from-double-to-5000-times-more-than-their-employees-2018-05-16.

4. "Learning from Failure (SSIR)," *Stanford Social Innovation Review*. Accessed March 23, 2019. https://ssir.org/articles/entry/learning_from_failure#.

5. "The Professionalization of Charities," *The Economist 424* (September 30–October 6, 2017): 55–56.

6. Brian Kay, interview, June 2018.

7. Stephen Fishman, "Reporting Nonprofit Operating Expenses." www.nolo.com. January 23, 2015. Accessed December 14, 2018. http://www.nolo.com/legal-encyclopedia/reporting-nonprofit-operating-expenses.html.

8. "What You Need to Know about Nonprofit Executive Compensation." Accessed December 14, 2018. https://www.guidestar.org/ViewCms-File.aspx?ContentID=3890.

9. "Exempt Organization Annual Reporting Requirements: Meaning of Reasonable Compensation, Internal Revenue Service," Internal Revenue Service. Accessed March 23, 2019. https://www.irs.gov/charities-non-profits/exempt-organization-annual-reporting-requirements-meaning-of-reasonable-compensation.

10. "What You Need to Know about Nonprofit Executive Compensation."

11. https://www.charitywatch.org/charitywatch-articles/charitywatch-hall-of-shame/63.

12. Wendy Maeda, "Nonprofits Push Back on Conventional Wisdom—The Boston Globe," BostonGlobe.com. January 15, 2015. Accessed December 14,

2018. https://www.bostonglobe.com/business/2015/01/15/nonprofits-push-back-conventional-wisdom/4CB4q1OTTZnxqkcYXEToHJ/story.html.

13. Dan Pallotta, *Uncharitable: How Restraints on Nonprofits Undermine Their Potential* (Medford, MA: Tufts University Press, 2010).

14. "What You Need to Know about Nonprofit Executive Compensation."

15. Stephan Katzbichler, *Historical Impacts on the Philanthropical American Tradition* (Munich: GRIN Verlag, 2013).

16. Alfie Kohn, "Why Incentive Plans Cannot Work." *Harvard Business Review*. August 1, 2014. Accessed March 24, 2019. https://hbr.org/1993/09/why-incentive-plans-cannot-work.

17. James Charles Collins, *Good to Great and the Social Sectors* (New York: Harper Business, 2011). Kindle Edition.

18. Simone Joyaux, "A Too-Sad Truth about the Nonprofit Sector." *Nonprofit Quarterly*. June 14, 2013. Accessed December 14, 2018. http://nonprofitquarterly.org/2012/08/17/a-too-sad-truth-about-the-nonprofit-sector/.

19. B. D. Galle, "Keep Charity Charitable." HeinOnline. Accessed December 14, 2018. https://heinonline.org/HOL/LandingPage?handle=hein.journals/tlr88&div=43&id=&page=.

20. Saul Mcleod, "Maslow's Hierarchy of Needs." *Simply Psychology*. May 21, 2018. https://www.simplypsychology.org/maslow.html.

21. Grace L. Chikoto and Daniel Gordon Neely, "Building Nonprofit Financial Capacity." *Nonprofit and Voluntary Sector Quarterly* 43, no. 3 (2013): 570–88. doi:10.1177/0899764012474120.

22. GuideStar, BBB Wise Giving Alliance, and Charity Navigator, http://overheadmyth.com/.

23. "World YMCA-Annual Report April 2011," *Human Rights Documents Online*. https://doi.org/10.1163/2210-7975_hrd-9843-0004.

24. "Ethics and Nonprofits (SSIR)," *Stanford Social Innovation Review*. Accessed December 17, 2018. https://ssir.org/articles/entry/ethics_and_nonprofits.

25. "2018 NFF State of the Nonprofit Sector Survey Results Warn of Danger," National Council of Nonprofits. June 20, 2018. Accessed March 24, 2019. https://www.councilofnonprofits.org/thought-leadership/2018-nff-state-of-the-nonprofit-sector-survey-results-warn-of-danger.

26. Ann Goggins Gregory and Don Howard, "The Nonprofit Starvation Cycle." *Stanford Social Innovation Review* 7, no. 4 (2009): 49–53.

27. Gregory and Howard, "The Nonprofit Starvation Cycle," 49–53.

28. Don Howard, interview, August 2018.

29. Marc J. Epstein and F. Warren McFarlan, "Nonprofit vs. For-Profit Boards: Critical Differences." *Strategic Finance* (March 2011): 28. *Academic OneFile*. Accessed December 20, 2018.

30. James A. Brickley and R. Lawrence Van Horn, "Managerial Incentives in Nonprofit Organizations: Evidence from Hospitals." *Journal of Law and Economics* 45, no. 1 (2002): 227–49. doi:10.1086/339493.

31. Jerry Y. Du, Alexander S. Rascoe, and Randall E. Marcus, "The Growing Executive-Physician Wage Gap in Major US Nonprofit Hospitals and Burden of Nonclinical Workers on the US Healthcare System." *Clinical Orthopaedics and Related Research* 476 (10) (2018): 1910–19. https://doi.org/10.1097/corr.0000000000000394.

32. William Landes Foster, Peter Kim, and Barbara Christiansen, "Ten Nonprofit Funding Models." 2009. https://ssir.org/articles/entry/ten_nonprofit_funding_models.

33. Matthew T. Journy, "Paying for the Best: Executive Compensation for Section 501(c)(3) Public Charities." Accessed December 21, 2018. https://www.venable.com/files/Publication/84527f21-29c3-4da2-a9dc-b16d21a323bf/Presentation/PublicationAttachment/29c08467-5b30-4668-9306-c287c537ac8d/Paying_for_the_Best_Executive_Compensation_for_Section_501(c)(3)_Public_Charities.pdf.

34. Peter D. Blumberg, "From 'Publish or Perish' to 'Profit or Perish': Revenues from University Technology Transfer and the § 501(c) (3) Tax Exemption." *University of Pennsylvania Law Review* 145, no. 1 (1996): 89–147. doi:10.2307/3312714.

35. Malin Burnham, interview, May 2018.

36. Collins, *Good to Great and the Social Sectors*, 11.

37. Nancy Jamison, interview, May 2018.

38. Sinek, Simon. "How Great Leaders Inspire Action." Ted. Accessed January 2, 2019. https://www.ted.com/talks/simon_sinek_how_great_leaders_inspire_action.

39. "County Pushes toward Elusive Goal of Treatment on Demand," Addiction Professional. Accessed March 24, 2019. https://www.addictionpro.com/article/management/county-pushes-toward-elusive-goal-treatment-demand.

40. Scott Greenstone, "One Way to Help Homeless in King County? Shorten the Wait for Treatment." *The Seattle Times*. November 24, 2017. Accessed January 2, 2019. https://www.seattletimes.com/seattle-news/homeless/one-way-to-help-homeless-in-king-county-shorten-the-wait-for-treatment/.

41. Greenstone, "One Way to Help Homeless in King County?"

42. John Grossman, interview, September 2018.

43. "County Pushes toward Elusive Goal of Treatment on Demand."

4. ARE THERE TOO MANY NONPROFITS?

1. "The Financial Health of the United States Nonprofit Sector: Facts and Observations," About Us. Accessed February 5, 2019. https://learn.guidestar.org/products/us-nonprofits-financial-health.

2. Tory, "The QSR 50." *QSR Magazine*. August 1, 2017. Accessed April 3, 2019. https://www.qsrmagazine.com/content/qsr50-2017-top-50-chart?sort=2016_us_average_sales_per_unit_thousands&dir=asc.

3. "The Financial Health of the United States Nonprofit Sector: Facts and Observations," About Us. Accessed February 5, 2019. https://learn.guidestar.org/products/us-nonprofits-financial-health.

4. Jan Masaoka, interview, June 2018.

5. Dace West, interview, October 2018.

6. Don Howard, interview, August 2018.

7. Clare Cooper, "Fuelling 'The Necessary Revolution,'" Grantmakers in the Arts. Accessed April 3, 2019. https://www.giarts.org.

8. "Strategic Partnerships." Accessed February 10, 2019. https://www.thearc.org/file/documents_nce/strategic-partnerships.pdf.

9. Gary Weitzman, interview, May 2018.

10. Jonathan Greenblatt, interview, August 2018.

11. John MacIntosh, interview, August 2018.

12. Willa Seldon, interview, September 2018.

13. William Foster, Alex Cortez, and Katie Smith Milway, "Nonprofit Mergers and Acquisitions: More Than a Tool for Tough Times." The Bridgespan Group. February 25, 2009. Accessed February 7, 2019. https://www.bridgespan.org/insights/library/mergers-and-collaborations/nonprofit-mergers-and-acquisitions-more-than-a-too.

14. John MacIntosh, interview, August 2018.

15. Alex Neuhoff, Katie Smith Milway, Reilly Kiernan, and Josh Grehan, "Making Sense of Nonprofit Collaborations." The Bridgespan Group. December 17, 2014. Accessed February 15, 2019. https://www.bridgespan.org/insights/library/mergers-and-collaborations/nonprofitcollaborations.

16. "Advice to Strengthen Strategic Mergers and Collaborations," Top Indicators of Nonprofit Financial Health, Nonprofit Finance Fund. March 27, 2017. Accessed February 12, 2019. https://nff.org/report/advice-strengthen-strategic-mergers-and-collaborations.

17. "Seed," SeaChange Capital Partners. October 10, 1970. Accessed April 3, 2019. http://seachangecap.org/glossary/seed/.

18. "A New Source for Funding Nonprofit Mergers and Collaborations (SSIR)." *Stanford Social Innovation Review*. Accessed February 11, 2019.

https://ssir.org/articles/entry/
a_new_source_for_funding_nonprofit_mergers_and_collaborations.

19. John MacIntosh, interview, August 2018.

20. "Our Grants," Our Grants, The Lodestar Foundation. Accessed April 3, 2019. http://www.lodestarfoundation.org/grants.

21. "Our Philanthropic Philosophy," Merger of Neighboring Big Brothers Big Sisters Affiliates. The Lodestar Foundation. Accessed February 12, 2019. http://www.lodestarfoundation.org/.

22. "How to Fund Nonprofit Mergers and Partnerships (SSIR)," *Stanford Social Innovation Review*. Accessed February 12, 2019. https://ssir.org/articles/entry/how_to_fund_nonprofit_mergers_and_partnerships#.

23. Bhakti Mirchandani, "How to Save a Nonprofit: The Care Steps Required in Mergers and Acquisitions." Non Profit News, *Nonprofit Quarterly*. September 26, 2018. Accessed February 13, 2019. https://nonprofitquarterly.org/2018/08/15/how-to-save-a-nonprofit-mergers-acquisitions/.

24. "Nonprofit Consultants, Nonprofit Strategic Restructuring—La Piana." La Piana Consulting. Accessed April 3, 2019. https://www.lapiana.org/.

25. "Nonprofit Consultants, Nonprofit Strategic Restructuring—La Piana."

26. "David La Piana," La Piana Consulting. Accessed February 13, 2019. https://lapiana.org/about-our-firm/our-team/partners/david-la-piana.

27. Neuhoff et al., "Making Sense of Nonprofit Collaborations."

28. "Collaborationists and Collectivists (SSIR)," *Stanford Social Innovation Review*. ssir.org/articles/entry/collaborationists_and_collectivists.

29. James M. Manyika, Roger P. Roberts, and Kara L. Sprague, "Eight Business Technology Trends to Watch." McKinsey & Company. Accessed February 20, 2019. https://www.mckinsey.com/business-functions/digital-mckinsey/our-insights/eight-business-technology-trends-to-watch.

30. "The Nonprofit World Becomes Flat: How Technology and Economic Needs May Shrink Our Globe (SSIR)," *Stanford Social Innovation Review*. Accessed April 1, 2019. https://ssir.org/articles/entry/the_nonprofit_world_becomes_flat_how_technology_and_economic_needs_may_shri.

31. "A Nonprofit Guide to Outsourcing." https://d2oc0ihd6a5bt.cloudfront.net/wp-content/uploads/sites/1482/2016/01/outsourcing.pdf.

32. NOC. Accessed February 20, 2019. https://noc.npccny.org/noc/.

33. "How Fiscal Sponsorship Nurtures Nonprofits," TSNE MissionWorks. December 7, 2018. Accessed February 20, 2019. https://www.tsne.org/blog/how-fiscal-sponsorship-nurtures-nonprofits.

34. "Our Vision, Mission and Approach," Tides. Accessed February 20, 2019. https://www.tides.org/about/vision-mission-approach/.

35. "FAQs," Tides. Accessed February 20, 2019. https://www.tides.org/faqs/.

36. Antony Bugg-Levine, interview, November 2018.

37. Robert Foster, interview, March 2019.

38. Joan Jacobs, interview, August 2018.

39. Eric Nee, interview, August 2018.

40. Dace West, interview, October 2018.

41. Carrie Hessler-Radelet, interview, November 2018.

42. John Vasconcellos, interview, June 2018.

43. Willa Seldon, interview, September 2018.

44. Dace West, interview, October 2018.

45. "Core WORKNOW Exceeds Goal with 200th Connection," Colorado Department of Transportation. August 14, 2018. Accessed April 3, 2019. https://www.codot.gov/projects/i70east/assets/worknow_press-release_200connection.pdf.

46. Willa Seldon, interview, September 2018.

5. THE TWIN ENGINES OF THE PLANE

1. "Board Responsibilities and Structures—FAQs," BoardSource. Accessed March 15, 2019. https://boardsource.org/resources/board-responsibilities-structures-faqs/.

2. Richard P. Chait, William P. Ryan, and Barbara E. Taylor, *Governance as Leadership: Reframing the Work of Nonprofit Boards* (New York: John Wiley & Sons, 2011).

3. Chait et al., *Governance as Leadership*.

4. Liz Shear, "Kaleidescope of Governance," University of San Diego, School of Leadership and Education. PowerPoint Lecture.

5. Inga Ingulfsen, interview, October 2018.

6. "Diversity on Nonprofit Boards," National Council of Nonprofits. March 8, 2019. Accessed March 20, 2019. https://www.councilofnonprofits.org/tools-resources/diversity-nonprofit-boards.

7. Malin Burnham, interview, May 2018.

8. "Leading with Intent—2017 National Index of Nonprofit Board Practices." Leading with Intent. Accessed April 25, 2019. https://leadingwithintent.org/wp-content/uploads/2017/09/LWI2017.pdf.

9. Ray Ashley, interview, September 2018.

10. Elizabeth Schmidt, "Rediagnosing 'Founder's Syndrome': Moving beyond Stereotypes to Improve Nonprofit Performance." Non Profit News, *Nonprofit Quarterly*. March 7, 2019. Accessed March 18, 2019. https://nonprofit-

quarterly.org/2019/03/07/rediagnosing-founder-s-syndrome-moving-beyond-stereotypes-to-improve-nonprofit-performance/.

11. George E. Reed, "Toxic Leadership." *Military Review* 84, no. 4 (2004): 67–71.

12. George Reed, interview, March 2019.

13. Mary Dowling, interview, December 2018.

14. Schmidt, "Rediagnosing 'Founder's Syndrome.'"

15. Tom Fetter, interview, May 2018.

16. "About Us," Fieldstone Leadership Network. Accessed July 18, 2019. https://fieldstoneleadershipsd.org/about-us/.

17. Janine Mason, interview, July 2019.

18. Peter M. Senge, *The Fifth Discipline* (London: Random House Business, 2006).

19. Trista Harris, interview, September 2018.

20. Pat Libby, interview, June 2018.

21. Trista Harris, interview, September 2018.

22. Malin Burnham, interview, June 2018.

23. Trista Harris, interview, September 2018.

24. Jonathan Greenblatt, interview, August 2018.

25. Phil Buchanan, interview, November 2018.

26. Jessica David, interview, August 2018.

27. Paul Brest and James E. Canales, "Let's Stop Reinventing Potholes." *Chronicle of Philanthropy*, August 9, 2007. https://www.philanthropy.com/article/Lets-Stop-Reinventing/178137 (subscription required to access full text).

28. Ray Ashley, interview, September 2018.

29. "Amit Patel," Accenture. Accessed March 22, 2019. https://www.accenture.com/us-en/company-amit-patel.

30. Amit Patel, interview, September 2018.

31. Preeta Nayak, interview, September 2018.

32. Preeta Nayak, interview, September 2018.

33. "Fresh Lifelines for Youth, FLY Program," Fresh Lifelines for Youth, FLY Program. Accessed March 14, 2019. https://www.ousd.org/Page/16336.

34. The Bridgespan Group, "My Experience with Investing in Future Leaders: Christa Gannon." YouTube. October 24, 2018. Accessed April 27, 2019. https://www.youtube.com/watch?time_continue=169&v=jomSWhUEEe0.

35. The Bridgespan Group, "My Experience with Investing in Future Leaders: Christa Gannon." YouTube. October 24, 2018. Accessed May 2, 2019. https://www.youtube.com/watch?time_continue=169&v=jomSWhUEEe0.

36. "Key Strategies for 'Social Startup Success': A Q&A with Spark Co-founder Kathleen Kelly Janus." NextBillion. January 17, 2018. Accessed April

27, 2019. https://nextbillion.net/key-strategies-for-social-startup-success-a-qa-with-spark-co-founder-kathleen-kelly-janus/.

37. Bill Drayton, interview, November 2018.

38. Belinda Luscombe, "Brené Brown: Reigning Expert on Feelings Talks Leadership." *Time*. November 1, 2018. Accessed April 27, 2019. http://time.com/5441422/expert-feelings-brene-brown-leadership/.

6. A BRIDGE TO SUSTAINABILITY

1. Nancy Jamison, interview, April 2018.

2. "Our Story," The Whitman Institute. Accessed June 20, 2019. https://thewhitmaninstitute.org/about/our-story/.

3. "The Whitman Institute, Trust-Based Philanthropy." The Whitman Institute Home Comments. Accessed April 18, 2019. https://thewhitmaninstitute.org/.

4. "Trust-Based Philanthropy: A Primer." The Whitman Institute. Accessed June 20, 2019. https://thewhitmaninstitute.org/wp-content/uploads/TBP-Primer.pdf.

5. "Trust-Based Grantmaking: What It Is, and Why It's Critical to Our Sector." *Nonprofit AF*. October 24, 2016. Accessed April 18, 2019. https://nonprofitaf.com/2016/10/trust-based-grantmaking-what-it-is-and-why-its-critical-to-our-sector/.

6. Trista Harris, interview, September 2018.

7. Ali Malekzadeh, interview, September 2018.

8. "Letting Go (SSIR)," *Stanford Social Innovation Review*. Accessed June 21, 2019. https://ssir.org/articles/entry/letting_go#.

9. "Letting Go (SSIR)."

10. John Esterle, "Putting Trust at the Center of Foundation Work." The Center for Effective Philanthropy. January 18, 2018. Accessed April 18, 2019. https://cep.org/putting-trust-center-foundation-work/.

11. "About," Robert Sterling Clark Foundation. Accessed June 21, 2019. https://www.rsclark.org/about.

12. "Approach," Robert Sterling Clark Foundation. Accessed April 18, 2019. https://www.rsclark.org/approach.

13. "The Ethical Argument for General Operating Funds," *Nonprofit AF*. Robert Sterling Clark Foundation. March 26, 2018. Accessed April 18, 2019. https://www.rsclark.org/blog/http/nonprofitafcom/2018/03/the-ethical-argument-for-general-operating-funds.

14. "Why We Accept Proposals Written for Other Funders." Exponent Philanthropy. January 8, 2018. Accessed May 9, 2019. https://www.exponentphilanthropy.org/blog/accept-proposals-written-funders/.

15. "Scaling Solutions toward Shifting Systems," Rockefeller Philanthropy Advisors. Accessed May 14, 2019. https://www.rockpa.org/project/scaling-solutions/.

16. Grant Recipients of OneWorld Boston, Grant Program, Cummings Foundation. Accessed May 20, 2019. https://www.cummingsfoundation.org/oneworldboston/grant_recipients.htm.

17. Weingart Foundation, Unrestricted Operating Support Grants. Accessed May 21, 2019. https://www.weingartfnd.org/Unrestricted-Operating-Support-Grants.

18. "GOS Assessment, The Sobrato Organization and Sobrato Philanthropies." The Sobrato Organization Sobrato Philanthropies. Accessed May 22, 2019. http://www.sobrato.com/sobrato-philanthropies/sobrato-family-foundation/gos-assessment/.

19. "GOS Assessment, The Sobrato Organization and Sobrato Philanthropies."

20. Steve Eldred, interview, June 2018.

21. "Deciding Together," GrantCraft. Accessed May 3, 2019. https://grantcraft.org/content/guides/deciding-together/.

22. Nancy Jamison, interview, April 2018.

23. "Great Funder–Nonprofit Relationships Toolkit," Exponent Philanthropy. Accessed May 13, 2019. https://www.exponentphilanthropy.org/publication/great-funder-nonprofit-relationships-toolkit/.

24. Ann Goggins Gregory and Don Howard, "The Nonprofit Starvation Cycle." *Stanford Social Innovation Review* 7, no. 4 (2009): 49–53.

25. Don Howard, interview, August 2018.

26. "Smart Money (SSIR)," *Stanford Social Innovation Review*. Accessed May 21, 2019. https://ssir.org/articles/entry/smart_money.

27. Ray Ashley, interview, July, 2018.

28. Stephen Kinzer, "As Funds Disappear, So Do Orchestras." *New York Times*. May 14, 2003. Accessed April 23, 2019. https://www.nytimes.com/2003/05/14/arts/as-funds-disappear-so-do-orchestras.html.

29. "Big Gift Still Floats Symphony 10 Years Later," *Voice of San Diego*. May 27, 2013. Accessed April 23, 2019. https://www.voiceofsandiego.org/topics/arts/big-gift-still-floats-symphony-10-years-later/.

30. "Big Gift Still Floats Symphony 10 Years Later."

31. "About, San Diego Symphony Orchestra, History and Mission," San Diego Symphony. Accessed May 20, 2019. https://www.sandiegosymphony.org/about-the-sdso/history-and-mission/.

32. Martha Gilmer, interview, May 2019.

33. Martha Gilmer, interview, May 2019.

34. "Is Grantmaking Getting Smarter?" Grantmakers for Effective Organizations. Accessed May 21, 2019. https://www.geofunders.org/resources/is-grantmaking-getting-smarter-968.

7. SHOW ME THE NUMBERS!

1. D. Neuhauser, "W. Edwards Deming: Father of Quality Management, Patient and Composer." BMJ Quality & Safety. August 1, 2005. Accessed July 11, 2019. https://qualitysafety.bmj.com/content/14/4/310.

2. "Strengthening Nonprofits." Accessed April 10, 2019. http://www.strengtheningnonprofits.org/.

3. https://www.gatesfoundation.org/Who-We-Are/Resources-and-Media/Annual-Letters-List/Annual-Letter-2013.

4. Organisation for Economic Co-operation, "Policy Brief on Social Impact Measurement for Social Enterprises: Policies for Social Entrepreneurship." Publications Office of the European Union. August 25, 2015. Accessed April 4, 2019. https://publications.europa.eu/en/publication-detail/-/publication/19c3e101-f673-437f-a9fe-4a6dc7ff1f6e/language-en.

5. "Lean Experimentation for the Social Sector: Build Smart to Learn Fast (SSIR)," *Stanford Social Innovation Review*. Accessed July 11, 2019. https://ssir.org/podcasts/entry/lean_experimentation_for_the_social_sector_build_smart_to_learn_fast.

6. William Landes Foster, Peter Kim, and Barbara Christiansen, "Ten Nonprofit Funding Models." 2009. https://ssir.org/articles/entry/ten_nonprofit_funding_models#

7. "What We're Learning," The James Irvine Foundation. Accessed July 11, 2019. https://www.irvine.org/learning/reports/what-matters-what-works.

8. Paul Brest and James E. Canales, "Let's Stop Reinventing Potholes." *Chronicle of Philanthropy*. August 9, 2007. Accessed August 7, 2019. https://www.philanthropy.com/article/Lets-Stop-Reinventing/178137.

9. "Ep 67: Busting the Overhead Myth [PODCAST]." Joan Garry Nonprofit Leadership. September 7, 2018. Accessed July 11, 2019. https://blog.joangarry.com/ep-67-busting-the-overhead-myth/.

10. Nelli Garton, interview, June 7, 2018.

11. https://www.undp.org/.../7%20Steps%20to%20Effective%20Impact%20Measurement.

12. "How Nonprofits Can Find Data-Driven Success (SSIR)," *Stanford Social Innovation Review*. Accessed July 11, 2019. https://ssir.org/podcasts/entry/how_nonprofits_can_find_data_driven_success.

13. Phil Buchanan, interview, November, 2018.

14. Mario Morino, "Leap of Reason: Managing to Outcomes in an Era of Scarcity." *Innovations: Technology, Governance, Globalization* 6, no. 3 (2011): 167–77.

15. Dace West, interview, October 29, 2018.

16. https://ssir.org/articles/entry/ten_reasons_not_to_measure_impact_and_what_to_do_instead.

17. Morino, "Leap of Reason," 167–77.

18. John Grossman, interview, September 17, 2018.

19. Kim Ammann Howard, interview, April 2019.

20. Laura Deitrick, interview, September 14, 2018.

21. "What's a Learning Culture and Why Does It Matter to Your Nonprofit?" Center for Nonprofit Excellence in Central New Mexico. May 29, 2014. Accessed June 6, 2019. https://www.centerfornonprofitexcellence.org/news/whats-learning-culture-why-does-it-matter-your-nonprofit/2016-5-11.

22. "The Nonprofit Dashboard: Using Metrics to Drive Mission Success." BoardSource. Accessed April 17, 2019. https://boardsource.org/product/nonprofit-dashboard-using-metrics-drive-mission-success/.

23. Carrie Stokes Holst, interview, June 2019.

24. Antony Bugg-Levine, interview, November 2018; and "Get the Book," About, What Matters: Investing in Results to Build Strong, Vibrant Communities. Accessed April 10, 2019. https://investinresults.org/about.

25. Kathleen Kelly Janus, "From Innovation to Impact: How Philanthropy Can Support Problem-Solving." Accessed July 11, 2019. http://www.kathleenjanus.com/blog/from-innovation-to-impact-how-philanthropy-can-support-problem-solving.

26. "Why Taking a Step Back from Social Impact Assessment Can Lead to Better Results (SSIR)," *Stanford Social Innovation Review*. Accessed April 17, 2019. https://ssir.org/articles/entry/why_taking_a_step_back_from_social_impact_assessment_can_lead_to_better_res.

27. "Strengthening Nonprofits."

28. "How to Measure the Social Impact of Museums?" MuseumNext. April 6, 2019. Accessed April 11, 2019. https://www.museumnext.com/2019/04/how-to-measure-the-social-impact-of-museums/.

29. "Media Kit," *USS Midway* Museum. Accessed April 11, 2019. https://www.midway.org/contact/media-kit/.

30. Interviews with selected board members and Report. Jacobs Institute for Innovation in Education, University of San Diego.

31. New Bedford Whaling Museum, "High School Apprenticeship Program." New Bedford Whaling Museum. Accessed April 15, 2019. https://www.whalingmuseum.org/learn/opportunities/apprenticeship.

32. "National Arts and Humanities Youth Program Awards," NASAA. Accessed July 11, 2019. https://nasaa-arts.org/nasaa_research/national-arts-humanities-youth-program-awards/.

33. Sara Rose, interview, March 2019.

34. Eillie Anzilotti, "How Mastercard's 'Data Philanthropy' Program Is Tackling the Global Financial Information Gap." Fast Company. August 29, 2017. Accessed July 11, 2019. https://www.fastcompany.com/40457902/how-mastercards-data-philanthropy-program-is-tackling-the-global-financial-information-gap.

35. "Is Grantmaking Getting Smarter?" Grantmakers for Effective Organizations. Accessed May 21, 2019. https://www.geofunders.org/resources/is-grantmaking-getting-smarter-968.

36. "W. K. Kellogg Foundation Evaluation Handbook." W. K. Kellogg Foundation. Accessed May 30, 2019. https://www.wkkf.org/resource-directory/resource/2010/w-k-kellogg-foundation-evaluation-handbook.

8. TELL ME A STORY

1. Eleanor Goldberg, "Group behind 'Kony 2012' Closing because of Funding Issues." HuffPost. December 7, 2017. Accessed June 18, 2019. https://www.huffpost.com/entry/invisible-children-closing_n_6329990.

2. "Why Nonprofits Need to Be Storytellers," Bridgespan. Accessed June 25, 2019. https://www.bridgespan.org/insights/library/leadership-development/why-nonprofits-need-to-be-storytellers?utm_campaign=ASCSept2019&utm_source=Google&utm_medium=cpc&utm_content=CIMgrants&gclid=EAIaIQobChMIm6mnmMa64wIVAZ-fCh1Xdwm8EAAYASAAEgLHNfD_BwE.

3. "Why Nonprofits Need to Be Storytellers," Bridgespan. Accessed August 2, 2019.

4. "How to Create Nonprofit Stories That Inspire," Bridgespan. Accessed June 27, 2019. https://www.bridgespan.org/insights/library/organizational-effectiveness/how-to-create-nonprofit-stories-that-inspire.

5. "Storytelling Projects," Freedom for Immigrants. Accessed August 2, 2019. https://www.freedomforimmigrants.org/storytelling-projects.

6. "Pallotta TeamWorks," Pallotta Teamworks, About Dan Pallotta. Accessed August 2, 2019. http://www.pallottateamworks.com/about_dan_pallotta.php.

7. Anthony Filipovitch, "Book Review: Pallotta, D. (2008). *Uncharitable: How Restraints on Nonprofits Undermine Their Potential*. Medford, MA: Tufts University Press. 340 pp. $35.00." *Nonprofit and Voluntary Sector Quarterly* 39 (2010): 371–73. 10.1177/0899764009338451.

8. Deloitteeditor, "Marketing Budgets Vary by Industry." *Wall Street Journal*. March 12, 2018. Accessed June 20, 2019. https://deloitte.wsj.com/cmo/2017/01/24/who-has-the-biggest-marketing-budgets/.

9. "How Much Should Companies Budget for Marketing?" FrogDog. October 27, 2017. Accessed June 21, 2019. https://frog-dog.com/how-much-should-companies-budget-for-marketing/.

10. "2017 Nonprofit Communications Trends Report," Nonprofit Marketing Guide.com. Accessed August 3, 2019. https://nonprofitmarketing-guide.com/freemembers/2017NonprofitCommunicationsTrendsReport.pdf?_ga=2.71702871.551848831.1563124247-2019382670.1563124247.

11. "Functional Expenses," Functional Expenses, Nonprofit Accounting Basics. Accessed June 25, 2019. https://www.nonprofitaccountingbasics.org/functional-expenses.

12. Steven Bellach, interview, May 2019.

13. Kathleen Kelly Janus, *Social Startup Success: How the Best Nonprofits Launch, Scale Up, and Make a Difference* (New York: Da Capo Press, 2018).

14. "Storytelling for Nonprofits," Network for Good, Storytelling for Nonprofits, Raise More Money. Accessed June 25, 2019. https://learn.networkforgood.com/storytelling-guide.html.

15. "The Nonprofit Storytelling Field Guide and Journal." Accessed June 25, 2019. https://nonprofitstorytellingconference.com/wp-content/uploads/2014/10/NonprofitStoryFieldGuide_v1.pdf.

16. Amit Patel, interview, August 6, 2018.

17. Chimamanda Ngozi Adichie, "The Danger of a Single Story." TED. Accessed June 19, 2019. https://www.ted.com/talks/chimamanda_adichie_the_danger_of_a_single_story.

18. "The Danger of a Single Story, by David Brooks—The New York Times," InconvenientNews.Net. April 19, 2016. Accessed June 19, 2019. https://inconvenientnews.wordpress.com/2016/04/19/the-danger-of-a-single-story-by-david-brooks-the-new-york-times/.

19. "Story Types," Working Narratives. October 6, 2016. Accessed June 25, 2019. https://workingnarratives.org/article/story-types/.

20. "Hone Your Craft: The Art of Nonprofit Storytelling," Nonprofit Hub. March 26, 2019. Accessed June 25, 2019. https://nonprofithub.org/nonprofit-marketing/the-art-of-nonprofit-storytelling/.

21. Nathalie Kylander and Christoper Stone, "The Role of Brand in the Nonprofit Sector (SSIR)," *Stanford Social Innovation Review*. Accessed June 27, 2019.

22. "Creating a Brand for Your Non-Profit," The Fundraising Authority RSS. Accessed June 27, 2019. http://www.thefundraisingauthority.com/strategy-and-planning/creating-a-brand-for-your-non-profit/.

23. "Sutton's Law," The Free Dictionary. Accessed July 1, 2019. https://medical-dictionary.thefreedictionary.com/Sutton's law.

24. Steven Bellach, interview, May 2019.

25. Julie Dixon, "Building a Storytelling Culture (SSIR)," *Stanford Social Innovation Review*. Accessed July 1, 2019. https://ssir.org/articles/entry/building_a_storytelling_culture.

26. Bruce Hoyt, interview, August 30, 2018.

27. Ray Ashley, interview, May 10, 2018.

9. CREDIT AND SUSTAINABILITY

1. "Ralph Waldo Emerson Quotes," BrainyQuote. Xplore. Accessed September 23, 2019. https://www.brainyquote.com/quotes/ralph_waldo_emerson_118865.

2. Board of Governors of the Federal Reserve System. Accessed September 23, 2019. https://www.federalreserve.gov/paymentsystems/check_commcheckcolannual.htm.

3. RPMG Research Corporation. Accessed September 23, 2019. https://rpmgresearch.net/Products-Report#.

4. "2017 AFP Payments Fraud and Control Survey," JPMorgan Chase. Association for Financial Professionals. Accessed September 23, 2019. https://commercial.jpmorganchase.com/jpmpdf/1320732417358.pdf.

5. Tim May, Interview, November 2018.

6. "Martin Luther King Jr. Quotes," BrainyQuote. Xplore. Accessed September 23, 2019. https://www.brainyquote.com/quotes/martin_luther_king_jr_109228.

7. "Loans: A Guide to Borrowing for Nonprofit Organizations," Propel Nonprofits. Accessed September 23, 2019. https://www.propelnonprofits.org/resources/using-loans-guide-borrowing-nonprofit-organizations/.

10. IT'S OUT THERE

1. "Nonprofit Finance Fund," Nonprofit Finance Fund. Accessed July 9, 2019. https://nff.org/.

2. "SeaChangeCap.org," SeaChange Capital Partners. Accessed July 9, 2019. http://seachangecap.org/.

3. Ben Paynter, "GuideStar and the Foundation Center Are Merging to Form the Definitive Nonprofit Transparency Organization." *Fast Company*. February 5, 2019. Accessed July 9, 2019. https://www.fastcompany.com/90301678/guidestar-and-the-foundation-center-are-merging-to-form-the-definitive-nonprofit-transparency-organzation.

4. "GrantSpace," GrantSpace. Accessed July 9, 2019. https://grantspace.org/.

5. "Collaboration Hub: Resources," GrantSpace. Accessed August 2, 2019. https://grantspace.org/collaboration/.

6. Rebecca Masisak, interview, October 2018.

7. "USD Nonprofit Leadership and Management Master's Program Best Practice Library." Accessed July 10, 2019. https://digital.sandiego.edu/npi-bpl/.

8. "About Us," National Council of Nonprofits. May 21, 2019. Accessed August 2, 2019. https://www.councilofnonprofits.org/about-us.

ACKNOWLEDGMENTS

1. "People," Nonprofit Finance Fund. Accessed August 6, 2019. https://nff.org/people.

2. "Home—The Giving Pledge," Giving Pledge. Accessed August 6, 2019. https://givingpledge.org/.ig.

BIBLIOGRAPHY

"2017 Nonprofit Communications Trends Report." Nonprofit Marketing Guide.com. Accessed August 3, 2019.

"2018 NFF State of the Nonprofit Sector Survey Results Warn of Danger." National Council of Nonprofits. June 20, 2018. Accessed March 24, 2019. https://www.councilofnonprofits.org/thought-leadership/2018-nff-state-of-the-nonprofit-sector-survey-results-warn-of-danger.

"About." Robert Sterling Clark Foundation. Accessed June 21, 2019. https://www.rsclark.org/about.

"About Us." National Council of Nonprofits. May 21, 2019. Accessed August 2, 2019. https://www.councilofnonprofits.org/about-us.

Adichie, Chimamanda Ngozi. "The Danger of a Single Story." TED. Accessed June 19, 2019. https://www.ted.com/talks/chimamanda_adichie_the_danger_of_a_single_story.

"Advice to Strengthen Strategic Mergers and Collaborations." Top Indicators of Nonprofit Financial Health, Nonprofit Finance Fund. March 27, 2017. Accessed February 12, 2019. https://nff.org/report/advice-strengthen-strategic-mergers-and-collaborations.

Albrecht, Leslie. "Americans Slashed Their Charitable Deductions by $54 Billion after Republican Tax-Code Overhaul." MarketWatch. July 11, 2019. Accessed July 25, 2019. https://www.marketwatch.com/story/americans-slashed-their-charitable-deductions-by-54-billion-after-trumps-tax-overhaul-2019-07-09.

Alliance for Children and Families. "Joining Forces to Strengthen Human Services in America." Authority and Institutions Challenged. Accessed January 28, 2019. http://www.alliance1.org/web/community/national-imperative-joining-forces-strengthen-human-services-america.aspx.

Amadeo, Kimberly. "Greed Is Good . . . or Is It?" The Balance Small Business. Accessed January 8, 2019. https://www.thebalance.com/greed-is-good-or-is-it-quote-and-meaning-3306247.

"Annual Impact Investor Survey 2018." The GIIN. Accessed January 15, 2019. https://thegiin.org/research/publication/annualsurvey2018.

Anzilotti, Eillie. "How Mastercard's 'Data Philanthropy' Program Is Tackling the Global Financial Information Gap." Fast Company. August 29, 2017. Accessed July 11, 2019. https://www.fastcompany.com/40457902/how-mastercards-data-philanthropy-program-is-tackling-the-global-financial-information-gap.

"Approach." Robert Sterling Clark Foundation. Accessed April 18, 2019. https://www.rsclark.org/approach.

"Arriving at 100 Percent for Mission: Now What?" *Stanford Social Innovation Review.* Accessed January 15, 2019. https://ssir.org/articles/entry/arriving_at_100_percent_for_mission._now_what.

"Basics." Utah High Quality Preschool Program, Pay for Success. Accessed January 7, 2019. https://www.payforsuccess.org/learn/basics/#what-is-pay-for-success.

"Bill Drayton on the Power of Collaborative Entrepreneurship in McKinsey's 'What Matters?'" Ashoka, Everyone a Changemaker. July 18, 2016. Accessed December 2, 2018. https://www.ashoka.org/en-US/node/3481.

Blumberg, Peter D. "From 'Publish or Perish' to 'Profit or Perish': Revenues from University Technology Transfer and the § 501 (c) (3) Tax Exemption." *University of Pennsylvania Law Review* 145, no. 1 (1996): 89–147. doi:10.2307/3312714.

"Board Responsibilities and Structures—FAQs." BoardSource. Accessed March 15, 2019. https://boardsource.org/resources/board-responsibilities-structures-faqs/.

"Boards." National Council of Nonprofits. March 8, 2019. Accessed March 20, 2019. https://www.councilofnonprofits.org/tools-resources/diversity-nonprofit-boards.

Bradley, Bill, Paul Jansen, and Les Silverman. "The Nonprofit Sector's $100 Billion Opportunity." *Harvard Business Review.* August 1, 2014. Accessed January 14, 2019. https://hbr.org/2003/05/the-nonprofit-sectors-100-billion-opportunity.

Brest, Paul, and James E. Canales. "Let's Stop Reinventing Potholes." *The Chronicle of Philanthropy.* August 9, 2007. Accessed August 7, 2019. https://www.philanthropy.com/article/Lets-Stop-Reinventing/178137.

Brickley, James A., and R. Lawrence Van Horn. "Managerial Incentives in Nonprofit Organizations: Evidence from Hospitals." *Journal of Law and Economics* 45, no. 1 (2002): 227–49. doi:10.1086/339493.

The Bridgespan Group. "My Experience with Investing in Future Leaders: Christa Gannon." YouTube. October 24, 2018. Accessed May 2, 2019. https://www.youtube.com/watch?time_continue=169&v=jomSWhUEEe0.

Buchanan, Phil. *Giving Done Right: Effective Philanthropy and Making Every Dollar Count.* New York: PublicAffairs, 2019.

"Business Thing." June 6, 2012. blog post, https://cep.org/author/philb/.

Candid. "The Financial Health of the United States Nonprofit Sector." The Financial Health of the United States Nonprofit Sector. Accessed July 25, 2019. https://learn.guidestar.org/products/us-nonprofits-financial-health.

Chait, Richard P. *Governance as Leadership: Reframing the Work of Nonprofit Boards.* New York: Wiley, 2011. Kindle Edition.

"The Charitable Sector." Independent Sector. https://independentsector.org/about/the-charitable-sector/.

Chikoto, Grace L., and Daniel Gordon Neely. "Building Nonprofit Financial Capacity." *Nonprofit and Voluntary Sector Quarterly* 43, no. 3 (2013): 570–88. doi:10.1177/0899764012474120.

"Collaborationists and Collectivists (SSIR)." *Stanford Social Innovation Review.* ssir.org/articles/entry/collaborationists_and_collectivists.

Collins, James Charles. *Good to Great and the Social Sectors: Why Business Thinking Is Not the Answer.* New York: Harper Business: 2011.

Cooper, Clare. "Fuelling 'The Necessary Revolution.'" Grantmakers in the Arts. Accessed April 3, 2019. https://www.giarts.org/article/fuelling-necessary-revolution.

"Core WORKNOW Exceeds Goal with 200th Connection." Colorado Department of Transportation. August 14, 2018. Accessed April 3, 2019. https://www.codot.gov/projects/i70east/assets/worknow_press-release_200connection.pdf.

"Council on Foundations Statement on Passage of the Tax Cuts and Jobs Act." Council on Foundations. December 21, 2017. Accessed July 19, 2019. https://www.cof.org/news/council-foundations-statement-passage-tax-cuts-and-jobs-act.

"County Pushes toward Elusive Goal of Treatment on Demand." Addiction Professional. Accessed March 23, 2019. https://www.addictionpro.com/article/management/county-pushes-toward-elusive-goal-treatment-demand.

"Creating a Brand for Your Non-Profit." The Fundraising Authority RSS. Accessed June 27, 2019. http://www.thefundraisingauthority.com/strategy-and-planning/creating-a-brand-for-your-non-profit/.

"The Danger of a Single Story, by David Brooks—The New York Times." Inconvenient-News.Net. April 19, 2016. Accessed June 19, 2019. https://inconvenient-news.wordpress.com/2016/04/19/the-danger-of-a-single-story-by-david-brooks-the-new-york-times/.

"Deciding Together." GrantCraft. Accessed May 3, 2019. https://grantcraft.org/content/guides/deciding-together/.

Deloitteeditor. "Marketing Budgets Vary by Industry." *Wall Street Journal*. March 12, 2018. Accessed June 20, 2019. https://deloitte.wsj.com/cmo/2017/01/24/who-has-the-biggest-marketing-budgets/.

Dixon, Julie. "Building a Storytelling Culture (SSIR)." *Stanford Social Innovation Review*. Accessed July 1, 2019. https://ssir.org/articles/entry/building_a_storytelling_culture.

Du, Jerry Y., Alexander S. Rascoe, and Randall E. Marcus. "The Growing Executive-Physician Wage Gap in Major US Nonprofit Hospitals and Burden of Nonclinical Workers on the US Healthcare System." *Clinical Orthopaedics and Related Research* 476 (10) (2018): 1910–19. https://doi.org/10.1097/corr.0000000000000394.

"Economic Impact." National Council of Nonprofits. October 18, 2017. Accessed October 2, 2018. https://www.councilofnonprofits.org/economic-impact.

"Ep 67: Busting the Overhead Myth [PODCAST]." Joan Garry Nonprofit Leadership. September 7, 2018. Accessed July 11, 2019. https://blog.joangarry.com/ep-67-busting-the-overhead-myth/.

Epstein, Marc J., and F. Warren McFarlan. "Nonprofit vs. For-Profit Boards: Critical Differences." *Strategic Finance* (March 2011): 28. Academic OneFile. Accessed December 20, 2018.

Esterle, John. "Putting Trust at the Center of Foundation Work." The Center for Effective Philanthropy. January 18, 2018. Accessed April 18, 2019. https://cep.org/putting-trust-center-foundation-work/.

"Ethics and Nonprofits (SSIR)." *Stanford Social Innovation Review*. Accessed December 17, 2018. https://ssir.org/articles/entry/ethics_and_nonprofits.

"Exempt Organization Annual Reporting Requirements: Meaning of Reasonable Compensation, Internal Revenue Service." Internal Revenue Service. Accessed March 23, 2019. https://www.irs.gov/charities-non-profits/exempt-organization-annual-reporting-requirements-meaning-of-reasonable-compensation.

"The Financial Health of the United States Nonprofit Sector: Facts and Observations." About Us. Accessed February 5, 2019. https://learn.guidestar.org/products/us-nonprofits-financial-health.

Fishman, Stephen. "Reporting Nonprofit Operating Expenses." www.nolo.com. January 23, 2015. Accessed December 14, 2018. http://www.nolo.com/legal-encyclopedia/reporting-nonprofit-operating-expenses.html.

Foster, William, and Jeffrey Bradach. "Should Nonprofits Seek Profits?" *Harvard Business Review* 83, no. 2 (2005): 92–100.

Foster, William, Alex Cortez, and Katie Smith Milway. "Nonprofit Mergers and Acquisitions: More Than a Tool for Tough Times." The Bridgespan Group. February 25, 2009. Accessed February 7, 2019. https://www.bridgespan.org/insights/library/mergers-and-collaborations/nonprofit-mergers-and-acquisitions-more-than-a-too.

Foster, William Landes, Peter Kim, and Barbara Christiansen. "Ten Nonprofit Funding Models." *Stanford Social Innovation Review* (2009). https://ssir.org/articles/entry/ten_nonprofit_funding_models.

Fottrell, Quentin. "Fortune 500 CEOs Are Paid from Double to 5,000 Times More Than Their Employees." MarketWatch. May 19, 2018. Accessed March 24, 2019. https://www.marketwatch.com/story/fortune-500-ceos-are-paid-from-double-to-5000-times-more-than-their-employees-2018-05-16.

Frailey, Kerstin. "What Does the Nonprofit Sector Really Look Like?" GuideStar Blog. Accessed January 28, 2019. https://trust.guidestar.org/what-does-the-nonprofit-sector-really-look-like.

"Functional Expenses." Functional Expenses, Nonprofit Accounting Basics. Accessed June 25, 2019. https://www.nonprofitaccountingbasics.org/functional-expenses.

Galle, B. D. "Keep Charity Charitable." HeinOnline. Accessed December 14, 2018. https://heinonline.org/HOL/LandingPage?handle=hein.journals/tlr88&div=43&id=&page=.

Gordon, Amanda. "Robin Hood Is Mum on Gala Haul, but It's More Than $54.5 Million." Bloomberg.com. Accessed July 10, 2019. https://www.bloomberg.com/news/articles/2018-05-16/robin-hood-is-mum-on-gala-haul-but-it-s-more-than-54-5-million.

GrantSpace. "Collaboration Hub: Resources." Accessed August 2, 2019. https://grantspace.org/collaboration/.

Grant Recipients of OneWorld Boston, Grant Program, Cummings Foundation. Accessed May 20, 2019. https://www.cummingsfoundation.org/oneworldboston/grant_recipients.htm.

"Great Funder—Nonprofit Relationships Toolkit." Exponent Philanthropy. Accessed May 13, 2019. https://www.exponentphilanthropy.org/publication/great-funder-nonprofit-relationships-toolkit/.

Greenstone, Scott. "One Way to Help Homeless in King County? Shorten the Wait for Treatment." *The Seattle Times*. November 24, 2017. Accessed January 2, 2019. https://www.seattletimes.com/seattle-news/homeless/one-way-to-help-homeless-in-king-county-shorten-the-wait-for-treatment/.

Gregory, Ann Goggins, and Don Howard. "The Nonprofit Starvation Cycle." *Stanford Social Innovation Review* 7, no. 4 (2009): 49–53.

Griswold, Alison. "Two Stanford Professors Have a Fascinating Theory of Why Businesses Succeed." *Business Insider*. February 4, 2014. Accessed January 28, 2019. https://www.businessinsider.com/scaling-up-excellence-robert-sutton-huggy-rao-2014-1.

GuideStar, BBB Wise Giving Alliance, and Charity Navigator. http://overheadmyth.com/.

GuideStar. "What You Need to Know about Nonprofit Executive Compensation." About Us. Accessed December 14, 2018. https://www.guidestar.org/ViewCms-File.aspx?ContentID=3890.

"Home—The Giving Pledge." Giving Pledge. Accessed August 6, 2019. https://givingpledge.org/.

"Hone Your Craft: The Art of Nonprofit Storytelling." Nonprofit Hub. March 26, 2019. Accessed June 25, 2019. https://nonprofithub.org/nonprofit-marketing/the-art-of-nonprofit-storytelling/.

"How Fiscal Sponsorship Nurtures Nonprofits." TSNE MissionWorks. December 7, 2018. Accessed February 20, 2019. https://www.tsne.org/blog/how-fiscal-sponsorship-nurtures-nonprofits.

"How Much Should Companies Budget for Marketing?" FrogDog. October 27, 2017. Accessed June 21, 2019. https://frog-dog.com/how-much-should-companies-budget-for-marketing/.

"How Nonprofits Can Find Data-Driven Success (SSIR)." *Stanford Social Innovation Review*. Accessed July 11, 2019. https://ssir.org/podcasts/entry/how_nonprofits_can_find_data_driven_success.

"How to Create Nonprofit Stories That Inspire." Bridgespan. Accessed June 27, 2019. https://www.bridgespan.org/insights/library/organizational-effectiveness/how-to-create-nonprofit-stories-that-inspire.

"How to Fund Nonprofit Mergers and Partnerships (SSIR)." *Stanford Social Innovation Review*. Accessed February 12, 2019. https://ssir.org/articles/entry/how_to_fund_nonprofit_mergers_and_partnerships#.

"How to Measure the Social Impact of Museums?" MuseumNext. April 6, 2019. Accessed April 11, 2019. https://www.museumnext.com/2019/04/how-to-measure-the-social-impact-of-museums/.

"Impact Investing." The GIIN. Accessed January 16, 2019. https://thegiin.org/impact-investing/.

"Is Grantmaking Getting Smarter?" Grantmakers for Effective Organizations. Accessed May 21, 2019. https://www.geofunders.org/resources/is-grantmaking-getting-smarter-968.

Janus, Kathleen Kelly. "From Innovation to Impact: How Philanthropy Can Support Problem-Solving." Kathleen Kelly Janus. Accessed July 11, 2019. http://www.kathleenjanus.com/blog/from-innovation-to-impact-how-philanthropy-can-support-problem-solving.

Janus, Kathleen Kelly. *Social Startup Success: How the Best Nonprofits Launch, Scale Up, and Make a Difference*. New York: Da Capo Press, 2018.

Journy, Matthew T. "Paying for the Best: Executive Compensation for Section 501(c)(3) Public Charities." Accessed December 21, 2018. https://www.venable.com/files/Publication/84527f21-29c3-4da2-a9dc-b16d21a323bf/Presentation/PublicationAttachment/29c08467-5b30-4668-9306-c287c537ac8d/Paying_for_the_Best_Executive_Compensation_for_Section_501(c)(3)_Public_Charities.pdf.

Joyaux, Simone. "A Too-Sad Truth about the Nonprofit Sector." (August 17, 2012). Retrieved November 8, 2015. http://nonprofitquarterly.org/2012/08/17/a-too-sad-truth-about-the-nonprofit-sector/.

Katzbichler, Stephan. "Historical Impacts on the Philanthropical American Tradition." Munich: GRIN Verlag, 2012. https://www.grin.com/document/262272.

"Key Strategies for 'Social Startup Success': A Q&A with Spark Co-founder Kathleen Kelly Janus." NextBillion. January 17, 2018. Accessed April 27, 2019. https://nextbillion.net/key-strategies-for-social-startup-success-a-qa-with-spark-co-founder-kathleen-kelly-janus/.

Kohn, Alfie. "Why Incentive Plans Cannot Work." *Harvard Business Review*. August 1, 2014. Accessed March 24, 2019. https://hbr.org/1993/09/why-incentive-plans-cannot-work.

Kramer, Larry. "Hewlett Foundation's Leader Makes a Case against Impact Investing." *The Chronicle of Philanthropy* (January 2019): 8–11.

Lane, Terry. "Can Nonprofit Corporations Issue Stock?" Small Business—Chron.com. November 21, 2017. Accessed January 5, 2019. https://smallbusiness.chron.com/can-nonprofit-corporations-issue-stock-65592.html.

"Leading with Intent—2017 National Index of Nonprofit Board Practices." Leading with Intent. Accessed April 25, 2019. https://leadingwithintent.org/wp-content/uploads/2017/09/LWI2017.pdf.

"Lean Experimentation for the Social Sector: Build Smart to Learn Fast (SSIR)." *Stanford Social Innovation Review*. Accessed July 11, 2019. https://ssir.org/podcasts/entry/lean_experimentation_for_the_social_sector_build_smart_to_learn_fast.

"Learning from Failure (SSIR)." *Stanford Social Innovation Review*. Accessed March 23, 2019. https://ssir.org/articles/entry/learning_from_failure#.

"Letting Go (SSIR)." *Stanford Social Innovation Review*. Accessed June 21, 2019. https://ssir.org/articles/entry/letting_go#.

Luscombe, Belinda. "Brené Brown: Reigning Expert on Feelings Talks Leadership." *Time*. November 1, 2018. Accessed April 27, 2019. http://time.com/5441422/expert-feelings-brene-brown-leadership/.

Maeda, Wendy. "Nonprofits Push Back on Conventional Wisdom—The Boston Globe." BostonGlobe.com. January 15, 2015. Accessed December 14, 2018. https://www.bostonglobe.com/business/2015/01/15/nonprofits-push-back-conventional-wisdom/4CB4q1OTTZnxqkcYXEToHJ/story.html.

"Making an Impact, Literally." Accessed February 27, 2019. Media2.Mofo.com/documents/npx-impact.pdf.

Manyika, James M., Roger P. Roberts, and Kara L. Sprague. "Eight Business Technology Trends to Watch." McKinsey & Company. Accessed February 20, 2019. https://www.mckinsey.com/business-functions/digital-mckinsey/our-insights/eight-business-technology-trends-to-watch.

"Market Making for Mission (SSIR)." *Stanford Social Innovation Review*. Accessed January 15, 2019. https://ssir.org/articles/entry/market_making_for_mission.

Mcleod, Saul. 2018. "Maslow's Hierarchy of Needs." *Simply Psychology*. May 21, 2018. https://www.simplypsychology.org/maslow.html.

Miller, Clara. "The World Has Changed and So Must We." http://www.frbsf.org/community-development/files/miller.pdf.

Mirchandani, Bhakti. "How to Save a Nonprofit: The Care Steps Required in Mergers and Acquisitions." Non Profit News, Nonprofit Quarterly. September 26, 2018. Accessed February 13, 2019. https://nonprofitquarterly.org/2018/08/15/how-to-save-a-nonprofit-mergers-acquisitions/.

Morino, Mario. "Leap of Reason: Managing to Outcomes in an Era of Scarcity." *Innovations: Technology, Governance, Globalization* 6, no. 3 (2011): 167–77.

Neuhauser, D. "W. Edwards Deming: Father of Quality Management, Patient and Composer." BMJ Quality & Safety. August 1, 2005. Accessed July 11, 2019. https://qualitysafety.bmj.com/content/14/4/310.

Neuhoff, Alex, Katie Smith Milway, Reilly Kiernan, and Josh Grehan. "Making Sense of Nonprofit Collaborations." Bridgespan. December 17, 2014. Accessed February 15, 2019. https://www.bridgespan.org/insights/library/mergers-and-collaborations/nonprofitcollaborations.

"A New Source for Funding Nonprofit Mergers and Collaborations (SSIR)." *Stanford Social Innovation Review.* Accessed February 11, 2019. https://ssir.org/articles/entry/a_new_source_for_funding_nonprofit_mergers_and_collaborations.

"NFF's Annual Survey: 3,000 and Counting." Top Indicators of Nonprofit Financial Health, Nonprofit Finance Fund. July 18, 2017. Accessed December 26, 2018. https://nff.org/blog/nff's-annual-survey-3000-and-counting.

NOC. Accessed February 20, 2019. https://noc.npccny.org/noc/.

Nonprofit AF. "The Ethical Argument for General Operating Funds." Robert Sterling Clark Foundation. March 26, 2018. Accessed April 18, 2019. https://www.rsclark.org/blog/http/nonprofitafcom/2018/03/the-ethical-argument-for-general-operating-funds.

"Nonprofit Consultants, Nonprofit Strategic Restructuring—La Piana." La Piana Consulting. Accessed April 3, 2019. https://www.lapiana.org/.

"The Nonprofit Dashboard: Using Metrics to Drive Mission Success." BoardSource. Accessed April 17, 2019. https://boardsource.org/product/nonprofit-dashboard-using-metrics-drive-mission-success/.

"A Nonprofit Guide to Outsourcing." https://d2oc0ihd6a5bt.cloudfront.net/wp-content/uploads/sites/1482/2016/01/outsourcing.pdf.

"The Nonprofit Storytelling Field Guide and Journal." Accessed June 25, 2019. https://nonprofitstorytellingconference.com/wp-content/uploads/2014/10/NonprofitStoryFieldGuide_v1.pdf.

"The Nonprofit World Becomes Flat: How Technology and Economic Needs May Shrink Our Globe (SSIR)." *Stanford Social Innovation Review.* Accessed April 1, 2019. https://ssir.org/articles/entry/the_nonprofit_world_becomes_flat_how_technology_and_economic_needs_may_shri.

O'Brien, Sarah. "Advocates: Cost of GOP Tax Bill Puts Entitlement Programs at Risk of Cuts." CNBC. December 6, 2017. Accessed July 19, 2019. https://www.cnbc.com/2017/12/06/advocates-cost-of-gop-tax-bill-puts-entitlement-programs-at-risk-of-cuts.html.

Organisation for Economic Co-operation. "Policy Brief on Social Impact Measurement for Social Enterprises: Policies for Social Entrepreneurship." Publications Office of the European Union. August 25, 2015. Accessed April 4, 2019. https://publications.europa.eu/en/publication-detail/-/publication/19c3e101-f673-437f-a9fe-4a6dc7ff1f6e/language-en.

"Our Philanthropic Philosophy." Merger of Neighboring Big Brothers Big Sisters Affiliates, The Lodestar Foundation. Accessed February 12, 2019. http://www.lodestarfoundation.org/.

"Our Story." The Whitman Institute. Accessed June 20, 2019. https://thewhitmaninstitute.org/about/our-story/.

Pallotta, Dan. *Uncharitable: How Restraints on Nonprofits Undermine Their Potential.* Medford, MA: Tufts University Press, 2010.

"Pallotta TeamWorks." About Dan Pallotta. Accessed August 2, 2019. http://www.pallottateamworks.com/about_dan_pallotta.php/.

Paynter, Ben. "GuideStar and the Foundation Center Are Merging to Form the Definitive Nonprofit Transparency Organization." Fast Company. February 5, 2019. Accessed July 9, 2019. https://www.fastcompany.com/90301678/guidestar-and-the-foundation-center-are-merging-to-form-the-definitive-nonprofit-transparency-organzation.

"The Payoff of Pay-for-Success (SSIR)." *Stanford Social Innovation Review*. Accessed January 7, 2019. https://ssir.org/up_for_debate/article/the_payoff_of_pay_for_success.

"People." Nonprofit Finance Fund. Accessed August 6, 2019. https://nff.org/people.

"The Professionalization of Charities." *The Economist* 424 (September 30–October 6, 2017): 55–56.

"The QSR 50." *QSR Magazine.* August 1, 2017. Accessed April 3, 2019. https://www.qsrmagazine.com/content/qsr50-2017-top-50-chart?sort=2016_us_average_sales_per_unit_thousands&dir=asc.

Reed, George E. "Toxic Leadership." *Military Review* 84, no. 4 (2004): 67–71.

Reich, R., and C. Wimer. *Charitable Giving and the Great Recession.* Palo Alto, CA: The Russell Sage Foundation and the Stanford Center on Poverty and Inequality, 2012.

"Report: Warehousing Wealth." Institute for Policy Studies. July 25, 2018. Accessed January 9, 2019. https://ips-dc.org/report-warehousing-wealth/.

"The Rise of Socially Responsible Investing." ETFdb.com. Accessed January 21, 2019. ttps://etfdb.com/practice-management/rise-of-socially-responsible-investing/.

"The Role of Brand in the Nonprofit Sector (SSIR)." *Stanford Social Innovation Review.* Accessed June 27, 2019. https://ssir.org/articles/entry/the_role_of_brand_in_the_nonprofit_sector.

Santana, Patrick. "Nonprofits and Tax-Exempt Bonds." Step by Step Guide for Starting a California Nonprofit—CalNonprofits. Accessed January 4, 2019. https://calnonprofits.org/resources/nonprofits-tax-exempt-bonds.

"Scaling Solutions toward Shifting Systems." Rockefeller Philanthropy Advisors. Accessed May 14, 2019. https://www.rockpa.org/project/scaling-solutions/.

Schmidt, Elizabeth. "Rediagnosing 'Founder's Syndrome': Moving beyond Stereotypes to Improve Nonprofit Performance." Non Profit News, *Nonprofit Quarterly*. March 7, 2019. Accessed March 18, 2019. https://nonprofitquarterly.org/2019/03/07/rediagnosing-founder-s-syndrome-moving-beyond-stereotypes-to-improve-nonprofit-performance/.

Schupmann, Will, and Matthew Eldridge. "Impact Securities: A New Twist on Pay for Success." Urban Institute—Pay for Success Initiative. June 14, 2018. Accessed January 14, 2019. https://pfs.urban.org/pay-success/pfs-perspectives/impact-securities-new-twist-pay-success.

Senge, Peter M. *The Fifth Discipline.* London: Random House Business, 2006.

Sinek, Simon. "How Great Leaders Inspire Action." Ted. Accessed January 2, 2019. https://www.ted.com/talks/simon_sinek_how_great_leaders_inspire_action.

Singer, Natasha, and Mike Isaac. "Mark Zuckerberg's Philanthropy Uses L.L.C. for More Control." *New York Times.* January 19, 2018. Accessed February 27, 2019. https://www.nytimes.com/2015/12/03/technology/zuckerbergs-philanthropy-uses-llc-for-more-control.html.

"Smart Money (SSIR)." *Stanford Social Innovation Review.* Accessed May 21, 2019. https://ssir.org/articles/entry/smart_money.

"Steps to Catalyze Private Foundation Impact Investing." National Archives and Records Administration. Accessed January 15, 2019. https://obamawhitehouse.archives.gov/blog/2016/04/21/steps-catalyze-private-foundation-impact-investing.

"Storytelling for Nonprofits." Network for Good, Storytelling for Nonprofits, Raise More Money. Accessed June 25, 2019. https://learn.networkforgood.com/storytelling-guide.html.

"Story Types." Working Narratives. October 6, 2016. Accessed June 25, 2019. https://workingnarratives.org/article/story-types/.

"Strategic Partnerships." https://www.thearc.org/file/documents_nce/strategic-partnerships.pdf. Accessed February 10, 2019.

"Strengthening Nonprofits." Strengthening Nonprofits. Accessed April 10, 2019. http://strengtheningnonprofits.org/resources/guidebooks/measuringoutcomes.pdf.

"Strengthening the Impact Investing Movement (SSIR)." *Stanford Social Innovation Review.* Accessed January 15, 2019. https://ssir.org/articles/entry/strengthening_the_impact_investing_movement.

"Sustainable Investing: The Millennial Investor." Ernst & Young. https://www.ey.com/Publication/vwLUAssets/ey-sustainable-investing-the-millennial-investor-gl/$FILE/ey-sustainable-investing-the-millennial-investor.pdf.

Sutton, Robert I., and Huggy Rao. *Scaling up Excellence: Getting to More without Settling for Less.* London: Random House, 2014.

Toffler, Alvin. *Future Shock.* London: Pan Books, 1970.

"Trust-Based Grantmaking: What It Is, and Why It's Critical to Our Sector." Nonprofit AF. October 24, 2016. Accessed April 18, 2019. https://nonprofitaf.com/2016/10/trust-based-grantmaking-what-it-is-and-why-its-critical-to-our-sector/.

"Trust-Based Philanthropy: A Primer." The Whitman Institute. Accessed June 20, 2019. https://thewhitmaninstitute.org/wp-content/uploads/TBP-Primer.pdf.

"USD Nonprofit Leadership and Management Master's Program Best Practice Library: University of San Diego Research: Digital USD." Accessed July 10, 2019. https://digital.sandiego.edu/npi-bpl/.

USA, Written By Giving. "Giving USA: 2015 Was America's Most Generous Year Ever, Giving USA." Accessed February 27, 2019. https://givingusa.org/giving-usa-2018-americans-gave-410-02-billion-to-charity-in-2017-crossing-the-400-billion-mark-for-the-first-time/.

Warfield, Zenobia Jeffries, Chris Winters, Tracy Matsue Loeffelholz, Ed Whitfield, Chuck Collins, Deonna Anderson, Ivy Brashear, Vicki Robin, New Economy Coalition, Working World, Southern Reparations Loan Fund., and Institute for Policy Studies. "The Good Money Issue." *YES! Magazine.* Accessed January 15, 2019. https://issues.yesmagazine.org/issue/good-money/theme.html#7thArticle.

Weingart Foundation. "Unrestricted Operating Support Grants." Accessed May 21, 2019. https://www.weingartfnd.org/Unrestricted-Operating-Support-Grants.

"What's a Learning Culture and Why Does It Matter to Your Nonprofit?" Center for Nonprofit Excellence in Central New Mexico. May 29, 2014. Accessed June 6, 2019. https://www.centerfornonprofitexcellence.org/news/whats-learning-culture-why-does-it-matter-your-nonprofit/2016-5-11.

"What We're Learning." The James Irvine Foundation. Accessed July 11, 2019. https://www.irvine.org/learning/reports/what-matters-what-works.

"What You Need to Know about Nonprofit Executive Compensation." Accessed December 14, 2018. https://learn.guidestar.org/news/publications/nonprofit-executive-compensation.

"The Whitman Institute, Trust-Based Philanthropy." The Whitman Institute Home Comments. Accessed April 18, 2019. https://thewhitmaninstitute.org/.

"Why Nonprofits Need to Be Storytellers." Bridgespan. Accessed June 25, 2019. https://www.bridgespan.org/insights/library/leadership-development/why-nonprofits-need-to-be-storytellers.

"Why We Accept Proposals Written for Other Funders." *Exponent Philanthropy.* January 8, 2018. Accessed May 9, 2019. https://www.exponentphilanthropy.org/blog/accept-proposals-written-funders/.

"Why Taking a Step Back from Social Impact Assessment Can Lead to Better Results (SSIR)." *Stanford Social Innovation Review.* Accessed April 17, 2019. https://ssir.org/articles/entry/why_taking_a_step_back_from_social_impact_assessment_can_lead_to_better_res.

"W. K. Kellogg Foundation Evaluation Handbook." W. K. Kellogg Foundation. Accessed May 30, 2019. https://www.wkkf.org/resource-directory/resource/2010/w-k-kellogg-foundation-evaluation-handbook.

"World YMCA Annual Report April 2011." n.d. Human Rights Documents Online. https://doi.org/10.1163/2210-7975_hrd-9843-0004.

WEBSITES

https://www.nytimes.com/2016/04/19/opinion/the-danger-of-a-single-story.html

http://www.payforsuccess.org/sites/default/files/pay-for-success.pdf

https://dealbook.nytimes.com/2013/11/11/plan-to-finance-philanthropy-shows-the-power-of-
a-simple-question

https://nonprofitmarketingguide.com/freemembers/2017NonprofitCommunicationsTrends-
Report.pdf?_ga=2.71702871.551848831.1563124247-2019382670.1563124247

https://ssir.org/articles/entry/
ten_reasons_not_to_measure_impact_and_what_to_do_instead.

https://www.charitywatch.org/charitywatch-articles/charitywatch-hall-of-shame/63

https://www.gatesfoundation.org/Who-We-Are/Resources-and-Media/Annual-Letters-List/
Annual-Letter-2013

INDEX

ABOUT THE AUTHORS

David J. O'Brien enjoyed a career in the for-profit sector over a span of forty-five years, with broad-based experience in multi-industry corporate development, finance, and management of organizations ranging from Fortune 500 conglomerates to startups. David has served as board chair, committee chairs, and director/trustee of numerous nonprofits in diverse fields including education, international health NGOs, social services, and the arts. He resides in rural San Diego county with his wife, Dr. Paula Cordeiro, and when not active in the nonprofit community, enjoys sailing his sixty-year-old sloop *Colibi*, cooking, oil painting, and accompanying Paula on her travels working with NGOs in Africa and Central and South America.

Matthew D. Craig is vice president and senior relationship manager with JPMorgan Chase, where he specializes in providing a broad range of services to governments and nonprofit organizations. With more than twenty years of experience in the financial sector, he has held positions in credit underwriting, commercial and small business banking, and private wealth management. Throughout his academic and professional careers, Matt has been an active volunteer and advocate for myriad social organizations. He is a philomath, teacher, traveler, and mediocre beach volleyball player. Matt currently lives in Escondido, California, with his wife Courtney and their twins, Kerrigan and Landry.